Worl

First published in Great Britain
by Bettany Press 2003.
8 Kildare Road, London E16 4AD.

Text © Margaret Moncrieff Kelly 2003.

The right of Margaret Moncrieff Kelly to be identified as
author of this work has been asserted by her in accordance
with the Copyright, Designs and Patents Act 1988.

British Library Cataloguing in Publication Data.
A catalogue record for this book is available
from the British Library.

This book is sold subject to the condition that it shall not,
by way of trade or otherwise, be lent, re-sold, hired out, or
otherwise circulated without the Publisher's prior consent in any
form of binding or cover other than that in which it is published
and without a similar condition including this condition being
imposed on the subsequent purchaser. All rights reserved.

ISBN 0-9524680-7-7

Designed and typeset by Bettany Press.

Printed and bound by CLE Print Ltd,
Huntingdon, Cambridgeshire.

Worlds Apart

Memoirs of Margaret Moncrieff Kelly
(Helen McClelland)

Bettany Press 2003

Acknowledgments

Warmest thanks are due to many people, and especially to:

Ju Gosling for having insisted that these memoirs should be written, as well as for all her help during the book's gestation, and to Bettany Press for publishing it.

All those who at different times have read the MS, or parts of it, and have given invaluable advice and suggestions. In particular, to: Sooty Asquith, Rosemary Auchmuty, William Bennett, Iain Burnside, Mary Cadogan, Fen Crosbie, Mary Firth, Gracie King, Judy Whale and Prue Wilson.

Joy Wotton, for being both a super editor and a tirelessly patient instructor in the habits of computers.

Also Michal Kaznowski, for so kindly supplying those computers we love to hate; and Antony Paton Walsh for unearthing and scanning family snapshots.

My daughters, Catriona and Alison Moncrieff Kelly, for help, guidance and unfailing support.

My late husband, Alexander Kelly, who could have shared so many of the memories with me.

Anyone who enjoys reading the book!

Contents

	PAGE
Foreword	vii
Part One: Growing Up in a Vanished World	1
I: Scottish Roots	3
II: Family Portraits	13
III: The World of Convent Schools	27
IV: Different Houses, Different People	39
V: Many Relatives	56
Part Two: A Slowly Changing World	71
VI: Reluctant Thoughts on Social Class	73
VII: Edinburgh Music	82
VIII: Random Wartime Memories	100
Part Three: New Worlds Beckon	111
IX: A Year at Lytton Grove	113
X: Scholarships to Paris	121
XI: Theatrical Interlude	146
Part Four: Meeting of the Worlds	153
XII: Alex	155
XIII: Two Worlds Meet	164
Part Five: Living in Three Worlds	179
XIV: World of Music/Performing and Teaching	181
XV: Brief Thoughts on Friendship	202
XVI: Kellys Cottage	206
XVII: World of Words	222
Afterword: Silver Wedding Greeting	248

Margaret Moncrieff Kelly (Helen McClelland), 1952.
Photograph: Yvonne Studio.

Foreword

BEING ASKED BY BETTANY PRESS to write an autobiography was flattering; but for me any temptation was resistible. Having always been what's called today 'a private person', I can't imagine wanting to give a factual blow-by-blow account of my life – still less envisage anyone wanting to read it.

On the other hand, when talking to younger friends, for whom it is impossible that World War II and the years before it can be even faint memories, I've come to realise that events in the early life of anyone who's now past seventy-five can be of interest to them. My growing-up years were lived in a world so different from theirs, and my circumstances have changed so remarkably, that it struck me it could be rewarding to record some memories of times past, and in particular of the many interesting people I've been lucky enough to know.

Hence, these memoirs; they are unashamedly selective and somewhat haphazard, and are not built around a time sequence but around people, places and ideas. I have tried for the most part to deal with things chronologically within each of the sections, but there is inevitably a good deal of moving back and forward and of overlapping in time between chapters.

Not every phase of my life is covered in detail, and there are many among my friends who are not mentioned by name. The omission of their names does not imply any lack on my part of affection, gratitude and admiration, but indicates only that the events described during the narrative did not happen to include them. And in testimony to this I should like to dedicate *Worlds Apart* to all my good friends, past and present, and most especially to those who have not been named.

Margaret Moncrieff Kelly (Helen McClelland)

Part One:
Growing Up in a Vanished World

(Overleaf) Me aged about 18 months, with my mother.

I: Scottish Roots

TO SELECT JUST ONE EVENT IN A LONG LIFE as having been the most significant, is an impossible task. But if for some reason compelled to do this, I'd name my marriage on 6 June 1957 to the Scottish pianist, Alexander Kelly. Many other happenings have been important, both before and after that — among them the births of our daughters, Catriona and Alison, and the arrivals of our grandchildren. But my reason for choosing our marriage is that, had it not been for the social upheaval brought about by World War II, it was a marriage that would probably never have taken place.

Any understanding of this requires some picture, not only of that incredibly different world, the Edinburgh of the 1930s and '40s, in which he and I grew up, but of our widely different backgrounds. For in pre-war days an upper-class girl with titled parents, and a young man, however talented, whose origins were not only working-class but even a little ambiguous, would have been separated by barriers more formidable than the Berlin Wall — that chilling monument to prejudice.

Fortunately things have changed; and to examine and illustrate the changes is among the main objectives of these memoirs. Even for me, many aspects of my early life now feel strangely remote. Not that I don't remember, and with clarity — having been gifted with an excellent memory. But parts of the story might almost belong to someone else.

By way of setting the scene, we'll begin with my parents. My father's family, the Moncrieffs, came originally from Perthshire. Although perhaps the word *originally* is not appropriate, since the earliest known bearer of the name, the twelfth-century Ramerus de Moncreiff [sic], is claimed by some authorities to have come from

Castille. And, as a musician, I rather like the idea of having Spanish ancestry.

In the more recent past, the particular branch of the family to which my father belonged was known as the Moncrieffs of Culfargie, named after a small estate near Bridge of Earn and a house that no longer exists. The family had through the years produced an astonishing number of Presbyterian clergymen, many of whom acted as ministers of Abernethy Church, where there is a large and impressive Moncrieff family tomb. They had also produced an equally remarkable number of lawyers, my paternal grandfather and great-grandfather both being among the latter group.

The Moncrieffs had frequently intermarried with cousins; in particular, during the nineteenth century, with the Pattisons, a family who came mainly from the region around Glasgow, having possibly originated in the north of England. (Two of the Pattisons were painted by Raeburn.) And amusing evidence of the particularly close links that existed between them and the Moncrieffs is provided in my father's immediate family: his mother, who had been a Miss Hope Moncrieff Pattison, became, following her marriage to my grandfather, Mrs Hope Moncrieff Moncrieff; his sister, Margaret Pattison Moncrieff, also married a cousin, then becoming Mrs Margaret Pattison Pattison.

My father, Alexander Moncrieff, was the youngest of nine children. He was born on 14 August 1870, and was a posthumous child, his father having died in the previous June at the relatively early age of 43. Sandy, as my father was always known, showed precocious intellectual gifts, and at fifteen he entered Glasgow University. Here he took an M.A. degree in 1888 (first degrees at many Scottish universities are known as M.A.s), going on to take an LLB at Edinburgh, where he was called to the Bar in around 1893.

He was to have a starrily distinguished legal career, both as a much-sought-after advocate (as barristers are named in Scotland), and later as a judge — or Senator of the College of Justice, to use the Scottish title. But the crowning point of his career was undoubtedly his appointment in 1947 as Lord Justice Clerk. This was a remarkable achievement from several points of view. My father was by then in his mid-70s, which would normally have been considered too old for the position. But, because the office of Lord Justice Clerk is usually a political appointment, the Labour Government who were then in power faced a dilemma, since none of their avowed supporters was thought

Two Pattison ancestors portrayed by Raeburn.

to be suitable for this high office (only the Lord President ranks above the Lord Justice Clerk). Now my father did not support the Labour Party — the Moncrieffs had always been Liberals, or in the old days, Whigs — but neither had he ever publicly espoused the Tories, or any other political party. Hence, the Attlee Government felt happy to appoint him, as a lawyer of unquestioned eminence and apparently neutral political views.

A vivid memory remains with me of attending his installation, which took place in Edinburgh's historic Parliament House in February 1947; and of being struck, not only by the ceremony itself but also by the measured beauty of the legal oath administered, which affirms that justice shall be dispensed '**Without fear or favour, affection or malice**'. Sadly my father was unable to fill the post for more than two years. In the spring of 1949 he was forced by ill health to resign, and he died a few months later, on the fifth of August.

My father in legal robes. Mid-1930s.

Later I shall be writing about him from a more personal angle, but for the moment I want to move to my mother's side of the family.

My mother, Helen McClelland Adams or Spens or Moncrieff — as she would be described in Scottish law, which gives first the maiden name and then in order any married surnames — was, like my father, the youngest of a long family. In her case she was her father's eighth child, although only the second of his second marriage. She too had lost a parent early in life, when her mother died of breast cancer at the age of only 37. At this time my mother was still a baby; and I often think that a psychologist could have a field day mulling over the significance in *my* life of having grown up, as I did, with a father who had never known a father, and a mother who had effectively never known a mother.

My maternal grandfather, John Robinson Adams, was yet another of the lawyers among my forebears, a highly successful family solicitor. He had been born and spent his early life in Kirby — now part of Liverpool — but had moved at some point to practise in London. His first wife, whom he married when very young, was the daughter of a local farmer — something I discovered for myself when doing family researches, for almost nothing appears to have been known in the family about Grandpapa Adams; and of course he died more than twenty years before I was born.

John Adams had been widowed for about seven years when on 19 July 1876 he married my grandmother, Helen Boyd McClelland, daughter of a well known and respected Galloway family, who would probably have qualified as 'County'. At the time of her marriage she was already 35, which was an unusually advanced age for a bride in those days. But then Helen McClelland was not an altogether usual person. As a young girl she was regarded as being, in a small way at least, an heiress, and was considered a matrimonial catch. And family legend relates that, when aged about twenty, she had actually been in the course of running away with some highly unsuitable man — clearly a fortune-hunter. Just in time the family was alerted, and the eloping couple had been stopped on the local station platform by the lady's two brothers, wielding the traditional horse-whips.

Grandpapa Adams. About 1885.

No one can tell how far the McClellands were able to hush things up. But perhaps this graphic episode explains why my grandmother appears to have spent more than fifteen of the ensuing years in obscurity; finally marrying a middle-aged man, a widower with six children, and one who came, moreover, from a rather lower rung of society. (Don't forget, these things mattered.)

As a stepmother, Helen Adams appears to have been remarkably well received. Certainly my mother's half-brothers and sisters clearly regarded her with real affection during the short time she was with them. Since the death of their own mother they had found life bleak, especially the boys, for my grandfather was apparently a rather autocratic type of Victorian father, who was ready to show some affection for his daughters, but had little empathy with his growing sons. As the result of a bitter disagreement that took place not long before his second marriage, the eldest of his family, Edmond, then about eighteen, had been unhappy enough to run away from home altogether. And a tale that could well have come from a novel of the times, is told about the first Christmas my grandmother spent with her new family. As they sat round the fire at tea-time in the gathering darkness, my grandmother looked up and saw to her initial fright a face staring in at the window. Keeping her calm — as it seems was characteristic of her — she went to investigate; and found that this was the runaway Eddie, who was in a desperate state and almost starving. My grandmother, refusing to listen to her husband who protested that the boy had made his choice when he moved out, simply insisted that Eddie must of course be immediately taken in and nursed back to health. No wonder that another of my mother's family, my Uncle Fred (to whom I was to be much devoted), once told her: "When your mother arrived, it was like an angel coming into the house."

Fate would leave her only a short time with them. At first things went well, and a year after her marriage she gave birth to a son, James McClelland Adams. But he was to live for little more than a year; the cause of death being described on the certificate as 'diarrhoea and syncope' (which apparently means constant sickness).

To add to the tragedy, the date of James's death on 3 September 1878 followed *only a fortnight after the birth of my mother* on the 19th of August, and it is not hard to imagine the feelings of my grandmother at this time. What is more, the breast cancer which would eventually cause her death fourteen months later may perhaps already have taken hold.

Today, it seems possible the little boy could have been saved, and that she herself might also have lived. Be that as it may, on 13 October 1879 Helen McClelland Adams died, aged not quite 38, leaving a motherless baby daughter, six motherless step-children, and her husband a widower for the second time.

For the nine or so years following my grandmother's death, my mother lived with her father and her half-sisters and -brothers, being looked after partly by her eldest sister, Alice, who was then past twenty, but mainly by nurses. (My mother didn't call them nannies — perhaps this term came into use later?) At first the family home was in Dulwich, but later an upmarket move was made to Queens Gate Terrace in South Kensington, where my mother would often point out to me as a child the room, at the top of this extremely tall house, which had been her nursery.

She was sent briefly to a small school in Barons Court, West Kensington, which she told me she had enjoyed — especially climbing ropes in the Swedish Gymnastics class. But around the age of nine she developed a serious heart condition. Apparently the specialists' prognosis gave her less than ten years to live, and her father clearly felt it too difficult for him and his youthful family to keep a possibly invalid child at home. (Fortunately that prognosis turned out to be in error by more than sixty years.) An advertisement was placed in the medical journals, seeking a doctor who would be willing to accept my mother into his family as a boarder, and to give her the expert care that might be needed. Through this my mother came to spend her next nine years living at Old Windsor, in the home of a Dr and Mrs Curwen; it was thought particularly suitable that the latter had a daughter by a previous marriage, Dorothy Riley, who was almost of an age with my mother.

Both Doctor Curwen and his wife were plainly most important in the formation of my mother's character and ideas. Both had strong though very different personalities. Doctor Curwen had suffered some illness (perhaps polio?) which left him wheelchair-bound, but he continued undaunted in his practice as a doctor. Mrs Curwen also had disabilities; but hers were of a social nature, for she was not widowed but a divorcee — something far more unusual and less acceptable then in the social climate of the late 19th century. She had, in many ways, the strictly conventional attitudes that often characterise those who feel themselves socially vulnerable. But she also had some surprisingly feminist ideas; and today, with hindsight, it becomes clear that many of the apparently contradictory aspects of my mother's social thinking had their origins in the years she spent with the Curwen family.

By the age of eighteen my mother must have been considered out of immediate danger, for at this point she returned to London to live at home with her father, who had now acquired a house in Hampstead. And, considering this was still the 19th century, the next step on her road seems remarkable, for at this point she was actually allowed to go and study for a time at Bedford College for Women — not then part of London University but an independent college. Never having taken the necessary London Matriculation exam, she wasn't eligible to study for a degree; and in any case it seems doubtful if her father would have approved of that. More probably he thought of her university studies as a pleasant hobby, something to keep her occupied until the right man came along — no one ever doubted that she would marry. Possibly he also shared the view of the renowned Professor Gregory Foster, whose lectures in English literature my mother attended, who apparently had once described her as "an intelligent butterfly".

Events of the next decade and more can only be filled by deduction, and by the scattered memories of things told to me by my mother and half-sister. No one today recalls how, when or where she met her first husband. However, it is known that John Gillespie Spens, who appears always to have been called Jack, was an Edinburgh lawyer with a flourishing practice as an advocate. At a guess — and judging by the age of his sister, Mrs Nelly Fellowes, whom I did know in childhood — he was probably a few years older than my mother. All in all, he would undoubtedly have fulfilled all of the necessary qualifications to be thought a suitable husband. As a member of the Spens family his social credentials were impeccable, for the Spenses can claim direct descent from the Sir Patrick Spens of the well-known Scottish ballad. There is, too, a famous portrait by Raeburn in the Scottish National Gallery of a more recent ancestor, Sir Nathaniel Spens, arrayed in his splendid uniform as Head of The Honourable Company of Archers (a historic society which still holds the honour of providing a bodyguard for the Royal Family when they visit Holyrood Palace). Added to all this, Jack Spens was himself a well-established advocate, who had enjoyed the benefits of a public school education at Rugby. The members of both families must have been delighted at the marriage; and, following an engagement of unknown duration, the couple's wedding took place in the summer of 1900 at the Church of St Mary Abbott in Kensington.

The newly married pair set up home in Heriot Row, a handsome street in Edinburgh's New Town; and during the next few years my mother gave birth to a son, Walter John McClelland Spens, and a daughter, Helen Patricia Spens. No details are available now about the years between this point and the sadly early death of my mother's first husband in about 1910. Nor do I know at what stage my mother

(L) My father aged about 40; (R) my mother at about 25.

became acquainted with her second husband — my father-to-be. But since both Jack Spens and Sandy Moncrieff were fellow members of the Faculty of Advocates, it is likely that they moved in the same circle of friends.

My father was always completely and obviously devoted to my mother. He could become exasperated with her — and she had a faultless knack of winding him up! But it was clear that she was the centre of his universe. I've sometimes wondered whether perhaps he may have carried a torch for her even before Jack Spens died. She was accounted very beautiful, and she clearly had enormous charm and no lack of admirers. However, regarding her feelings towards him I never had quite the same impression. At the time of their marriage my mother was a widow with two young children, and she was always a great pragmatist. I'm sure she loved him sincerely, so no doubt it would have seemed ideal to link her fortunes and those of her children with such an eligible man who plainly adored her. All that can be said for certain is that, in March 1913, my parents were married — not in Edinburgh, but at the little Catholic church of Our Lady Star of the Sea in North Berwick, my mother having converted to Roman Catholicism a few years previously.

In the course of the next five years my two brothers, Hugh and Philip, were born; but the 1920s were rolling along by the time I arrived, my mother in the mean time having had at least one miscarriage. (My husband-to-be was also a 1920s' baby, just squeezing in towards the end of the decade.) That my birth may have occasioned some anxiety is suggested by a remark my father apparently made at the time. It seems both he and my mother had been greatly hoping for a daughter; but, when my father was told by a smiling doctor that the baby was indeed a girl, his brusque response was: "I don't care if it's a giraffe so long as it's born."

Hugh, Philip and I completed the family, both my parents being now well into middle age. It's possible I was a 'change of life baby', and the little sister I sometimes longed for was never to be. But perhaps this was just as well, for it turned out that both my brothers had learning difficulties — a situation that overshadowed our family throughout my early years, and one that for many reasons was harder to cope with in those days than it would be now.

More of this later; here, I want to begin giving some detailed portraits of the most important members of my family.

II: Family Portraits

Monica Bond

STRICTLY SPEAKING THIS SECTION SHOULD NOT BEGIN with Monica, since she was not a blood relation. But, when I think back to my very earliest memories of people, the one who comes first to mind is not my mother, nor yet my father or any of my other relatives, but my nanny, Monica Bond. Monica was engaged by my mother when I was a baby of a few months, and she remained with us until just before my sixth birthday. She is there in the background to all my scanty recollections of those early days. Not only that: it was Monica who in many respects became my role model. In particular she was the person from whom I learnt the capacity to show affection. Not that my parents were lacking in affection as a quality — far from it. But my mother, who would unhesitatingly have lain down in the road and died for any of us, was never in my memory physically demonstrative; and my father, whom I now think would often have liked to show affection more openly, was inhibited, not only by the conventions of the time, but by personal circumstances (as will emerge).

Monica had been trained at the Norland Nurses School — a good old-fashioned institution that still flourishes today in the 21st century (though now its nannies are probably employed as often by working mothers as by society families). In any case, Monica — trained or untrained — would always have been a wonderful nanny; she had warmth and innate charm, and relating to children came naturally to her. When she had to leave — being dramatically summoned late one night to return home to Hampshire where her mother was dangerously ill — it was the second great loss of my short life, and by far the more serious. The first was when my beloved puppy, a Scotch terrier, was stricken with canine distemper and had to be put to sleep — something I never knew at the time, for I was simply told that he had gone "to live in the country", which at around three years old I found puzzling but acceptable.

At the time Monica left I always hoped she would come back, but for reasons which aren't clear to me she never did. However, after she had moved on to other families I was able to go and stay with her a couple of times; and we kept in touch over the years, even though at fairly long intervals. The last time I saw her was in 1965, when she had retired to live at Budleigh Salterton in Devon; and in the course of a return journey from one of the Dartington Music Summer Schools I was able to take my small daughters to visit her.

Me at about 3 with my adored Puppy 'Mutt'.

Thinking of Monica brings a picture to mind of the way she would often make a little ritual, holding her hands at first only a few inches apart and saying in her attractively deep voice: "I don't love you a tiny little bit like this! But . . ." now stretching her arms out to their fullest extent — "I love you a great huge enormous bit, like THIS!" And the lesson conveyed was to remain with me for life. Later on in childhood, and even as a young adult, I was to become wary of showing my feelings, other than in music and acting. But later still Monica's gifts to me were to bear fruit, and the affectionate relationships I have enjoyed with my own children and grandchildren owe much to her.

My mother

For me it is only possible to judge from photographs how beautiful my mother must have been in her youth. Before I was able to have any clear appreciation of her looks she was already pushing fifty; and although still handsome she was growing a little grey-haired and a little plump. As a girl, and in her twenties and thirties, she had been willow-slim, the possessor of a fashionably small waist, with regular features and bright flaxen hair that contrasted vividly with her lively dark brown eyes.

Highly intelligent, she had a good sense of both fun and humour, although the latter was of an entirely different kind from my father's. My mother never had much use for fantasy, always maintaining that she had no imagination; and whether or not this really was the case, her attitude to life was unflinchingly realistic. She once avowed that she could never understand the concept of being "crossed in love" — because, surely, if the other person wasn't interested you just forgot about them . . . And certainly she was a most practical capable person — one who took considerable pride in being so.

Oddly enough, in view of this down-to-earth approach, it appears that my mother was unusually sensitive to psychic phenomena. On many occasions, all well attested, she had visited places where quite unknown to her some tragedy had happened, or which had a reputation for being haunted, and had unerringly picked out the particular room or site in question, although she could never explain how she did this. There is even independent evidence to suggest that she had once actually seen a ghost when visiting Christchurch Priory in Hampshire. All rather unexpected in someone so pronouncedly commonsense; but then there were many contradictions in my mother's personality. Probably that was part of the spell she exerted, for she was unquestionably gifted with remarkable charm. A person who throughout life could, as the saying goes, 'get people eating out of her hand'.

Always active, indeed almost hyperactive, my mother until the outbreak of World War II had occupied part of her time with the inevitable charity work that used then to fill the lives of most so-called ladies of leisure. She had also been involved in the running of several women's organisations, political and social — among them, the National Council of Women and the Catholic Women's League. In addition, besides making regular sorties to work in the garden — a hobby she particularly enjoyed and in which she was quite knowledgeable — she had used an aptitude for dress-making to provide many of her own clothes, and all of mine apart from school uniforms. (She continued to do this even after I was grown up; and when I became a professional cellist she made many strikingly beautiful concert dresses for me.) At one point she took up weaving and spinning; and, to the end of her life, she was rarely to be seen without some piece of knitting — or of embroidery, in which she excelled. Today, most members of our extended family still have at least one chair delightfully covered by her in a variety of petit point and other stitches.

My mother also read extensively, and not only in English; she had a good knowledge of French and was fluent in German, having spoken it regularly as a child during the nine years she lived with the Curwens, when a German governess had looked after her and my honorary aunt, Dorothy Riley. She was in fact greatly interested in languages, and at some point in the 1930s had bought herself a set of Linguaphone records for learning Russian and had even made some progress. I still recall one or two of the phrases I picked up when the records were playing in the background. She had moreover some talent for painting in water-colours, possessed a pleasant mezzo-soprano voice, and, although her piano playing was not of a high standard, she was undoubtedly musical. Into the bargain, she was a tireless letter-writer.

This much is easy to describe. To highlight the reasons why I was so devotedly attached to her is much harder; and I'm sadly aware that some of the things to be related in these memoirs will show her in a decidedly unfavourable light. Without question she was a dominating person; distinctly managing and perhaps rather inflexible. But she had, for her generation, an extraordinarily broad-minded outlook; from quite early on I found it possible to discuss almost anything with her, for she often seemed far more in tune with modern days than, for example, my half-sister who was mathematically much nearer my age. Even before I was grown up, my mother began in many ways to treat me, if not quite as an equal certainly not as a child. (How many mothers of her period would have shared with even a grown-up daughter this naughty little rhyme that had gone the rounds of the legal fraternity in her early years? — "They said she preferred Mr Hewitt to Mr Commissioner Grant, Because Mr Hewitt can do it, Whereas the Commissioner can't.") All round, I think it could be said that by about my mid-teens she and I had become friends. We shared so many interests and enjoyed each other's company. One thing that could never have been questioned at any time was the depth of my mother's love for all her family. Not only were they the centre of her life — her family was her life. And by around the age of sixteen I began to be aware that I, as her youngest child and constant companion, was at the centre of that centre. It was a heavy responsibility.

Today, from the perspective of old age, I begin to understand that when my mother made dictatorial pronouncements — and insisted on their being carried out — this happened because of her intense desire that everything for her family should happen in the very best possible way. Perhaps she was a little too inclined to know best; but there was absolutely nothing she would not have done to help any of us.

None of this, though, can really account for the enormous affection my mother inspired in so many people: my father; all her children and grandchildren without exception; and hosts of other relatives and friends, including many of my contemporaries. Only the magic that lies in some kind of personal chemistry can explain that.

My father

To write about my father is not easy for me. Our relationship was In many ways an unhappy one, for reasons that I am slowly coming to understand a little better today. I have been told that we were close when I was a small child, and the body language shown in early photographs would suggest this. But I never remember feeling other than a certain antagonism towards him, which later was exacerbated by his attitude to my involvement with music. Not that he was against music in itself — and in its proper place. It was noise to which he strenuously objected. All the Moncrieffs were considered abnormally sensitive to noise. And of course children practising caused noise. (On this theme, there is a delightful anecdote of my aunts Constance and Georgina Moncrieff, who when on holiday in the French countryside went sallying forth at midnight armed with shawls, in a vain effort to muffle the cowbells that were disturbing their slumbers.)

Looking back, though, I've no doubt now that my mother in a curious way contributed to this antagonism. Undoubtedly this was quite unconscious on her part, but she had a habit of saying crossly, whenever I did or said something that displeased her: "Oh, you're exactly like your father." And, since I absolutely adored her, this immediately set up jangling vibrations. She would also use my father as a kind of scapegoat when disagreeable decisions had to be made — perhaps about such matters as my having to spend another year at school when I was dying to leave. It was never "We think . . . " — or "We have decided" — always "Your father wants you to do this . . . or that . . . or whatever".

By my mid-teens I had already begun to have some inkling about how this worked. But by then it was too late. My relationship with my father had been irrevocably set.

This was painfully brought home to me on one occasion towards the end of the war, when I was beginning to make plans for leaving home to study the cello in London. At this point a family friend, Mrs Claudia Shelley, mother of one of my childhood contemporaries, was living with us while negotiations for the house she had bought in Edinburgh were completed. Claudia was in her middle fifties, a woman of strong character, who as a single parent had for many years run a school in order to support herself and her daughter. She had known me from a small child, and was in the privileged position of being an old friend of all the family (in particular of my Aunt Georgina, my father's youngest sister). Besides, she was by nature outspoken. And I shall always recall one evening when she and I were sitting by the drawing-room fire after supper. My mother must have been away at the time, and my father would have retired long since to his study. I was raking the embers in the fire when Claudia suddenly asked: "Margaret, what is the matter between you and your father?" I remember being completely taken aback and saying in a dazed way "Why, is it so obvious?" To which the answer was simply: "Oh, my dear . . . ," accompanied by a compassionate shake of the head.

Today, I can see all too clearly how difficult life must have been for my father in so many ways. As a posthumous child, the youngest of a long family and gifted with both charm and talents, he had plainly been much cosseted at home by his mother and sisters. He was well past forty when he married, and he then had also to fill the difficult position of stepfather to my mother's son and daughter from her first marriage. The transition cannot have been easy. Nor can it have helped matters that the first two children of his own marriage — my two older brothers — both turned out to have learning difficulties.

At no time would this have been easy to handle. But at that period it was unimaginably harder than it might be nowadays. Intellectual impairments may still not be fully understood today, or accepted as they should be, but at least the subject is not completely taboo in the way that it was. Nor, I think, are people nowadays made to feel, to the same extent anyway, that having intellectually impaired children is a kind of social disgrace, which it undoubtedly was in earlier days. Apart from anything, people then were often frightened at any suggestion of 'mental problems'.

Even in post-war Edinburgh a wariness of attitude persisted, as illustrated by a curious happening when my godmother, Miss Isabel Maxwell — a lady of unimpeachable social standing — offered to sponsor me for the Queens Club, then one of the two important ladies' clubs in Edinburgh. (The other was the Ladies Caledonian Club to which my mother belonged.) This was in the summer of 1946; I was just beginning my cello studies in London and my godmother thought it could be useful for me to have somewhere independent to entertain friends when returning to Edinburgh on holiday. She duly submitted my name to the committee as a suitable member of the club; and was both horror-struck and mystified when I was turned down — 'black-balled', as it was known. No one could think of any possible reason; no rational objection could have been made, from a personal or social angle, against either me or my godmother. The explanation — although this was learnt only from hearsay — seemed to be that certain members of the committee were afraid I might bring my brothers to the club, which was something my mother was known to do from time to time at the Ladies' Caledonian.

The difference in attitude of more recent generations came home to me with particular clarity when in the 1970s some friends of ours, whose youngest child was born with Downs Syndrome, related how their twelve-year-old daughter had given a talk to her class at school about growing up in a family with a Downs Syndrome child. This, quite simply, could never have happened in the world of my childhood. In the first place, 'mental handicap' in the family would not have been considered a suitable subject at that time for young schoolchildren to discuss. Yet more important: at no point in my childhood did I ever breathe a word about my brothers to anyone, not even to my then 'best friends' (some of whom are still my good friends today). What is more, I would have suffered agonies of mortification had I dreamt that anyone knew about our problems. Now, so many years on, it's funny to think of this, because — as I soon learnt in later life — most people in Edinburgh were well aware of the situation.

One of the hardest things for my father must have been the knowledge that, whereas my mother already had two normal and successful children, he, until after my arrival several years later, had fathered only two boys who both, in the unkind terminology of the times, were 'mentally defective'.

The fact that my father had a prominent position in society only made things more difficult. Everything contributed to making him conspicuous: as a judge he held the courtesy title of Lord Moncrieff — with my mother being Lady Moncrieff. (The latter may seem obvious, but at one time in Scotland only the judges themselves were accorded the title 'Lord', while their wives remained plain 'Mrs'; this system had to be abandoned after certain judges who had chosen to take a title other than their surname, as was their right, experienced problems when staying at hotels. One can imagine the scandal aroused in those days if, say, Lord Bruntisfield and Mrs Brown were to request a double bedroom . . .)

It also singled out my father that he was a Roman Catholic, for at that time in Edinburgh this was considered unusual for someone in his position and — I hate to mention it — social class. On all counts he inevitably attracted publicity, as did his family; even to the extent that when, for example, my brother Philip or I played golf on the children's links at North Berwick we were frequently photographed, and the pictures would appear in newspapers, or such glossy magazines as the *Queen* or the *Tatler*.

However, in my father's dealings with his two disabled sons, the question of personal chemistry was also a most important factor. Over the years he did become genuinely attached to my brother Hugh, who was the elder of the two, but his relationship with his younger son, Philip, was always uneasy and often stormy, for my father had an explosive temper.

One thing that particularly irritated him was unpunctuality in arriving at meals; and it must be stressed that the latter in pre-war days were extremely formal occasions. Until 1940 there was always in our house a maid waiting at table, and even after that meal times still had a kind of ritualistic aura. Distressing scenes inevitably took place if any of us younger people arrived late; and these occurred with particular frequency during our annual family holidays at North Berwick.

Life was in many ways fairly free during these summer months, and Philip used to spend much of his time at the open air swimming pool, where he was accounted quite a character, making many friends as well as arousing a fair amount of amusement — most of it good-natured. Now, Philip had a bicycle, and there was no reason in the world why he should not have been able to get home in time for the evening meal at seven o'clock — or whenever it was. But time after time, when the family assembled, Philip would be missing. Then, when he eventually arrived stammering terrified apologies, a tempest would rage with words like 'disgraceful' and 'outrageous' filling the air, while the rest of us sat round, our heads bowed in helpless misery.

To me as a child it always seemed incredible that any adult could make such a fuss about what seemed a relatively trivial matter. And from quite an early age I can remember making a silent impassioned vow that never, but never when I was grown up, would anyone complain if people were late for meals. (Here, of course, fate got its revenge on me, for my beloved husband used to arrive in the evenings at a range of times that varied between about six o'clock and half-past ten! — though, to be fair, seldom without warning.)

On the whole I was less often the object of my father's wrath, although I was incessantly scolded for not being sufficiently respectful and polite. It always struck me as unfair that comments that were perfectly in order if made by adults to children, were considered rude if it was the other way round. And trouble often arose because my father, no doubt from genuine interest, would like to cross-question me in a style that belonged more to his legal life. In particular, when a subject was under general discussion, he would turn to me and ask: "Now, what do young people of your age think about this?" And I, thrawn little creature that I was, would reply: "I can't tell you what other people of my age think, only what I think" — which was of course accounted extremely rude.

And occasionally there were more serious breaches. One happened on an Easter Sunday when I was about twelve. The family had attended High Mass at Edinburgh's Roman Catholic Cathedral in Broughton Street; and when we emerged, and were standing on the steps in full view of the large crowd assembled outside, my father had insisted on embracing us all. As a self-conscious pre-teenager I found this so acutely embarrassing that when it came to my turn I actually ducked. And this caused a row of unbelievably monumental proportions. I was ordered to apologise; and, when I refused to do so, I was told that my father would not speak to me again until I did. Even at the time I could see that this was a foolish tactic on the part of my parents, because they were boxing themselves into a corner. Sad as it may seem now, I didn't really care whether he spoke to me or not, and was quite ready to leave things like that. And I'm ashamed to say that after about a week it was my parents who eventually gave way: the avowed reason being that a very old friend was coming to visit us, and that it would be uncomfortable for him to see me in disgrace. (At the time, I secretly swore another of those fervent oaths, to the effect that I would never make a similar threat to my children. Nor did I.)

All this gives such a depressing picture that I should like to try to redress the balance a little. For there are happier memories: among them of my father reading aloud to me from a variety of books. Early on these were often 19th-century children's classics, such as R.M. Ballantyne's *Coral Island* and *Masterman Ready*, the books of Captain Marryat, or *The Swiss Family Robinson*. The latter we used sometimes to enjoy sending up; in particular, the invariable way in which the narrator, the family's Papa, never misses the opportunity to point a moral. On the lines of: "See, Fritz, how the Almighty has arranged for this insignificant-looking plant to grow, just where its juice can provide all the nourishment required to meet our family's present needs, while your mother will be able to make sun-hats out of its leaves. Truly we must all give thanks to God for His Providence."

Later we turned to Kipling and Stevenson — including not only the inevitable *Treasure Island* and *Kidnapped* but the much less well known *Weir of Hermiston* and *St.Ives* — and to Dickens. Here I remember my father particularly relishing the American scenes in Martin Chuzzlewit; these he may have rendered in a quite inauthentic transatlantic accent, but I was perfectly happy. And one interesting point about these reading sessions is that they were among our relatively few shared family activities, for my mother also loved reading aloud. Her choice of books was in some ways different from

**Me aged about 18 months with
my father (then well into his fifties).**

his — it included the books of George Eliot, Mrs Gaskell and Charlotte M.Yonge — but they were both great lovers of Dickens and would often take turns in reading when we were in the midst of one of his novels.

One childhood enthusiasm of mine that, rather surprisingly, my father fully shared was for A.A.Milne's Winnie-the-Pooh books. He must have been over sixty when he first met them, but he had succumbed completely to their magic, and I think he read the stories almost as often as I did. My dearly adored teddy bear was needless to say called 'Pooh'; and I still have a letter, stamped and postmarked, that my father wrote and despatched at some point to: "Pooh Bear Esq., c/o Miss Margaret Moncrieff, 8 Abbotsford Crescent, Edinburgh." My father also liked listening to music in the evenings — from time to time, that is, and when the mood so took him. When I was a small child the music was provided by the wind-up gramophone — a smart red model that was possibly the latest thing at the time; and there was quite a large collection of records, all of course the old '78s', which had to be turned over or changed at approximately four-and-a-half minute intervals.

Beethoven was among my father's favourites; especially the Kreutzer Sonata slow movement, which at about the age of eight I can remember hearing in the distance as I lay in bed, and being even at that age entranced by its beauty. Chopin was another composer he particularly enjoyed; and he also liked to hear great stretches of Wagner's Lohengrin and Tannhauser — despite being almost fanatically anti-German in his sympathies. Later, when my piano playing reached a certain standard, I would sometimes be required to play from the piano transcriptions of these and other operas — a task that I actually enjoyed.

Turning to something more unexpected: my father as a much younger man had been an active and accomplished mountaineer and, along with one of his oldest and life-long friends, had tackled many of the major peaks in the Scottish Highlands. The two used to go off together for several days on end; and there is an amusing tale of their arrival for supper at some Highland farm where they were spending the night. Here they had quickly demolished large platefuls of scrambled eggs and, still hungry, had enquired if there could be a second helping. To which the good lady had kindly agreed, simply asking: "Would you be needing another dozen each, or maybe a dozen between you?"

This mountaineering activity had of course ceased long before I was born; but I remember that until near the end of his life my father enjoyed walking, and especially at night. This my mother found rather strange; but occasionally I was allowed to accompany him. And I know that it was he who first pointed out to me the beauties of the night sky, and taught me the names of some of the constellations.

Looking back, I realise that unquestionably my father was a good, generous and deeply kind man. Sensitive, highly intelligent and possessed of a lively sense of humour, he had a considerable gift for writing poetry — including translations from Greek, Latin and French; he played golf until quite late in life, and one of his preferred leisure-time occupations was reading detective stories. Here, the novels of Dorothy L.Sayers would have been at the top of his list. He also was a great admirer of P.G.Wodehouse.

Today it often strikes me that, had things turned out a little differently, he and I might have been friends. And even at the time I realised that he commanded, not only respect, but much affection from friends and colleagues and from relatives in the wider family. Among them my cousins Agnes, Hope and Noel, who were the daughters of his eldest brother Hugh Moncrieff. They, as children in the early years of the 20th century, were devoted to 'Uck-Sa' — the contraction of 'Uncle Sandy' which was their special name for him. And I remember in more recent years, probably in the late 1980s, talking about this to Noel, the youngest sister (born 1896), who of the three was my special friend. She spoke of her great and abiding affection for my late father, whom she described as "A darling"; adding, however, with a wry smile "But he was a very difficult man!"

A specially poignant memory of my father is of a remark he made to me during his last illness. I had been summoned by telegram to hasten back home from Paris where I was studying, and one afternoon I was standing awkwardly by his bedside, uncertain what to say or do. He opened his eyes, reached out a hand and murmured "Oh, it's you, dear" — having obviously expected it to be my mother. After a pause he added unexpectedly: "I've always admired you very much." And the only reply I could think of was "and I, you." Which was true. But it struck me even at the time as being such a sad exchange between a dying father and his only daughter. His was the first death I had ever witnessed. He had been in a coma for some days, and the characteristic death-rattle breathing had begun. But then, barely a minute before he died, his eyes suddenly opened wide and he looked round at us all with apparent recognition. It seems this is not uncommon in the actual moment of death.

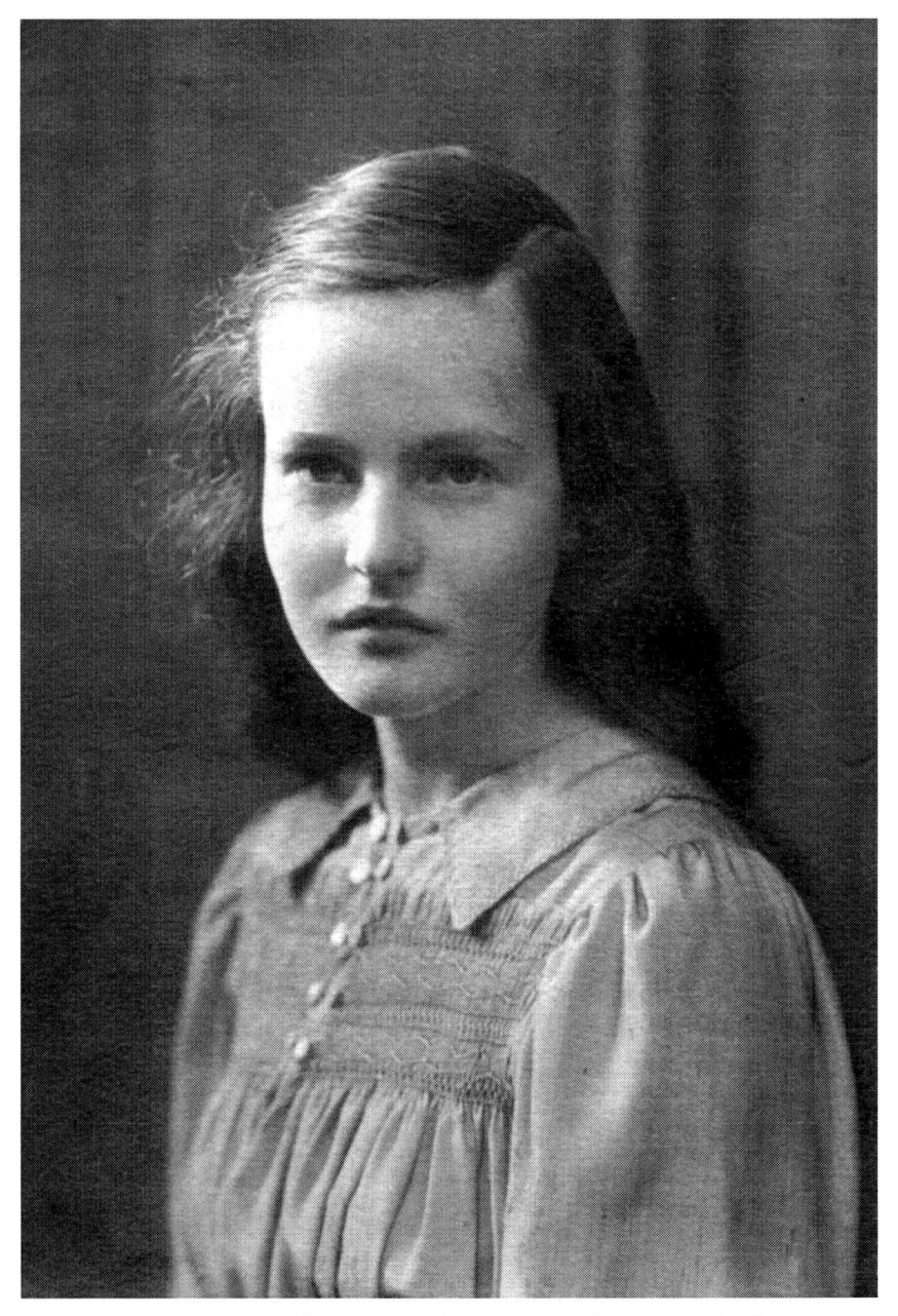

Me at around 13 (the smock was made by my mother).

III: The World of Convent Schools

TURNING BACK NOW TO THE EARLY STAGES of my education: my mother had decided that I was too fragile a blossom for school at the statutory age of five, and to begin with I was taught at home by governesses. Nor was I exactly pushed: I must have been seven before I was taught to read and write. To read and write *words*, that is. At less than five I had begun learning to read music in a small class, run by a formidable old lady with elastic-sided boots — or so my father always described her. She was named Miss Marian P. Gibb, and she taught by a method known as *Chassevent*, called after the French woman who had devised the system. For these classes we had to climb countless stairs to Miss Gibb's flat, perched high among the rooftops of Dundas Street in north Edinburgh; and I have vague memories of sitting at a cream-coloured table with music staves painted on it, and putting little black metal notes of various rhythmic values onto the staves. *Chassevent* had things in common with the much better known *Solfa* system, but differed from this in using not only the moveable *Doh* but the *Doh minor* scale — something considered highly controversial in certain quarters.

Since this is not a musical treatise it would be pointless to discuss the ins and outs of the matter here. But Mademoiselle Chassevent's method did unquestionably work. By five I was already reading music with fair fluency; although when it came to the singing which concluded all our sessions, I always, to my extreme embarrassment, had to be taught the *words* of the songs beforehand. (More than fifty years later I discovered that another, slightly older member of the little group had also been unable to read, but neither of us had the comfort of knowing about the other at the time.)

My schooldays as such didn't begin till I was almost eight years old.

Then, during the next eight-and-a-half to nine years I attended three different Edinburgh convent schools, though two of them only briefly; and I also spent a short period boarding at St Mary's Convent, Ascot. The time there was a mixed experience, but I did learn much of value; and by extending my horizons beyond the rather narrow Edinburgh scene, this undoubtedly played a significant part in my all-round development. (Later I was to establish a genuinely affectionate relationship with St Mary's, where I taught cello between 1952 and 1958, and frequently gave concerts with my husband and our piano trio.)

As well as gracing these various institutions, I also at one point, before the war when my parents were travelling abroad, was sent for a short while to board at a small school that was situated on the East Lothian coast near Dunbar. The head of this was Mrs Claudia Shelley, who (as mentioned in a earlier section) had chosen, when left as a single parent, to run a school in order to support herself and her young daughter Jean, who was my friend. This was my first real-life encounter with any kind of boarding-school, but it was hardly typical since the school numbered barely twenty pupils, only a handful being boarders. On the other hand, St Columba's, with its near-family atmosphere, bore a certain resemblance to the early stages of Elinor Brent-Dyer's fictional Chalet School — of which I had become a devotee at that time. The fictional and real-life schools did share various characteristics, including a similar touch of old-fashioned formality in, for example, the relationship between staff and pupils. It would never have crossed the mind of any girl to use a teacher's first name, though some did have nicknames in accordance with school-story traditions; I feel sure, too, that the staff always addressed each other in public as 'Miss' or 'Mrs'. My memory of lessons, sitting round a table with a group of not more than eight or nine girls of mixed ages, also fits very much into the world of the early Chalet School stories. And on one occasion we actually held one of those typical school-story events, a midnight feast. Ours, however, was not unauthorised but official: it was attended by both Mrs Shelley and her assistant-mistress, as well as by numerous day-girls who were invited to spend the night on a random array of mattresses, lilos and camp-beds. We were all sent to bed at the normal time — probably not later than 8.30pm in those days — to be awakened on the stroke of midnight in order to don dressing-gowns and slippers and join in the fun.

On a different level, a memory endures of the evening when

Claudia Shelley, who always made a goodnight visit to the boarders, read aloud Francis Thompson's poem, *The Hound of Heaven*, to Jean and me as we lay in bed. She prefaced her reading by saying that, even if we did not understand it all, she thought we would gain something from hearing the poem. And the fact that I still recall this vividly, more than sixty-five years on, suggests she was right.

All round, I found this brief boarding-school experience enjoyable, and learnt quite a lot from it; especially from contact with Jean, who was a stimulating, if occasionally abrasive character. An only child, who had spent most of her early life with adults and had for some years lived abroad, Jean was a little younger than me, being barely ten and a half; but in the modern phrase she was far more street-wise. She had considerable self-assurance and a complete lack of shyness, along with a splendid capacity for plain speaking. If Jean didn't approve of your clothes or hair-style, or your course of conduct, she would tell you so with total frankness, yet in a matter-of-fact way that, somehow, was not offensive. She is one of the childhood friends with whom I much regret having lost touch after we grew up.

One way and another I had the opportunity during more than eight years of formal education to sample quite a wide spectrum of scholastic establishments, and to wear four or five different school uniforms. At an early point these even included the archetypal navy-blue gym tunic, with its loose girdle, flat yoke, and box-pleats back and front; it was worn with a plain white blouse, and stockings of heavy black cotton, in what was known as 'gym length' — viz. reaching almost to the top of the thigh, and meeting up with one's navy-blue cotton knickers. The stockings were held in place by suspenders, attached to the rubber buttons on a white liberty-bodice (and whoever named it a *liberty*-bodice showed a curious sense of humour, as it was a decidedly constricting garment — especially for someone who began to develop a bust as early as ten years old).

The wearing of hats was another thing compulsory at almost all girls' schools in those days (and the custom persisted until many years after the second World War). Hats inflicted on me included the standard black velour (pudding-basin type) that was worn in the winter and spring terms; then in summer it was the panama straw (ditto). Both were wide-brimmed, of a depth akin to giant candle-snuffers, and were encircled round the crown with a band in the school colours, ornamented with a badge or crest. Fortunately the hat-styles were common to many schools and the bands and school-badges could be changed, which saved my mother from having to buy new hats every time I moved to another establishment, as seemed to happen quite frequently at the early stages. It seems I was removed from the first school because I'd begun to acquire an Edinburgh accent . . . while the second school moved away from Edinburgh a year after I went there.

Viewing my education as a whole, the school where I spent longest, and continued to visit regularly until leaving home in 1946 to study in London, was that run by the Sacred Heart nuns at Craiglockhart Convent in the suburbs of Edinburgh (the premises now form part of Napier College).

On the surface this school was not particularly distinguished in either social or academic terms. But it must be remembered that my parents were restricted in their choice by the fact that we were Roman Catholics. Both my father and mother were converts: my mother, who had grown up in the Church of England, was received into the Catholic Church around 1911, a year or so after the death of her first husband; my father who, like all the Moncrieffs, was brought up a Presbyterian, did not join the Catholic Church until more than ten years after he married my mother. Of the two, my mother wore the change more easily — probably it was a less radical upheaval for her. My father had previously been decidedly anti-Catholic, and seemingly had fought a tough personal battle before making the change. Afterwards, as can sometimes happen, he tended to be, perhaps not *more* but at least *as* Catholic as the Pope. In other words, fairly hard line.

Other parents belonging to the upper middle class might have chosen to request the necessary dispensation for me to attend a non-Catholic and more socially upmarket school. This permission could have been obtained without much difficulty; but they had finally decided on Craiglockhart — simply taking for granted at the time that I should, like my much older half-sister, be going on to boarding school when I was twelve or thirteen. And of course Craiglockhart was convenient — the bus that ran through the part of Edinburgh where we lived to the gates of the convent passed the end of our road, barely two minutes walk from the house. Even as a nine-year-old I was allowed, overprotected as I undoubtedly was in childhood, to make the journey to school alone.

Craiglockhart was probably typical of the *day*-schools run by the nuns of the Sacred Heart order at that period. (There were then significantly different aspects to their far more fashionable boarding-schools, and those who have read Antonia White's acclaimed *Frost in May* should remember that it describes a convent boarding-school in the years **before** World War I.) The regime at Craiglockhart was fairly strict; but I, unlike some of those who've written about convent schools in the past, remember nothing to indicate that it was specially repressive. I did spend much of my first year at the school being, as I saw it, regularly picked on by the nun in charge of our class, who appeared to have taken a particular dislike to me and often managed to make life quite unpleasant. But this is something by no means peculiar to convent schools: it can, and does happen in schools of every kind and period (both my daughters had similar experiences in more recent times, and neither of these involved nuns).

However, there were in those days accepted formalities that might strike today's children as extraordinary. For instance, we always curtsied to the Reverend Mother and to other high-ranking dignitaries, both from inside and outside the convent; and it goes without saying that doors were punctiliously held open for any teacher entering or leaving the classroom, while pupils would stand to attention by their desks. Girls progressing from one place to another did so in line — or rather, in what was called a file. This file would wait silently (at least, that was the theory) until the superintending nun gave the signal to move, which she did by clicking the small wooden box that was carried by all the nuns (I've no idea what its specific function was).

Then each week, on Monday morning, a ritual took place known as Notes. For this the whole school assembled in the hall; and there, before all, a verdict would be read out, class by class, summarising the conduct of each girl during the previous week. There were three categories: the first and second, Very Satisfactory and Satisfactory, were ordinary enough, but the third was the dreaded Indifferent — a term that may arise in the French origins of the Sacred Heart order (along with others, e.g. files and Notes, as already mentioned). And on these occasions it wasn't just conduct that was signalled out for comment: each week, distinctions called *The Cross for Class* were awarded, two in each form, one for English and one for French. These were real silver crosses, Celtic style; but whether they were allotted on the basis of the highest standard of work, or of the greatest effort made, remains a mystery to me.

There were too the 'Orals' — public examinations, which happened twice-yearly. Here, each class in turn, and every pupil, would be questioned in every subject. Standing up before the entire school was quite an ordeal; but the experience provided was valuable (especially for anyone later entering a performing career).

None of this was unusual for a convent school of the period. But at Craiglockhart we were unexpectedly favoured in some respects: for one, the building had originally been a hydropathic hotel, and although the older part betrayed its age, there were modern additions, and both building and grounds were extensive. The facilities even included a gymnasium of reasonable size and an indoor swimming-pool. More importantly, the convent also ran a teacher-training college in the same premises, and a number of the highly qualified lecturers on the college staff also did some teaching in our school (which must have been 'slumming it' from their point of view). Among them was a learned nun, author of several books, whose methods of teaching history were far ahead of her time. Not for her pupils the conventional syllabus restricted to *English* history: nor did we suffer the fate of poor Elfrida in Nesbit's *The House of Arden*, who was "always having to go back to the Wars of the Roses, because of the new girls". Instead, from quite an early stage, and following some glimpses of the ancient world, we learnt both European and Scottish history — the latter, oddly enough, was seldom taught in any detail at Scottish schools of that era (as later on my husband would testify). Of course our teacher, belonging as she did to an order of nuns that was then strictly enclosed, was unable to accompany us on expeditions round historic Edinburgh; but her lessons did inspire many of us to go off and explore our native city with much enthusiasm, and even a certain amount of knowledge.

We were also fortunate for some years in being taught both English and Latin (a good combination) by a lay teacher of remarkable personality. Stella Urquhart was one of those teachers who seem never to have a problem with discipline. She could capture the attention of the most apathetic class, and she was notably gifted in the making of nicely turned deflating comments. The memory still lingers of one, in her immaculate handwriting, below an exercise I had probably dashed off without much care: it ran: "Apparently your main concern is to complete your homework with the least possible trouble to yourself" —

ouch!

Never, that I can recall, did Miss Urquhart use the term 'Good' — let alone 'Very Good'; her highest praise being 'Promising', or the still more rarely achieved 'Very Promising'. Her English lessons were always stimulating and they contributed significantly to my interest in writing; while her punctilious training in grammar and construction (in English as well as in Latin) undoubtedly laid excellent foundations, greatly influencing my own ideas. I owe her a lot.

To digress for a moment: the whole approach to teaching English in schools was to undergo wholesale changes during the decades that separated my own schooldays from those of my daughters in the late '60s and 1970s, and to alter yet more drastically in recent years. Not only have those little matters of grammar, spelling and punctuation become ever less important, but the teachers of my day would have reeled in astonishment at the choice of certain titles among the set books that are now considered appropriate for GCSE and A-level students. **We** had even been provided with specially edited *school* versions of Shakespeare which, although by no means totally Bowdlerised, did have many of the saucier bits removed. And topics that are now the subject of open discussion in English classes would have been categorised in earlier times as quite *unsuitable* — the word always spoken with a certain intonation. However, let no one think that the children of my generation all grew up in total ignorance of the facts of life, or that we never discussed them together in private. At around ten years old I had already learnt the basic facts — though not from my mother, and not, it must be said, with total accuracy. The full details were only revealed later in a book I found buried high up in my father's library, when on one occasion I had been sent up a ladder to dust the top shelves — a task that took rather a long time . . .

Turning back to Craiglockhart: the school had no magazine to provide writing opportunities, but we did, about once a term, hold what was grandly called a 'Literary Meeting'. Before these occasions, a theme was set and we were required to submit papers under pseudonyms. These were read aloud at the meeting by one of the nuns (she also produced our plays, and she had the most amazingly mobile eyebrows, which used to disappear completely into the headband of her veil at dramatic moments). Votes were then taken and the winner announced. And the future **Helen McClelland** was twice awarded the most votes: on the first occasion it was for a Christmas story; on the other, for a piece on the unlikely sounding subject of *Civium Vires Civitatis Vis* (the strength of a city lies in the strength of its citizens). Here, I had baulked at the idea of a serious essay, and had turned it all into an allegorical story, which, in the event, was much preferred by the audience to the more sober contributions!

As regards other subjects, memory would suggest that the teaching of French at Craiglockhart was above average for a small Scottish school of that era. With the result that, unlike some of my Edinburgh contemporaries who had attended more fashionable schools, I felt reasonably at home when first visiting France after the war. However, the teaching of Maths was fairly disastrous! Only by having outside coaching did I manage to struggle through the papers in Arithmetic, Algebra and Geometry, that were compulsory then for candidates taking any examination that would admit them to university.

Craiglockhart's facilities for games were also limited. In the winter and spring terms we played netball, a game which I, unlike many of my contemporaries, rather enjoyed. And we had regular matches with other Edinburgh schools — which we usually lost. Then, in the summer, we played rounders, and we could in theory play tennis, for there were several courts in the convent grounds. But since the school had no official games-mistress we never had any proper coaching; and we were only occasionally allowed to use the swimming-pool referred to earlier, for this was mainly the territory of the training-college students.

Altogether things were quite amateurish as regards any form of sport or athletics. On the other hand we were given plenty of scope in drama; the convent premises included a little theatre with a proper stage, and plays were regularly produced by a nun of both enthusiasm and some expertise. We were also encouraged — in fact expected — to memorise and speak poetry aloud.

At no point in my schooldays was I ever a model pupil. Indeed, my daughters recall gleefully that when, many years on, I was giving a concert at St. Mary's School in Ascot, an elderly nun sitting beside them was heard to murmur: "Well, well — and to think she's turned out like this, when she was always *such* a naughty little girl!" Not that my transgressions were spectacular, especially when compared with those of some tearaway pupils today. But I had a certain non-conformist streak, and individualists don't always fit comfortably into a school regime. I was continually in trouble for such things as failing to hand in work on the appointed day, or for talking at the wrong time and in the wrong place; and, if ever it happened that a group of girls was enjoying an illicit bout of giggles, without fail I would be the only one who was still laughing when the teacher walked in. It also took me many painful years to acquire the art of phrasing things diplomatically, and my remarks and comments often sounded more unvarnished than I intended; with the result that I was forever being scolded for rudeness.

There was, too, the occasion when I was caught playing quite unsuitable music on the chapel organ (I think it was *Somewhere Over the Rainbow*). But many of my misdeeds fell only into the category of relatively harmless mischief; of a type that can seem pretty silly from an adult perspective, though sometimes quite entertainingly described by school-story authors. Many years later I was to write a story, *Visitors for the Chalet School*, that would include a fake nose-bleed episode and a duel with needles that are both events founded on real life. One, however, that has not appeared in fiction, and had led at the time to the most appalling row, occurred when a friend and I decorated one of the convent staircases with festoons of toilet paper — purloined from a WC on the nearby landing. Sadly, we were quite unable to convince an outraged nun-headmistress that the fact of its being *lavatory* paper had simply not entered our heads — it had just been such fun to see the rolls unwinding over the banisters. She clearly didn't believe us, and I recall the word **disgusting** being freely used.

Of course I did also have a fiery temper; and among my worst crimes was to storm out of a singing class, noisily banging the door, when I'd been wrongly accused by the nun in charge of causing some minor disturbance. That episode had dire consequences, and I was excluded from all singing-classes for the next two terms. And yes — I did mind, because although that particular nun could be a pain, she was an excellent teacher, and to date I'd always enjoyed her classes.

Not surprisingly my school-fellows would have collapsed in raucous laughter had anyone suggested that I was in any way 'religious'; but I can now see clearly that firm foundations of religious belief were being laid throughout those years at Craiglockhart. No one goes through life unscathed, but I have often been grateful for the strong grounding we were given in the basic doctrines of the Roman Catholic Church. Of course, certain observances have changed since the Second Vatican Council in the 1960s — many of them to my mind greatly for the better. I am for instance an enthusiastic supporter of Mass in English, and of Saturday and Sunday evening Masses. Also, having spent much of my early life among non-Catholics, I appreciate the far more tolerant attitude shown today by the Catholic Church towards those of different religious faiths and denominations.

On the other hand, I'm glad to have grown up at a time when it was always stressed, in relating to the clergy, that it was not the individual personality of a priest that mattered. Certainly the maxim current in those days that one reverenced the *office*, not necessarily the man, has made it possible over the years to accept with equanimity many priests who were not in themselves particularly sympathetic or enlivening characters.

It's true that I would in my youth have seen little to be said in favour of nuns; and true that we convent schoolgirls would quite often scoff at the various pious customs we were encouraged to observe. One that's frequently derided nowadays is the practice of 'offering up' to God disappointments, pain or whatever, for some good cause. Here, I would today agree that when 'offering up' becomes an excuse for inertia and for not taking action to change those things that can and *should* be changed, it will be a negative force. But with those inevitable things in life that can *not* be changed, the attitude engendered can be entirely positive. Certainly the way in which religion and prayer were woven into daily life at Craiglockhart (also, in a different way, at St Mary's Ascot) was something we absorbed unconsciously. Something that, for many of us, would remain there in the background throughout our lives, out of sight at times, but never quite forgotten.

Today it is hard to visualise how isolated a Roman Catholic child from the upper-middle class could sometimes feel when growing up in the Edinburgh of that period. Few of the Edinburgh friends I was encouraged — you could say *allowed* — to know socially were Roman Catholics. Certainly none of my musical friends were, and by the time I was twelve music was becoming increasingly important in my life. Besides, at that far-gone time, attitudes in Edinburgh were often pronouncedly anti-Catholic, and to an extent that now seems incredible. One of my early memories concerns a Roman Catholic priest, a family friend, who used often to stay with us; one day he returned to the house with bruised and bleeding shins, having been assaulted in the street and kicked by a gang who allegedly belonged to an anti-Catholic group called the 'Protestant Action Society'. I can't date this incident exactly, but it was probably around 1935, hence not all that long ago in historical terms. I can recall, too, that around the same time one of our religious processions at Craiglockhart — in the convent's *own private grounds* — actually had to have police protection. We children found it immensely amusing to see police officers popping up behind the bushes at every turn while we made our way singing demurely around the grounds, but I doubt if the adults shared our amusement.

No wonder, perhaps, that I was moved at one point in my early life to write in enormous chalk letters, unbelievably high up on the convent wall, the words "**TO HELL WITH CORMACK!**" (The leader of the Protestant Action Society, who always received a lot of publicity in the newspapers, was a Mr Cormack. I hope he would have forgiven me.) The actual writing of this slogan was quite a feat, as I had to hang perilously out of a second floor window, reaching down as far as possible and writing upside-down, while my classmates hung tightly onto my legs. And I've always had a great respect for Reverend Mother Gleeson, the head at that time of the convent community: in my innocence I had assumed that, since no one took me to task over the crime, no one could have known who was the culprit. On the contrary it turned out, as Mother Gleeson confided later to my mother, that she had known exactly who was responsible but had considered it wiser to let things lie. (Maybe she had even sympathised secretly . . .)

In a number of ways I benefited from my years at Craiglockhart. And quite enjoyed many things about them; or at least as much as I'd have enjoyed being at any school. For me, schooldays seemed so far from being the best years of my life that, by the age of fourteen or fifteen, I couldn't wait to leave and begin serious musical studies. Not that my parents were enthusiastic about the idea of my taking up music professionally. On the contrary, much head-shaking and tut-tutting took place, and it was incessantly pointed out to me what a dismally insecure life I should have. The importance of my being financially self-supporting in the future was always underlined, as my brothers, in the thinking of those days, were considered to be incapable of earning their own living; and it was heavily stressed that, since no one in our circle of friends and relatives had the smallest influence in the musical world, no one would be able to help in any way to advance my career. Whereas, if only I'd chosen to enter the legal profession, things could have been so different . . . This was a source of particular worry to my mother; but in later life, it actually brings me satisfaction to know that, having arrived on the London musical scene as a complete unknown, anything I may have achieved in music has been gained without the string-pulling of relatives or family-friends — although I gladly acknowledge much invaluable help along the way from teachers and colleagues.

The pressure to take up a more respectable and financially secure career than music might have been even greater, had it not been for an established tradition that existed at the time I was growing up in Edinburgh. This quite approved of nicely brought-up young girls going to study music at the university — a compromise between the artistic and academic worlds that offered advantages from both my own and my parents' points of view. But before coming to the university days, I want to fill in some more general background to that vanished world of my early life.

Self-portrait — my pigtails held up by two friends.

IV: Different Houses, Different People

8 Abbotsford Crescent, Edinburgh

UNLIKE THE POET THOMAS HOOD, I do not "remember the house where I was born". But every detail of our next family home, where I lived consecutively during the time up to September 1946, and returned to regularly throughout the next fifteen years, remains indelibly in my memory.

No 8 Abbotsford Crescent was a typically Edinburgh Victorian villa, solidly built in grey stone, and set in a large garden that was surrounded by six-feet-high stone walls. To attempt a circular tour of the garden by walking along the top of these was a favourite childhood pastime — decidedly hazardous in places, due to overhanging branches.

The house was situated in the residential part of south Edinburgh known as Church Hill — a not surprising name, for there were at that tIme at least fIve churches of various different denominations within quite a small area, the local tram-stop being known as 'Holy Corner'. To present-day ideas 8 Abbotsford Crescent was a huge house: there were seventeen rooms, not counting bathrooms, kitchen, cloakroom, pantries and so on; and the drawing-room was a double room large enough to accommodate, in just one half, two grand pianos and, on one occasion, an entire string orchestra. This room and the other rooms on the south side of the house, including my own bedroom, had the most superb view of the Pentland Hills; and my parents always alleged that they had bought the house for the view alone.

The garden was also extensive, and to me as a child it seemed enormous. The back part was divided into two sections, with that nearest the house containing a lawn considerably bigger than a tennis-court, surrounded and punctuated by gravel paths and flower-beds. There was an abundance of colourful shrubs that included three glorious lilac bushes. Numerous large trees lined the walls and paths — among them sycamores, yew trees, willows, hawthorn, laburnum and holly; and a weeping ash was picturesquely placed on a small hillock which, come springtime, would be carpeted with snowdrops and multi-coloured crocuses.

Behind this main part lay a further stretch of ground, not quite as large, but of a size that would later, in the 1960s, provide the site for an independent house to be built with its own garden of comfortable proportions. Here, too, there were trees along the back wall; mainly white poplars and limes, as well as the inevitable sycamores that were a feature of all the local gardens. Also a number of apple trees, which regularly each autumn were stripped of their fruit by local lads, who would climb over the back wall during the family's absence on holiday (suggesting that some minor forms of juvenile delinquency are not confined to the present day).

At the back of the main garden, and bordering on the road behind, were some extensive stone outbuildings; including, besides a garage, a sizeable block that had originally been the stables. This contained a large area with two loose boxes, a harness-room, and a coach house complete with grooves on the floor to accommodate the carriage-wheels. The garage was of a later date, and had a pit to enable examination of a car's nether regions. In our day, though, it was used only for storage, as my parents never owned a car. It was rather dank and spider-ridden; but the stables were a children's paradise, and provided the setting for endless imaginary games. Some of these were shared with my friends, but due to family circumstances a good deal of my childhood was spent alone, and many happy though solitary hours were passed in the Abbotsford Crescent garden.

To this day I cannot smell new-mown grass without immediately being carried back there: at that time the grass was always cut with a hand-propelled lawn-mower, which must have taken ages; and the gardener would empty out the cut grass as he went along and pile it up in heaps, rather like little hayricks. These would then be left until all the grass was finished, when they would be bundled into a wheel-barrow and taken to the compost heap at the far back of the garden.

Until World War II the running of the Abbotsford Crescent

household had required not only three resident maids — designated respectively cook, table-maid and housemaid — but also the daily services of a man to stoke the wonderfully old-fashioned boiler, a twice-weekly gardener, and weekly visits by a man who wound the clocks. Hard to believe in the latter, but I remember him well — he always came on Wednesdays. Nor is he the only relic of a bygone age to figure in my early memories: a less attractive recollection is of the chamber-pots that used in those days to lurk under every bed. They were regularly used too, by both adults and children, and it was an accepted part of the housemaid's daily routine to empty them each morning. Then, in addition to this large house in Edinburgh, the family, or to be more exact my mother, owned a house at North Berwick on the East Lothian coast. This wasn't at all grand, but it too was remarkably commodious; our extended family used to foregather there every summer and the house was capable of squeezing in around fourteen people.

Now, the above descriptions may well give an exaggerated idea of my parents' wealth. They were of course not badly off: my father, as a Judge of the Court of Session, had what was probably for those days quite a handsome salary, but it amounted to far less than the sums earned by, for example, successful barristers or business men. My mother did have some money of her own, inherited from *her* mother, but my father had nothing apart from his salary (when he died in 1949 there was less than a hundred pounds in his bank account), and he had few material possessions of any value. Both the Edinburgh and North Berwick houses belonged in fact to my mother — the latter having been her property before she and my father married. But the crucial point to remember is that, throughout their lives, my father and mother were constantly agonising about the future of my two brothers, since they were thought in those days to be incapable of earning any kind of living for themselves. Certainly much of my parents' income must always have gone towards the cost of supporting these two in various establishments. (That their lives in the end turned out so much better than anyone could ever have hoped, happy as they were in the enlightened care of the St. Aidan's Community near Melrose, was something that, sadly, my parents didn't live to see.)

Going back to No 8 Abbotsford Crescent: before the war my parents had led quite an active social life, and I can remember the dinner-parties that used to take place regularly. Everyone of course

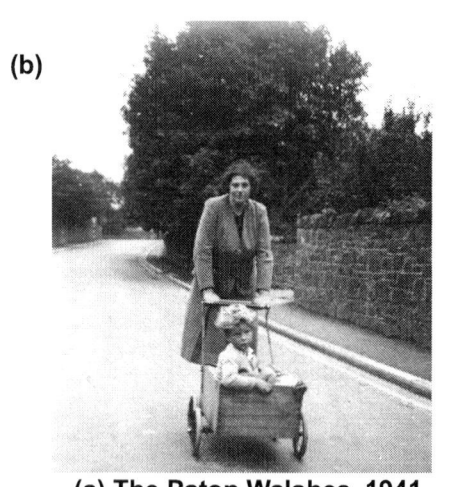

(a) The Paton Walshes, 1941.
(b) Meecie with John in trek-cart, 1945.
(c) and (d) 'Ghillie Dhu' and 'Wisp'.
(e) My mother in the garden, mid-1930s.
(f) 1939 Family production of 'Snow White' — me as the wicked witch.

used to change for dinner — not just for dinner parties, either, but *every evening*; the men were resplendent in dinner-jackets and what were known as 'boiled shirts' (stiff-fronted white shirts); the ladies wore long evening gowns, complemented by their jewellery. As a child, I used to hang pyjama-clad over the banisters on the top floor where my bedroom was to watch the grown-ups arrive in their finery. Also to await the delicious morsels from the evening's menu that one of the maids would always smuggle upstairs for me. Among them such delights as *Devils on Horseback* (prunes encased in bacon), and home-made loganberry ice cream, which was one of the cook's specialities.

During my childhood, the inhabitants of the house also included a number of cats and dogs. Both my parents were specially attached to a breed of dog that's not much seen nowadays, the Dandy Dinmont; and two of these — known respectively as 'Wisp' and 'Dusty Puff' — are among my early memories. The former showed a curious predilection for eating sweet peas: in summer my father often wore a small nosegay of these in his buttonhole, and when he was reclining on a deck-chair in the garden, Wisp, to the astonishment of visitors, used to jump on top of him in order to seize and gobble up the flowers.

The cats were a mixed bunch. One in the mid-1930s was originally given the name *Hitler*, due to the small oblong black moustache that stood out strikingly on its white muzzle. But 'Hitler' then went and produced kittens . . . (an interesting thought). Later — in fact during the war — we had a very beloved black cat whom I insisted on naming *Ghillie Dhu* — at the time I had a huge enthusiasm for all things Celtic, and this is of course the Gaelic for Black Boy. Ghillie used to sleep on, and in winter frequently *in* my bed, which would probably have horrified my mother had she known. Sadly, he developed some kind of internal blockage and died at less than four years old; he was buried in the garden by a tearful group which was even joined by my father.

(Today, having grown up as I did in a household where pets were important, I've always regretted that it wasn't practicable for our children to enjoy this valuable experience. But, with professional engagements quite frequently taking both my husband and myself away from home, it was often hard enough to make reliable temporary arrangements for two little girls, without complicating the matter with animals.)

Right through the first months of the war the same pattern of life continued. Then, with the summer of 1940, everything changed. The three maids departed, probably to do war work, but in any case I remember being told we could no longer afford to keep them. They were replaced by an 20-year-old girl whose job it was to clean the house as far as possible, while my mother took over the cooking, catering and everything else. I think a gardener must still have come occasionally, even if it was only to mow the very considerable amount of grass; and of course my mother was herself an enthusiastic gardener. Efficient, too: at one point, in response to the national appeal to "Dig For Victory", she launched into growing onions, cabbages and lettuces in some of the former flower-beds. But I think things were left to run fairly wild in the extensive back part of the garden, which was mercifully well out of sight from the house.

Characteristically, my mother tackled her new life with undaunted energy and a willingness that was totally admirable. She was by this point in her sixties, and she had not been brought up to lift a finger for herself around the house. Unless she wanted to, that is. Not that she had ever been idle. Inactivity was something she positively disliked, and, as described earlier, she had always found plenty of occupations to fill her days. (Interestingly, though, and un-typically of her generation and class, she had never shown the smallest interest in playing Bridge — a favourite pastime then for well-born ladies, with Afternoon Bridge Parties, at which discreet small amounts of money would change hands, being a regular feature of social life.)

With the coming of war, my mother had immediately joined the Women's Voluntary Service (now WRVS); and very smart she looked in the Norman Hartnell-designed uniform — a tailored coat and skirt in green herringbone tweed, worn with a dark pink blouse and a stylish green hat. She had also, by the spring of 1940, become much involved with the Polish Relief Fund and other Polish organisations. As a result of this our house soon became a meeting place for Poles of all sorts, ages and descriptions. In those days tea-time on Sunday afternoon was generally considered to be a sort of open house; and both during and before the war — indeed as far back as I can remember — we had a stream of regular callers who used to descend at about four o'clock.

Even as a child I was expected to take part in these (frequently rather dreary) gatherings, and to make polite conversation to the visiting adults. These ranged from representatives of the legal profession of varying degrees of distinction or otherwise to clerics (ditto) from several of the Roman Catholic churches in Edinburgh; relatives, who either lived in or were visiting Edinburgh; ladies who perhaps worked on committees with my mother; and the occasional caller who was actually under thirty, including one young man with an unusually high-pitched voice, unkindly known behind his back as "Squeaky Boy".

The Polish visitors also encompassed a wide variety: one who came with particular regularity was a worthy middle-aged Colonel, a colleague of my mother's on the Polish Relief Fund Committee; but another was a glamorous and highly entertaining Count, a man of both practised and natural charm, with whom conversation presented no problems. He once made a splendid analogy to illustrate the diametrically opposed thinking-processes (as he saw things) of Russians and other nations. "You and I . . . " he said, gesturing expressively with his hands . . . "We may disagree about whether two and two actually make four, but we shall argue in numbers. Now, for a Russian two and two may make anything . . . " he glanced round the room and pointed towards the fire . . . "Perhaps, the mantelpiece?"

My mother was to keep on the Abbotsford Crescent house until her death in October 1961. And although after I departed from Edinburgh in 1946 to study — first in London and then in Paris — it was never again my permanent home, I used regularly to visit it; latterly with my husband and our elder daughter, and sometimes to spend quite long periods there. In the meantime the house saw many changes, for in 1949, when my mother was left alone after my father's death, she was advised to re-arrange things so that each of the three floors in the house could provide independent living-quarters. From then onwards the middle and lower floors were let as furnished flats to various tenants, while my mother occupied the top floor. This scheme helped to provide her with a regular income, while enabling her to retain the use of the handsome double drawing-room and of four other sizeable rooms in addition.

In many ways this was a good arrangement; although, as my mother approached her eighties, the house not surprisingly became more and more dilapidated, with the staircase wallpaper parting company with the wall in many places, cracked and faded paintwork everywhere, and a long-outdated electrical installation. On my last visit there, at Christmas 1960, I actually received a mild shock when I knelt inadvertently on an exposed place in the wiring to one of the drawing-rooms lamps! Altogether that was a somewhat anxious Christmas, for as well as worrying about my mother, I was constantly afraid that disasters would overtake my small daughter Catriona — then an exceedingly active fourteen-month-old toddler.

Picturing the sad state into which the house had declined reminds me of an occasion when I overheard a friend, who had visited my mother towards the end of her life, subsequently giving a highly coloured account of how the whole place had become exactly like Miss Havisham's room in *Great Expectations*, and declaring in particular that the red brocade curtains in the drawing-room had been hanging down in tattered strips. Now, her description was strong on atmosphere and the Dickens reference was entirely apposite. But for me it was invalidated, because it so happens the drawing-room curtains were not red but moss-green, made not from brocade but from heavy furnishing material with stout linings. Moreover that *they*, unlike most things around the house, were still in surprisingly good condition! No — I didn't bother to correct her. But took it as a hint about the importance of not letting imagination run away with the facts.

Eventually, a few months after my mother's death in October 1961, the house at No 8 Abbotsford Crscent was sold to a builder, who then converted it into six flats. Today it's a sobering thought that the smallest of those flats might now sell for about fifteen times the £4000 that was paid in 1962 for the whole house.

Cairnbank, North Berwick

As a child I often envied those families who went on holiday somewhere different each year. For us, the summer months brought a regular repeat of the same ritual: around the middle of July our entire household, domestic staff included, would move in a block from Edinburgh down to the house in North Berwick that my mother had owned since the days of her first marriage. (Perhaps it should be mentioned here, for the benefit of readers south of the border, that *North* Berwick has no direct connection with the English Berwick-on-Tweed, but is a small town about twenty-two miles down the coast from Edinburgh.) Here at North Berwick we would remain throughout the summer until, late in October, there would be a mass return to Edinburgh.

This pattern was tailored to my father's timetable at the Parliament House. The sessions there finished quite early in July, and although they began again well before the end of October, he always spent the first weeks of the new session travelling daily in and out of Edinburgh — a train journey of less than a hour.

But what — someone might ask — happened about my attendance at school? A good question, but not one that anybody who knew my mother would have dreamt of asking. The authorities at Craiglockhart were simply told that "Margaret will not be returning to school until the end of October". Perhaps, had things been as they are today, she would not have been allowed to get away with such dictatorial pronouncements, but no one seems to have objected at the time. (My mother also insisted throughout my first years at Craiglockhart that I should attend school only in the mornings — one result being some noticeable gaps in my geographical knowledge, since Geography for some reason was always timetabled as an 'afternoon subject'.)

Clearly the arrangements for the North Berwick holidays had presented no problems from my parents' point of view. For me, things looked very different. No child likes to be singled out for special treatment; and in the early part of each school year I used to feel hideously conspicuous when I sidled into the classroom more than six weeks after the Christmas term had begun. Catching up with the lessons wasn't in itself a great problem — work used in any case to be set for me to do during the weeks at North Berwick. But socially I was placed in an extremely uncomfortable position. Indeed, it seems that my school-fellows must have been remarkably tolerant, because I've no memories of anyone being unpleasant to me on this score.

To ensure that I didn't fall behind in school-work my mother sometimes made arrangements, especially in the later years, for me to have occasional coaching from a Mr Robin Weir, who was then acting as tutor on a regular basis to the family of North Berwick's local 'Laird', Sir Hew Hamilton-Dalrymple, and could fit me in for a few hours between times. A splendid teacher, and an interesting man who obviously had considerable intellectual gifts, he had suffered the sad experience of having to resign a lectureship at St Andrews University during World War I, simply because his wife was of German origin which had apparently caused much ill feeling. As a result he had buried himself in North Berwick, although it must for him have been an intellectual backwater. For us who were fortunate in being his pupils — and Elsie Hamilton-Dalrymple, now Gibbs, is a lifelong friend — he brought a breadth of vision that could not ordinarily have been expected in a small-town tutor. Not that his methods were orthodox — and I can't help thinking that he might nowadays incur censure for his habit of accompanying his often used phrase, "Let me stimulate you to further efforts!", by jogging one in the ribs with a pencil. But he was unfailingly interesting, and I owe it entirely to him that I was able to pass the necessary mathematics papers when sitting the School Certificate examination (forerunner of today's GCSE). Into the bargain Mr Weir's lessons were always fun, and I enjoyed flirting with him shamelessly — something else that might be discouraged nowadays.

Returning to the North Berwick house itself: Cairnbank (named after the Mr Cairns who had built it towards the end of the 19th century) was remarkably roomy. There were three floors, each containing five or six rooms, those on the top floor being attic-style, with dormer windows and what are called in Scotland comb-ceilings — i.e. sloping. A brick path led to the front door, and this was flanked on either side by hedges of sweet-brier and borders filled with lavender — providing a vivid, undying 'scent memory' for all of us who ever stayed at Cairnbank during the summer months. Another is that of the dark red, wonderfully perfumed roses (a variety known as *Étoile d'Hollande*, that's less frequently seen nowadays) which used to flourish at one side of the front garden; another, of the wallflower and sweet-scented stocks in the border at the other side. Yet another, of the magnificent hedge of multi-coloured sweet peas on the west side of the house, which had to be culled daily to keep it within bounds, the fragrant products then filling vases in all the living rooms.

Undoubtedly the house itself would have struck a present-day family as primitive. Until about a year before the war there was only one bathroom for the entire house; and no electricity, which meant that the only lighting was by gas lamps and candles. Hot water was provided by a large old-fashioned kitchen range, which was also the sole means of cooking. It was fired on solid fuel and the ovens were notably temperamental. Not until some point around 1938 was electricity finally laid on. Then about three years later — probably as a result of the family now having to cope on their own with that kitchen range — a gas cooker and gas-fired water heater were installed.

Needless to say there was no fridge. The one place where perishable food could be stored was a small larder with a stone floor and a fair-sized stone shelf. All right in itself, but since the larder faced south west it didn't remain really cool if the temperatures rose anywhere near the twenties — or seventies, take your choice — as they sometimes do even in the east of Scotland. However, there was a large old-fashioned ice-box: this was worked by the simple method of inserting a huge block of ice into a special compartment, after which the perishables were placed alongside the ice in a sort of roomy cupboard, with a heavy insulated lid being then closed to seal in the cold.

In pre-war days the ice was probably delivered to the house by what is known in Scotland as a message-boy; but later it became one of the tasks allotted to younger members of the family to bicycle into the town and collect the enormous frozen block from the fish shop. And rarely did these blocks fit exactly into the ice-box compartment, often needing to be tailored by hand with a hammer and knife — a somewhat cold, wet task.

Before the war North Berwick had been a thoroughly upmarket resort, favoured by members of the aristocracy and other prominent people. Golf was then one of the great attractions, and North Berwick itself possessed two excellent courses. The championship golf course at Muirfield was only about four miles up the road towards Edinburgh (my father was a member of this); and a mile or so beyond that at Gullane (pronounced by the masses as spelt but by the cognoscenti as *Gill-un*) there were a further three courses.

In the pre-war days we children used often to congregate at the first tee on North Berwick's West Links, watching goggle-eyed as the great ladies and gentlemen, with their clipped accents and smart clothes, set off on their rounds. Names that I still vaguely recall include Lady Diana Duff Cooper, the Duke of Rutland, the Earl of Wemyss, Sir John Simon, Lady Violet Bonham Carter, and her step-mother, the colourful — though by then elderly — Margot Countess of Oxford and Asquith. The latter was rudely nicknamed by my brother Philip "Lady Ox and Ass", which at the time — mid-1930s — we thought hugely amusing.

For children, one of the greatest assets of North Berwick was — and I imagine still is — its dramatic coast. The sea there is thronged with rocks, and islands large and small, but there are also two splendid beaches — the West Bay and the East Bay — which lie on either side of the picturesque old harbour and the rocky peninsula that leads from it. In my young days each bay had its devotees; some preferred the East Bay, with its mixture of smaller sandy stretches and rock pools; our family favoured the West Bay, which has a long unbroken stretch of sand curving round towards the massive rocks at Point Garry, where there used at that time to be the added attraction of a small cave, accessible at low tide.

That the North Berwick coast is without question scenically beautiful is something of which I became consciously aware only in later life. During my childhood, the main attraction for me of our holidays there was the annual arrival of what could almost be called my surrogate family. These were the children of my half-sister and brother-in-law, the Paton Walsh family, and they undoubtedly represented a near equivalent in my life to siblings. There was some age difference, but it was far less than the gap between me and my half-sister and half-brother; and throughout the years this family became my closest and most loved relatives. I used to look forward longingly to their arrival, and shed tears (unusual for me in childhood) when they departed.

There were eventually five of them: Barbara, Petronilla, Veronica, Antony and John; although the last named did not arrive until November 1941, and after a more than five-year gap. With him, and to some extent with his elder brother Antony and with Veronica, — always known as 'Tigger' — it wasn't perhaps until 1946, the year I spent with the Paton Walsh family in their Putney house, that we had the opportunity to become really close. But the eldest two — Barbara and Petronilla — I looked on from their earliest days as particularly cherished sisters.

Barbara was allowed to share my attic bedroom — apart, that is, from one year when we were separated for having apparently talked too long into the nights the previous summer. As a small child she was known as my "little shadow"; and as time passed she and I and Petronilla were able to do many things together. At first this was limited to such gentle pastimes as making sand-pies on the beach, or collecting shells, or hopefully trawling with shrimping nets at low tide. But North Berwick offered plenty of occupations at all sorts of levels, and as time went on we made full use of them. Swimming, of course (intensely cold even during summer in those dark green North Sea waters, but gloriously stimulating). Golf, tennis, cycling and riding (although I think this last probably stopped during the war); rock-scrambling, digging immense sandcastles to be demolished by the incoming tide, exploring the wonderfully varied seashore; and playing all the different beach games that families enjoy. One special favourite was 'French and English' — a splendidly fast team game involving forays across No-Man's land to steal the enemies' 'treasure' (an agreed number of pebbles) and the taking and rescuing of prisoners; and in this we used to be joined by gangs of other children whose families were holidaying in North Berwick. Another ploy used regularly to be organised by one of the parents, an Edinburgh doctor who prided himself on his skills in throwing a ball to impressive heights, and who liked to arrange concentrated sessions of practice in catching. In our family he became known as 'The Black Bat' — a name that obviously originated in Tennyson's poem *Maud*, though I've now forgotten the reason for its choice. It should be mentioned too, in case all this presents a rather over-strenuous picture, that quite a lot of time was spent just sitting on the beach and reading.

At home, we played vicious games of croquet in the garden (croquet brings out malicious streaks in people); and on wet days there were equally high pressure bouts of Racing Demon, or table-tennis matches on the huge dining-room table. Much time was also occupied, both inside and out, in practising hand-stands, particularly in trying to perfect the arts of 'staying-up' and 'going over'. Petronilla and Tigger were the stars.

As the years passed the younger children joined in more and more (these summer holidays continued until 1949); and by the time Barbara and Petronilla were teenagers, the three of us were even allowed to go off on our very own for short expeditions further afield. Looking back this rather astonishes me, for we were in many ways vastly over-protected, and to me this still appears quite daring (perhaps a comment on how life in some respects was safer at that time?). Our first voyage of discovery was in August 1945, when we spent a magical few days in the West Highlands — an area I had always longed to visit. Here we were based at Fort William, in a boarding-house that would fall within the pink-blancmange category — one particularly memorable specimen appeared at High Tea on the first evening — and we made our way around on foot and by public transport. The high points of the trip were two memorable train journeys: first, that between Glasgow and Fort William, when having left Edinburgh at 4.30 a.m. on a morning of heavy rain, and mist that wrapped the carriages in a cotton-wool blanket, there came a dramatic moment. For suddenly, like the curtain rising in a theatre, the mist lifted to reveal a glorious vista of Loch Lomond, which we just happened to be passing at the time. The other was the wonderful West Highland line from Fort William, alongside Loch Eil, past the Jacobite memorial at Glenfinnan where Bonnie Prince Charlie first raised his standard in 1745, and up the west coast to Morar. We'd always heard about the beauty of the white sands of Morar and the view across to Skye. At that time Petronilla and I were both devoted to D.K.Broster's *Flight of the Heron* trilogy, and we could picture the scene as Keith Wyndham lay dying, his life's blood ebbing out across those white sands. We also visited the inland Loch Morar — one of the deepest in Scotland — with its strangely mournful atmosphere. Altogether a memorably enjoyable day; although we had one of the coldest bathes in that lovely jade-green sea that I can ever remember. So much for the supposedly milder climate of the west coast.

On the second occasion — the following year — we were despatched to Orkney to stay with an elderly second cousin who had for many years been the Sheriff of Orkney. In Scotland the office of resident Sheriff is an important one; and although Uncle George, as we called him, had then been retired for a considerable time, he was still a much respected local figure. He was obviously delighted to show off his beloved Orkney to newcomers and tirelessly drove us around, making full use of the impressive network of causeway-roads that had been built during the war to link many of the islands. Through his influence we not only were given a private tour of the magnificent red-stone Cathedral of St Magnus, and were allowed to wander freely among the Standing Stones of Stenness, but had many of the prehistoric tombs and other sites specially opened up for us. This meant that we were able to crawl along the narrow square passage that leads to the interior of Maes Howe and to see its extraordinary domed burial chamber and the runic graffiti; and we were allowed actually to explore the houses and the little winding streets in the Stone Age village of Skarra Brae, which can normally be viewed only from behind a parapet.

We were overawed by the landscapes — especially that amazing three-hundred-feet stack, the Old Man of Hoy. However, much as we were struck by these historical and natural wonders, perhaps the greatest impression of our visit was made by the joint of beef that appeared at Sunday lunchtime: it was enormous by any standards, of proportions that in those days of strict rationing had become a dim memory even to me, and something the younger two could barely recall. Goggle-eyes were also caused at tea-time by the thickness of the butter spread on the slices of home-made fruit loaf. Plainly Uncle George had friends among the farming community.

During our earlier North Berwick holidays the family's beach hut often became our main residence, and a large part of the day would be spent there. We were all extremely hardy and used to swim every day, sometimes right into October — a training in immunity to cold which has stood me in good stead throughout life, for even at its warmest the sea temperature seldom reaches sixteen degrees, and is often substantially lower. But we didn't go to the beach just to swim.

In the very early days we had always returned home for lunch, but later a remarkable person entered our lives who used to organise things so that we were able to spend whole days unbroken on the beach. This was Miss Grace Randall, a woman of enormous character and kindness who had come in 1938 to act as mother's help or nursery governess to the Paton Walsh family. And it seems most appropriate that Grace Randall should have a place of honour in this part of my memoirs, as she always particularly loved the North Berwick holidays and made them very much her own.

To begin with we addressed her politely as Miss Randall, which in no time had been shortened to Meecie; at first only by Antony, who, at the age of two, was then the baby of the family, but soon the name was adopted by everyone, and Meecie she was always to remain.

Grace Monica Randall was not at all the typical mother's help. When she first arrived in the family she was only about 32, but she had already followed several contrasting careers. At one time she had been a social worker at a settlement in the East End; at another had acted as companion to Lady Wood — the second wife of the celebrated Sir Henry Wood, founder of the Promenade Concerts. Meecie had spent a number of years living with the Woods in their house at Chorley Wood in Hertfordshire, and ever afterwards they remained for her Uncle Henry and Aunt Muriel.

Always a colourful raconteuse, Meecie would give vivid pictures of life at the settlement and of Sir Henry Wood's household. Perhaps her stories could be said to have lost nothing in the telling — but they were most amusing. She had, in spite of notably poor health, such a zest for life, which was probably among the secrets of her happy relationships with children. When Meecie was around, nothing was ever allowed to become irksome. Even on the occasion when there was a flood in the back kitchen at Cairnbank, this domestic disaster was somehow transformed into a lively game. My mother used to describe being met by a party of excited children, clad in waterproofs and wellies and bearing mops, lead by a beaming Meecie who assured her: "Don't worry Granny — we're all going to have such fun clearing it up." And if that sounds almost unbearably 'Pollyanna-ish', it was in Meecie's case absolutely spontaneous — and it worked.

Above all Meecie was a notably kind person — though she was quite human enough to enjoy a bout of family gossip from time to time, especially if it was a trifle scandalous! She was to be a mainstay of the extended Paton Walsh family for many years; continuing to take a close interest in everyone's doings until the end of her life. (I'd like to record here, too, the wonderfully devoted way in which Meecie helped to care for, first my father and later my mother, all through their last illnesses — in, respectively, 1949 and 1961.)

During her time at the settlement, Meecie had been an active member of the Girl Guide Movement and had run Brownie packs, Wolf Cubs (as they used to be called), Guide companies and Rangers. Her accounts of taking her East End Guides to camp could have made an entertaining book, and the skills she had herself acquired were put to good use during our North Berwick days. It was she who suggested that instead of just taking a tea-time picnic to the beach as we had always done, it would require only a little organisation to provide and transport a hot lunch every day, that could be eaten either out of doors or in the beach hut, according to the weather.

She set about constructing a wooden trek-cart, with wheels taken from an ancient perambulator she'd found in the garden shed. This splendid little vehicle was then used daily to carry the materials for a full meal for hungry children down to the beach, with the various pots, pans, casseroles or whatever carefully stacked in rows. At the front, there was also just enough room in the early years for John, the youngest of the family, to ride in state — although before long he became too big, being always well-grown for his age.

One other thing should be mentioned — the plays that Meecie

used regularly to organise in the Cairnbank garden. All the younger members of the household took part in these, with even the two- and four-year-olds having some kind of walk-on part. The performances would begin with a series of tableaux, usually on historical themes, followed by a more extended play. All round the most successful production was probably a version of *Cinderella*, in which Meecie and I played the Ugly Sisters, Barbara was the Prince, Petronilla took the title role, Tigger was the Fairy Godmother (in a specially designed dress created by Meecie from blue crepe paper); and Antony, aged about three, was the driver of Cinderella's coach — a wheelbarrow drawn by Meecie, doubled-up and enveloped in a huge brown tablecloth, representing the horse.

The last of the North Berwick holidays took place in the summer of 1949, the year of my father's death; and during the following winter the house was sold. In the ensuing years I have often driven past it, but Cairnbank has now been converted into several flats and the exterior looks quite different today, with modern extended windows replacing the old-fashioned dormers, and a block of garages at the side, occupying what was formerly a large herbaceous border. Sad to say, the lavender bushes and the sweet-brier hedge have vanished from the front garden.

Petronilla (9) and Antony (5) on North Berwick West Beach, 1941.

V: Many Relatives

My father's relatives

EVEN AS A SMALL CHILD I never really knew an aunt or uncle who hadn't already reached their sixties. Both my parents had been the youngest of long families — in my father's case of nine children, in my mother's of eight — and although my own immediate family numbered only five, the span of age difference was similar, or possibly a little wider.

Another result of this elongated family structure was that I never even met my grandparents. Not surprisingly, either, for had they lived all four would have been somewhere in their nineties at the time I was born, with my paternal grandfather not so far from a hundred!

Coming to my father's immediate family: among his five sisters, neither of the two eldest — Jessie, who forsook Presbyterianism to become an Anglican nun, and Hope who married a Mr Haig-Brown and had three children — was alive in my day. Nor did I ever see either of my father's older brothers, Hugh and Frederick (both family names). Hugh had died in about 1917, and Fred had emigrated towards the end of the 19th century to South Africa where, having originally been considered rather 'unsatisfactory', he had settled down, married and fathered eight children. Today most of his family have many descendants, which means that the particular branch of the Moncrieffs to which my father belonged — the Moncrieffs of Culfargie — is now far more represented in the new world than in the old, where the branch has almost died out.

Then there was Aunt Margaret, who had followed the Moncrieff tradition of marrying a Pattison cousin. She had no children, and I only dimly remember her as a bundle of shawls lying on an invalid chair in the back garden of our house at North Berwick. It seems she had been quite a lively character in her day; but my one recollection is of being regularly sent, as a very small child, to carry out to her the glass of Kümmel that she used to enjoy before lunch. This drink completely fascinated me: it *looked* exactly like water, but — as I discovered by secret and repeated experiment — it smelt and tasted quite different.

One way and another, it was only with the three youngest of my father's sisters — Emily Lina, Constance Sarah Louisa, and Georgina Grace — that I had any real contact; and of the three the only one whom I had much opportunity really to know was my Aunt Georgina, the youngest of the three, and hence the nearest in age and probably the closest of all his siblings to my father.

Both Aunt Lina and Aunt Constance spent much time living abroad: the former mainly in South Africa, the latter in France. Aunt Lina, who married quite young and had four children (rather nearer in age to my parents than to me), did return to Britain at some point in the 1930s, and she then set up house at Shamley Green, near Guildford in Surrey. I never knew her well, but I have happy memories of making occasional visits to the Shamley Green house during holidays from school and later university, and recall that she was a most delightful person, notably gifted with both charm and warmth.

Aunt Constance, who was unmarried, was even more elusive in my early days, for she had made a permanent home at Pau in the Pyrenees. She was a committed Francophile and her spoken French was absolutely fluent — though I was always intrigued as a child to hear that it sounded exactly the same as her English, with no concessions to a 'French accent'. During the war she was forced to leave France — being indeed among the last Britons to be evacuated from Bordeaux in June 1940. She then spent the war years with her sister, Lina, at Shamley Green; but at the earliest opportunity she was off on her way back to Pau, and she continued to live there until her death in about 1950. She was another outsize Moncrieff personality, with a handsome aquiline profile, dark brown eyes, luxuriantly beautiful white hair and a deep, almost gritty voice — attributed by some to her incessant smoking (note, however, that she lived into her late eighties).

Aunt Constance stays in my memories principally as one of the interesting wartime household at Shamley Green that included, among other refugees from the bombing in London, Aunt Lina's daughter, the writer Hope Mirrlees, and the poet T.S. Eliot, who was a close friend of hers. I have a proud memory of being invited on one of my occasional visits to play the piano for Mr Eliot; and an even more important recollection of his reading aloud to us one evening a poem he had finished earlier that day. Of Eliot himself the enduring picture is of a quietly courteous man, of whom I felt in considerable awe; in company he always appeared shy and even a little withdrawn — but perhaps that was partly by contrast with my cousin Hope, who was exactly the opposite.

Hope Mirrlees is no longer a well-known name, but in her day she was a writer of some reputation, a member of the Bloomsbury set who had published a variety of successful novels — including one, *Lud-in-the-Mist* (1927), that was serialised by the BBC as recently as the 1980s. In appearance and manner everything about her was on the largest of scales; and as a teenager I found her distinctly overwhelming, with her loud booming voice and boisterous exaggerated manner. A memory still lingers of Hope, seated at the foot of the wooden staircase in the Shamley Green house, addressing her beloved pug dog, Mary, in tones which rang throughout the house and might have been heard echoing in the farthest corner of the three-acre garden.

Aunt Georgina, like her sisters Lina and Constance, had also lived abroad at various times and in a number of different places; including France, South Africa and China — the last named a decidedly unusual place at that time for a single woman to visit on her own. But then it should be stressed that Georgina Grace Moncrieff was in no way the standard type of person. Born on 6 March 1868, she had spent her childhood partly in Glasgow, but mainly in Edinburgh. No information exists now about her early life, but, as the family's youngest unmarried daughter, she had been the one to remain at home and care for my grandmother, and to some extent also for my father, who lived at home until his marriage. Not that this task, in the handsome Edinburgh house near the Dean Bridge where the family lived at the time, would have involved any practical domestic work: Aunt Georgina belonged to an era when well-bred women usually had everything done for them. There would have been no housework, no bed-making, no cooking of meals; no washing of garments — let alone of sheets and towels; no ironing or shopping. Hers was that vanished generation who were often said to be "unable to boil an egg" (though it's odd that that partic-

Growing Up in a Vanished World 59

(a) My father (centre) with his mother and sister, Georgina.
(b) Aunt Dorothy (pre WWI).
(c) Aunt Georgina with her Celtic cross.

(a)

(b)

(c)

ular example should have been chosen as a stereotype, since cookery experts, Delia Smith among them, have pointed out that the successful boiling of an egg is by no means a simple art).

Perhaps Aunt Georgina did occasionally, during and after the second World War, tackle such tasks as making a cup of afternoon tea; but only on the housekeeper's day out, of course, and before sitting down in the evening to the cold supper left carefully prepared for her. And to the end of her long life she would invariably ring the bell if the fire needed attention and ask her housekeeper to put on more coal — or whatever. She would also, when she'd finished a letter, summon the same long-suffering housekeeper with a request that the letter be immediately taken to the post. All this, too, was happening, not in the 19th century but during the time I personally remember from the mid-1930s, through the '40s and '50s!

In looking after her mother's home in Lyndoch Place, Aunt Georgina's actual duties might have involved a certain amount in the way of organising domestic matters, but they would have consisted mainly in acting as a constant companion to her mother — in the old phrase, "dancing attendance on her".

No one now can say how demanding my grandmother was; but she too was plainly a woman of character, and many of the anecdotes about her would suggest she had a way with words. The story goes that on one occasion the rabbits supplied by the local butcher had been of inferior quality, and a note was despatched — in her name, but doubtless written by my aunt — to this effect: "Dear Sir, Kindly send two rabbits, **different in every respect** from those last sent." She had also been renowned for her quiet self-control: once when she had leant too near a lighted candle, and an agitated gentleman exclaimed in horror "Madam, Madam — your cap is on fire!", she had simply replied in a stately way: "Then may I trouble you, sir, to put it out."

All available evidence suggests that the relationship between my grandmother and her youngest daughter was extremely close; but it could be that my aunt, while unfailing in her filial duties, had always held fast to certain purposes of her own. For it is significant that, after her mother died, Aunt Georgina did not fade into the anonymous genteel retirement that would so frequently overtake single ladies of that period when bereaved of their parents. Instead she set about realising her lifetime ambition to work as a Church of Scotland missionary in China. By this point she must have been over fifty; but nothing daunted she undertook on her own the long and hazardous journey to China, where she joined two medical friends at a mission station, and spent a considerable period helping with their work among blind Chinese people. Unfortunately no one today can give me any details about this important phase in her life. Not even the name of the place in China where she lived, or the length of time she spent there. The bare facts were part of family legend, but sadly I know nothing more. An example, this, of wasted opportunities; for when young I never thought to ask about her experiences. Now, when I should so much like to know more, it's too late.

Nevertheless, a picture emerges of a woman of personality and determination. And at least Aunt Georgina did live until 1957, which gave me some opportunity to know her in my adult life. In my early days she had appeared to me noticeably eccentric — as I think she unquestionably was. Everything about her seemed then to personify the two qualities 'old' and 'old-fashioned'. Certainly her clothes and general appearance, with her long flowing garments and voluminous shawls, and the beautiful Celtic cross she always wore, belonged to a bygone era. Her dark hair, which contained little grey even at the end of her long life, was worn in a severe bun at the back of her elegant head, but due to its extreme fineness it always appeared untidy; and her most striking physical characteristic was her intensely blue eyes — they truly could have been described in the adjective beloved of romantic novelists as 'gentian-blue'.

Aunt Georgina was deeply religious; and she was one of the few among my father's eight siblings who remained true to the Presbyterian faith in which they were all brought up. My father's conversion to Roman Catholicism had apparently been a particular shock to her; and, although her attitude to me and to all our family was unfailingly affectionate, it was always clear that there were barriers here and territory that could not be entered.

However, while my aunt never wavered from strict Presbyterianism, one of her lifetime passions was for Dante — a rather unexpected choice of poet for a loyal daughter of John Knox. Not only did she throughout her life read and study Dante's poetry in the original Italian, she also devoted much time to making translations and commentaries, and at the age of 84 she actually published a book entitled *Lyrical Meditations on the Paradiso of Dante*.

Her reading covered French and German as well as Italian and a huge range of English literature, older and newer. The classics, of course, including many now-forgotten 19th-century writers; as well as contemporary novels, biography and other non-fiction (using the word contemporary to cover the first half of the 20th century). And, unusually for those days, she did not confine herself to books written for adults, but took an open and unashamed delight in reading children's books, with a particular leaning towards girls' school-stories.

Like my mother and father, Aunt Georgina enjoyed reading aloud; and I owe to her my first introduction to innumerable books. Among others, those of Mrs Molesworth and Mrs Ewing, the lesser known books of Louisa Alcott (such as *Eight Cousins*), and the Chalet School stories of Elinor M.Brent-Dyer — which would later open up my own path as a writer. Aunt Georgina's reading aloud from the Brent-Dyer books, and from two of Mrs Ewing's — *Jan of the Windmill* and *Mrs Overtheway's Remembrances* — remains a particularly vivid memory of this time.

Perhaps, if I had been born thirty or forty years earlier, I might have been able to know Aunt Georgina on a more personal level. She did I think have, not exactly a closer, but a more equal relationship with my much older cousins, Agnes, Hope and Noel Moncrieff, who were partly responsible for creating the remarkable variety of nicknames by which she was known to family and friends. These included 'La Chine' (for obvious reasons), 'Chintz', 'Tulip' and 'Yani' (reasons unknown); as well as the more to be expected 'G.G.', and Aunt George — the latter being the name I most often used.

When grown up, I came to enjoy her company and her quirky sense of humour; and I always had both fondness and admiration for her, but there was no really intimate bond between us. A certain constraint existed; and it can't have been just the age gap, for around the same time (the last years of the war and through the 1950s) I numbered among my real friends a wonderful old lady in her seventies, Mrs Lucy Laurie, who was almost exactly Aunt Georgina's contemporary. Most probably my aunt was someone who showed her real self to very few people — perhaps not to any. My main memories of her are both affectionate and grateful (indeed, it was her legacy to me of her Edinburgh flat that enabled us in 1961 to purchase our home in Barnes). But the enduring picture is of a rather secret person.

Cousins

To round off this section on my father's family I'd like to record some memories of my Moncrieff cousins — Agnes, Hope and Noel. They were the daughters of my father's eldest brother, Hugh, and his wife Emily; which made them technically my first cousins, but they belonged to another generation, having reached their thirties when I was born. Nevertheless, with the younger two, and especially with Noel, I was able over the years to have a close and affectionate relationship, for both lived into the 1990s — and well into *their* nineties.

Of the eldest sister, Agnes, who sadly had died of a brain tumour at the relatively early age of 54, my memories are more restricted and less personal, but clearly she had been a remarkable person. Born in 1892 into a well-off and socially well established family, she had worked as a nurse during the first World War; and afterwards she had taken a step that was almost unknown at the time for a young woman of her upbringing and social class. For, instead of returning to the life of a county lady, Agnes had made up her mind to go off and study medicine seriously, with the object of actually becoming a doctor. And this must have been a dramatic decision for her to take in that very different era, the 1920s: financially there was no need for her to have worked in any paid capacity, and at that time women of her class were not generally encouraged to have careers.

On the other hand, Scotland, unlike some other parts of the United Kingdom, already had a long tradition of women entering the medical profession — going right back to the 19th century and the feisty ladies, Elsie Inglis among them, who had campaigned so hard, and in the end so successfully, to be accepted in Edinburgh's prestigious medical school. Agnes was to prove herself a worthy successor to these women, obtaining first all the degrees and diplomas necessary for a practitioner of traditional medicine, and later taking further courses in order to qualify in homeopathy. Here she undoubtedly would have had the encouragement of Dr John Weir, later Sir John, a key figure in the establishment of homeopathy in Britain, for it seems the latter was a family friend. There is no one alive to explain the connection, but certainly he and my father had known each from their youth; and since Weir, like Agnes, had worked in Glasgow, it seems highly probable that the two became acquainted quite early in Agnes's medical career.

To digress for a moment: John Weir, who could be regarded as a founding father of British homeopathy, was one of various larger-than-life personalities who figured in my early days. Born around 1880, he had risen from humble beginnings to be not only internationally famous in homeopathy, but, during the 1920s, to be appointed personal physician to the then Duke of York — later King George VI — and his family, eventually becoming one of the official doctors to Queen Elizabeth II.

All through the years at North Berwick Sir John used to visit us regularly each summer, when he always took a month's holiday at the golfing resort of Gullane. Here he stayed in Bissett's Hotel, and spent hours each day (not Sundays, of course at that time) in devoted — though by no means very expert — pursuit of the Royal and Ancient Game, in which he was quite often joined by my father. He was a genuinely kindly man, not above taking a certain innocent delight in his own fame and success; and he had a large fund of anecdotes — including some *very discreet* tales of the Royal Family — which he so much enjoyed telling that no one could complain if, as could happen, he rather tended to repeat himself.

The last time I saw him was in April 1960, when I and my six-month-old daughter, Catriona, were spending some weeks in the Royal London Homeopathic Hospital. And it caused quite a stir in the hospital one evening when Sir John, in an act of kindness that was entirely typical, announced that he wished to visit me and the baby in our little cubicle off the children's ward. Especially as he was at the time *literally* on his way to Buckingham Palace! — and resplendent in full formal dress, with the blue and red sash denoting his rank as K.C.M.G. draped around his not inconsiderable form.

Returning to Cousin Agnes — as I always called her in early life, in accordance with the old-fashioned Scottish custom of using a respectful form of address for relatives in an older age group (I could never imagine calling any of my aunts by her first name). She, after qualifying in both traditional medicine and as a homeopath, went on to have a notably successful career and to become a much loved G.P. Her practice was mainly in North London, where she had settled in Hendon during the 1930s; but she also consulted once a week in Harley Street, as well as working regularly at the Homeopathic Hospital and giving lectures to students of homeopathy up and down the country. She was accounted a great loss to the medical profession and to the cause of homeopathy when she died in 1948 at the age of only 56.

Cousin Hope, the second of the three sisters, was a completely different kind of person. Where Agnes had been brisk and efficient — though her underlying kindness could not have been questioned — Hope was sensitive and artistic. Her talents lay mainly in music; and, although not a pioneer like her elder sister, she too had broken out of the social mould in which the family were brought up, to the extent of going in the 1920s to spend a couple of years in London, studying piano and singing at the Royal Academy of Music. She never had any pretentions, or indeed ambition to make a career as a professional musician, but music always remained important to her; and during her time at the Academy she also made a number of friends with whom she kept regularly in touch to the end of her long life.

Hope had considerable charm in both looks and manner, enjoyed social life and the theatre, and gave time both to helping with charitable organisations and to playing a supportive part in the local Conservative party. Her appearance was always immaculate, and testified to her interest in buying and wearing nice clothes (something that my vague memories suggest was not the case with Agnes, who always looked neat and competent, but just a trifle dowdy).

Both Hope and her younger sister Noel were notably generous people (and doubtless Agnes was also). They had been brought up to believe that those who enjoy good fortune should try to share this with others; many charities benefited from their regular and lavish generosity, as did numerous of their friends and relatives. Typical of this was the occasion in 1954 when I had to go into hospital for an operation, and for various reasons needed to have a private room. No sooner had the news reached Hope and Noel than two cheques arrived, one from each, which covered the entire cost. And the wonderful presents they heaped on me at the time of my marriage in 1957 would have made any bride's jaw drop. They included — *as just one item* — four pairs of king-sized sheets and matching pillowcases, with embroidered monograms, in the best quality Irish linen, which even at that time must have cost a vast amount. Yet another example: when in 1961 Alex and I acquired our house in Barnes, further cheques arrived towards carpets and furnishings.

Between Hope and me, music always provided a strong link. But it was mainly with Noel, the youngest of the family, that I was able to form a real friendship. She, like her sisters, had worked as a V.A.D. during part of the first World War; and, although she returned afterwards to the lifestyle of county-lady and didn't aspire to a career, I rather think that things might have been different had she been born in another period. Not that Noel didn't enjoy social life: dances, tennis, bridge-parties and going to race meetings were all things she found congenial. She loved to take part in amateur dramatics; and by temperament she was by far the most domesticated of the three sisters, and was an outstandingly good cook — her blackcurrant jam was specially delicious. She was also, right into her nineties, a devotedly enthusiastic and knowledgeable gardener.

At no point was she ever idle: Noel had a most active social conscience and supported many charities, her own special favourite being 'Save the Children'. Each year, right up to the point when she and Hope, by then both well over ninety, had been obliged to retire to a nursing home, Noel had unfailingly assisted in the charity shop run every Christmas by 'Save the Children' in Ayr, the small West-of-Scotland town where the sisters had made their home since the early 1950s.

When she died Noel was around 96, but she had the gift of being to some extent ageless. She had always taken an immense interest in every aspect of life, and, while herself holding strong moral and religious principles, she showed a broad-minded, non-judgemental attitude, and a lively sense of humour that made it not only possible but enjoyable to discuss anything with her. On paper she belonged to a much earlier generation than mine, but this never seemed important. Not that I've ever myself been much concerned about ages, having throughout life enjoyed friendships in many age groups, but with some people age always seems to matter. Never with Noel. She was without question one of my favourite relatives.

My mother's relatives

Turning now to the other side of the family: my mother had had six half-brothers and sisters; but the eldest, Edmond, had left Britain to live in the Far East, in the country we now call Malaysia, and had died at quite an early age. I doubt if she herself ever knew him. And of course her only full brother, James, had died when she was just a fortnight old.

Her eldest half-sister, Alice, must have been at least twenty years older than she was; and although Aunt Alice may just have lived into my lifetime I have no memory of her. However, I did as a child see a certain amount of the other two half-sisters, Fanny and Mary. Not that I had the chance to know either of them well, since both lived in southern England, and didn't in my memory visit us in Scotland. The same applied to the middle brother, my Uncle Charlie, who had been given the splendidly Jacobite name of Charles James; he inhabited a bachelor bed-sitting-room somewhere in South Kensington, where I can vaguely recollect visiting him with my mother on a couple of occasions.

These relatives remain only shadowy figures in the background of my memories. But throughout my childhood I was regularly taken to stay with Uncle Fred, the youngest of my mother's half-brothers, who was at a guess her favourite relative and was to become for me a most beloved uncle.

Children can have mercenary characteristics — I certainly did. And Uncle Fred was, to our family standards, *rich*. He was a self-made man, who completely unaided had made his way up the commercial ladder; and by the time I remember him in the 1930s he was living in a large Hampstead villa with seven or eight bedrooms and a full staff of servants, had a period-gem country house at West Mersea in Essex, a Rolls Royce in which he was driven around by a uniformed chauffeur, and a beautiful sailing yacht based at Brightlingsea — a one-hundred-and-forty-foot schooner with a professional crew. All this was deeply impressive to a child brought up in a style that, while in no way poverty-stricken, was relatively simple (my parents had always felt obliged by their heavy family responsibilities to practise a certain economy, and this was constantly emphasised to me from my earliest days). From a materialistic point of view, staying with Uncle Fred and his gentle wife, Aunt Bina (short for Sabina), was a thoroughly gold-plated experience.

Into the bargain Uncle Fred was a notably generous man, who took immense pleasure in giving presents to his friends and relatives. I still treasure some of those he gave me — among them a lovely little brooch showing a replica of his sailing yacht, *Tamesis*. I wouldn't have been a human child if I hadn't enjoyed the experience of such an unwontedly luxurious lifestyle. But my fondness for Uncle Fred went far beyond this. He was a most lovable man; humorous in a dry way,

Uncle Fred and Aunt Bina aboard 'Tamesis', 1937.

charming and kind; attractive-looking too, with his deep-set dark brown eyes, snowy white hair and neat white imperial beard. He was always exceedingly good to me, and in any list I should ever compile of favourite men he would come in the top category.

Perhaps it gives some measure of Uncle Fred's remarkable balance of temperament that he survived the appalling financial disaster that befell his business at some point just before World War II, when his trusted partner embezzled most of the firm's assets and absconded, leaving him almost bankrupt. Everything had to be sold: the houses in Hampstead and West Mersea along with much of the furniture, the Rolls Royce, and his beloved sailing yacht. He and Aunt Bina retired to a small house in Brightlingsea, situated in a respectable but undistinguished road, where they were to spend the rest of their days (both lived into the late 1940s). They had enough to survive and to live modestly, but the contrast was dramatic.

At no point did Uncle Fred express any bitterness about the change in his fortunes. In the good days he had never shown the smallest touch of ostentation; now he simply accepted his changed life in a completely philosophical manner. Here he was faithfully supported by his wife, my Aunt Bina, who like him had made the full circular tour from humble beginnings to riches and back. For Aunt Bina had started life as a barmaid — something that was never mentioned, and that no one ever told me till well after I was grown up. Nor would anyone ever have guessed it. Aunt Bina, with her beautifully made and quietly stylish clothes, and her gentle voice and manner, always appeared to embody in the best and most genuine sense the word 'ladylike'. But that wasn't the only secret in Aunt Bina's story: Uncle Fred had in fact been married first to her sister, Emmie; the latter had lived for only a short time, but in those far gone days marriage with a deceased wife's sister was still illegal in England. In order to marry the two had been obliged to go to the Channel Islands and hold their wedding in Jersey, where there was no law against it. Uncle Fred was in so many ways an impressive person; and he is among those relatives — my Aunt Georgina is another — whom I would dearly like to have known better, and to have known in my more adult life.

Aunt Dorothy

The gallery of family portraits began with Monica Bond; and to round it off another person should be mentioned who was, like Monica, of great importance in the family though not a blood relation. Dorothy Riley was the daughter of Mrs Curwen and stepdaughter of Dr Curwen — the couple who, as related in an early section of these memoirs, had taken my mother into their home and been responsible for looking after her between the ages of nine and eighteen. And perhaps because Aunt Dorothy, as she was always known in the family, had grown up with my mother, she was in many ways more like a sister to her than any of the three half-sisters who were actually blood relatives.

She and my mother always remained close friends, and kept constantly in touch although their lives were to follow very different paths — for one thing, Aunt Dorothy never married. I know little about her early life, but it seems that at some point she had been stricken with tuberculosis, and had been obliged to spend a long period in a sanatorium. Fortunately she had recovered, living indeed to be past ninety. But to the end of her life she suffered from a paroxysmal cough, and the rasping sound of Aunt Dorothy having one of her regular coughing bouts must figure in the memory of anyone who knew her. She herself would describe this noise with characteristic dry humour as "my barking fits".

Unquestionably Aunt Dorothy was a most independent person, and before the second World War she had spent a lot of time travelling abroad, including sojourns in different continents and many remote countries. Various tales about her journeys were part of family legend; in particular about the time when she had encountered a certain Major Armstrong during some kind of group tour to France. In those days Aunt Dorothy had a reputation for her skill in palmistry, and one evening in the hotel she was persuaded to read the hands of several people in the group, among them a Major Armstrong. Now by nature Aunt Dorothy was extremely rational, even sceptical, and she had always regarded palmistry as a bit of fun. So, when she saw in this gentleman's hand a sign that was supposed to denote death on the scaffold, she simply thought that this just proved what nonsense the whole thing was. Needless to say Aunt Dorothy didn't reveal to the subject himself or to anyone in the group what she had seen, though she did on her return home mention the episode laughingly to my mother. But then a few months later she was to learn from the newspapers that this same Major Armstrong had been tried and convicted for the murder of his wife, and that he was indeed to be hanged. Her astonishment and horror can be imagined. And thereafter she refused ever again to read anyone's hand.

Nor was the Armstrong affair the only murder case to impinge on Aunt Dorothy's life, for in an odd way she seems to have been a focus for dramas. On this second occasion — at some time during my childhood — she was actually staying with us in Edinburgh when she was contacted by Scotland Yard, with the shocking news that not only had her London flat been broken into, but that her housekeeper had been brutally battered to death by the intruder (who turned out to have been the housekeeper's son-in-law). His weapon had been the old-fashioned flat-iron she was using at the time. And it gives some indication of Aunt Dorothy's totally matter-of-fact attitude to life that she insisted, despite all that my mother and various friends could do to dissuade her, on returning to the flat and resuming her daily life there just as before.

To finish on a gentler and more personal note: one of the things that most struck me as a child about Aunt Dorothy was her habit of talking aloud to herself in perfectly audible tones as she went around the house. Probably it was because she had spent so much of her life living alone. I often think of her nowadays when I catch myself doing the same thing.

Part Two: A Slowly Changing World

(Overleaf) Me aged 10 with my first (half-size) cello.

VI: Reluctant Thoughts on Social Class

THIS SECTION SHOULD REALLY BEGIN with one of those disclaimers often seen in magazines, to the effect that: "Opinions expressed here are not necessarily those of the editor." Because I should hate anyone to think that I share some of the views on social class that have to be discussed.

Ideas on class have changed so much during the past century. My mother, for example, would have been most surprised at one time had anyone described her or her family as *middle*-class, for the meaning of this term has altered radically since the earlier decades of the twentieth century. As my mother saw things, we were unquestionably *upper*-class. Not aristocracy, but belonging to a section of society where any man would always have described himself on the census form as 'Gentleman'.

My much older half-sister, who was born before World War I, used also to comment on this change; remarking once that in her younger days the term 'middle class' had even carried a slightly pejorative tinge. Apparently people would sometimes pass such comments on a young girl as "She's a nice little thing, but of course very *middle-class*". (In *my* youth, a deplorable equivalent was the four-letter **N.O.C.D.**, meaning, Not Our Class Dear.)

Edinburgh in the pre-war days was a decidedly snobbish place, with strictly demarcated social barriers. 'East-windy, West-endy,' so went the tag. And it is here that the split between my mother's natural temperament and her social conditioning can be most clearly seen. It was epitomised in her ambivalent attitude to a friend I made through the *Chassevent* music classes, described earlier.

Gracie, then Dods, now King, is one of the friends I have been lucky enough to keep right through life; we are still regularly in touch and, although she now lives several hundred miles away from me in Perth, we usually manage to meet at least once a year. She was a little older than me — still is, for that matter, although these differences disappear once childhood is over! — and even in those early days she was a forceful character, decidedly someone to be reckoned with. Both my parents had a great liking for her; as a person, that is. The problems arose because Gracie came from what was considered in those pre-war Edinburgh days to be the 'wrong background'; in other words, from the wrong social class. And one side of my mother's attitude is exemplified in a pronouncement that I hate to remember her making, to the effect that much care would have to be taken because, if people got to know that I had the *wrong sort of friends*, then when I grew up and went to the various Edinburgh parties and dances — balls, as they were known — no one would want to dance with me.

I can't have been more than ten at the time, but I remember thinking venomously that, if it came to a choice between being friends with Gracie and going to these stupid dances, I'd have no problem in choosing. And I'm happy to be able to redress the balance on behalf of my mother. In the pronouncement quoted above it was not her true self that spoke, but the social mores in which she had been brought up. Truer by far of her real self was her reaction some years later during the war (for Gracie and I had managed always to remain friends, partly because we had many regular links through music). On this occasion my mother had learnt that Gracie's parents and family were completely ignoring her birthday and making no attempt of any kind to celebrate it. This my mother thought incredibly unfeeling, for she always liked to make much of birthdays and other family events. And her immediate reaction was to lay on a party in our house, at which Gracie was invited to be the guest of honour. My father, who was fully in sympathy with the project, even presented her with a gift — probably the one pound note that was such riches to us in those days. And I like to think that the kindness behind these actions was far more typical of them both than their outward pronouncements could sometimes appear.

Nevertheless it must be faced that, when it came to deciding whether or not I should be allowed to associate with certain people, my mother could sometimes act in an authoritarian way that appears unacceptable today. And at times her embargoes were not just for social reasons. On one dreadful occasion I had been invited to tea by a girl with whom I'd become friends when playing on the children's golf links — one of the great institutions of pre-war North Berwick. Here, even before the war no one bothered much about formality; people mixed freely and the youthful golfers came from a wide social span. According to my fading memories, this included a sprinkling of Lords and Ladies (with capital 'L's) and even one Romanian princess — North Berwick being at that time quite a fashionable resort — but there were also numerous children from a variety of local families.

The girl who had issued my invitation lived quite near us, and I had anticipated no problems. But when I told my mother about it she professed extreme horror, announcing that I could not possibly be allowed to go to tea with "those horrible people". I protested in vain that this girl was not in the least horrible, that I had already accepted her invitation, and that she would be upset if I didn't turn up. All to no avail: my mother simply went to the telephone and cancelled the invitation. What she said, I never knew. Nor did I ever learn what these people had done that was stigmatised as so 'horrible'.

Perhaps from one point of view this kind of happening did me no ultimate harm. It certainly removed any danger of my becoming infected with similar ideas. No one likes to think of themselves as a snob; and I've often been grateful that various things along the way helped to insure that, hopefully, I didn't become one. Going to school at Craiglockhart was an important factor. Here, not many of the pupils — I cringe to say it — would have passed muster with my mother as socially acceptable. In fact, the only school-fellows I was ever actually encouraged to invite home were the daughters of two senior officers at Redford Barracks in Colinton — just up the road from the convent — who were relatively short-term pupils at Craiglockhart. (One of them, Prue Wilson, was to become one of my most valued and life-long friends.) Then an exception was also made for a girl whose mother happened to have been at school with my half-sister — a curious piece of reasoning, that. And already as a child I was rebelling against these and many other ideas. With the result that all this, instead of indoctrinating me, had the opposite effect. Since I liked many of my school-fellows at Craiglockhart, I simply resolved that when I had the choice I would know whom I pleased.

Another wonderful learning experience was being asked during the war to help with running the Brownie Pack connected with St Patrick's

R.C. Church. This was a complete revelation, for St Patrick's was situated in what was then the heart of the Edinburgh slums. The Brownies all came from the tenements around the High Street — not then the gentrified district it is today but a really deprived quarter. And part of my apprenticeship included visiting the children's parents — or, at least, their mothers. Up to this point my life had in some ways been remarkably sheltered; and this experience taught me amongst other things a respectful admiration for the women who, despite living in these sordid surroundings, worked so hard to look after their homes. The buildings were without exception dilapidated and the stairways dark and often smelly, as were the streets, but the actual living quarters were usually clean and neat.

The children themselves were lively and not particularly easy to control, but completely endearing in their enjoyment of the various Brownie activities. And their total artlessness was demonstrated on one occasion when they came dancing up to me on my arrival, all chanting: "Miss! — Miss! — you'll not see Susie Meighan again, Miss!" Thinking Susie's family must have gone to live somewhere else I enquired casually: "Why, what's happened to her?" Only to be totally floored when the reply came, again chanted in chorus: "She's *deid*!" Apparently there had been a dreadful accident in the previous week and the eight-year-old Susie had plunged to her death over the banisters on the fourth floor where they lived. It was my first experience of the perfectly innocent if ghoulish delight that small children can sometimes take in dramatic tragedies.

Going back to my mother's attitude as to who was, or was not, a 'suitable' acquaintance for her family, this of course stemmed in part from a kind of anxiety complex which could be named the 'Caesar's Wife Syndrome'. For much was always made of the crucial necessity that my father, as a judge of the Court of Session, should preserve a dignified distance from ordinary people. A convoluted theory used to be explained to me that if, say, the greengrocer's children came to our house to play this could pose a danger; because, should an adult in their family ever be brought up in court before my father, it might appear that he was biased in their favour. Such people might even expect favourable treatment. This same theory was also responsible for my being allowed to visit the homes of so few among my schoolfellows. Here, the ironic thing is, that it seemingly never occurred to anyone that the parents of my *upper-middle-class* friends would ever dream of taking advantage in a similar way! Maybe the thought that people from these higher rungs of society would ever stand charged in a court of law simply didn't cross anyone's mind . . .

Another curious anomaly struck me only recently when writing these memoirs. For although I was so rarely allowed to visit the homes of my school-friends, my parents did not apparently object to my being taken, as I quite often was in early childhood, to spend a Sunday afternoon with the working-class families of either our housemaid or our table-maid. And yet, why should the 'Caesar's Wife Syndrome' not have applied here? However that may be, I used greatly to enjoy these expeditions; especially the visits to our table-maid's family, despite the long walk — a good two and a half miles from our North Berwick house — to where they lived in the picturesque village of Dirleton, with its imposing ruined castle. Their cottage was charming in appearance, but must have been totally inadequate to house all the family. It consisted of only about three quite small rooms, with a kind of large shed at the back of the cottage; and the family of our table-maid, Agnes, had numbered six children. Of course, by this point three of them were grown up and living elsewhere, but the only water-supply was provided by a pump in the yard, and today it's impossible not to wonder how in the world Agnes's parents had managed. I think that eventually the cottage was condemned and the family moved elsewhere. Not that any such thoughts occurred to me as a child. I simply enjoyed my visits, in particular being given tomatoes for tea — I can't recall at that stage ever having them at home.

Life did become a good deal more relaxed during and after the war. And although the social changes that were sweeping across the world came late to Edinburgh, at least they were in time to save me from the kind of restricted existence that could perhaps have been mine had I been born just a few years earlier.

I sometimes try to picture how life might have turned out had it been my misfortune (as I would see it) to be grown up and launched in society before World War II. Certainly the life that my parents would originally have pictured for me was very different from the way things eventually developed. Their plan would undoubtedly have been for me to take the same path that my half-sister, Patricia, had trodden in the mid-1920s. She, after nearly seven years at boarding school, where she became Head Girl, followed by two years 'finishing' in Switzerland, had returned to Edinburgh to make a formal debut in society. This traditionally included a busy round of parties, luncheons, dances and other jollifications, and culminated in a Presentation Evening, either at Holyrood or at Buckingham Palace. For this great occasion the customary garb was a formal evening gown with a long train and an elegant feather head-dress. Arrayed in this finery, the debutantes, ushered by their escorts, would each in turn file slowly up the Throne Room, making full curtseys — that is, right to the ground — when they arrived in front of the King and Queen. (A dress, complete with green velvet train, that my mother must have worn when presenting a debutante at one of these parties, survived to become an asset of my children's dressing-up box.)

The ideal next step on a debutante's road was marriage. My sister had duly become engaged and was married by about the age of twenty-three. Her husband, Edmund James Paton Walsh, was at that time a Captain in the Royal Artillery; he had an irreproachable family background, was around thirty years of age, and a practising Roman Catholic — all of which would have been considered most suitable. He was also tall and good-looking.

In my case, my mother and father would almost certainly have visualised my eventually marrying and settling down in Edinburgh, ideally with some nice, successful young lawyer. Either that, or just possibly joining the ranks of the Moncrieff maiden ladies, of whom there were quite a few. Bearing in mind my parents' constant anxiety about the future of my brothers, they might have anticipated the need in future years for the services that had been taken for granted from single women by their generation.

Of course, my brothers were themselves victims of the social attitudes that dominated the pre-war era. In today's world there might have been many possibilities for both of them to lead more normal lives. Both were perfectly literate and numerate; they were well able to tackle many practical jobs; both actually enjoyed work in the garden; and, at one of the establishments where my brother Philip spent some years, he showed a considerable ability for working with animals on the community's farm. The sad thing is that it was thought in those days to be out of the question for *Lord Moncrieff's sons* to have a job as either gardener or farm-hand.

However, on a certain level, there were some privileges associated with being the offspring of Lord Moncrieff. For example, whenever members of the Royal Family visited Holyrood Palace my parents

A Slowly Changing World 79

My half-sister, Patricia, in traditional dress for a Presentation party at Buckingham Palace. About 1926.

would always be invited to attend various functions, and after the war I was eligible to be included in the invitations; among them, royal events not only at Holyrood but at Buckingham Palace. The most memorable were two relatively small-scale evening parties. One at Holyrood in the summer of 1953, held in celebration of the present Queen's coronation, when she wore her coronation dress and it was possible to view its gorgeous damask and jewel-encrusted beauties from close quarters. The other, five years earlier, when in April 1948 King George VI and Queen Elizabeth held a small gathering at Buckingham Palace to mark their Silver Wedding; here, an unforgettable and amusing recollection is of the King and Queen sailing out to open the dancing — on their own of course — while the band played Rodgers and Hammerstein's *Anything you can do I can do better.*

But in fact this latter occasion does not belong purely to my 'social' memories: in order to attend that party I had to travel by sleeper between London and Edinburgh on two successive nights, because on the following evening I was performing Haydn's D major Cello Concerto with the Edinburgh Chamber Orchestra! Thus vindicating my regular claim to my family to be considered, not a social butterfly, but a serious young musician.

In any case, my most special moment with royal connections did not come about through my parents, but through an invitation to me personally. This happened in the early 1940s when Sir Ian Colquhoun of Luss was acting as High Commissioner for the annual General Assembly of the Church of Scotland. As Commissioner, he enjoyed the privilege of residing with his family for a week in the Palace of Holyrood. And to my great delight Sir Ian's teenage daughters, Robina and Mary, whom I'd got to know when they were holidaying at North Berwick, invited me to come and have tea with them in the private apartments at Holyrood (the Colquhouns being among the friends who **were** considered to be suitable acquaintances for me . . .).

This was on a Sunday, which meant the palace was closed to the public, and we were able to wander everywhere, unsupervised, and even to go up and down the little staircase between Queen Mary's bed-chamber and her reception room, which is never accessible to ordinary visitors. At the time I was history-mad, and particularly obsessed with Mary Queen of Scots, so this was a fascinating experience. However, another memory of that visit is quite unconnected with either royalty or history: a picture of Sir Ian, seated in the corner of one of the unexpectedly small drawing-rooms, happily occupied in embroidering a tapestry. Before that I can't recall ever meeting a man who knew one end of an embroidery thread from the other.

Me with Robina Colquhoun and their nanny
in forecourt of Holyrood Palace. Mid 1940s.

VII: Edinburgh Music

RETURNING NOW TO EARLIER DAYS: the *Chassevent* classes that marked my first introduction to music have already been recorded in a previous chapter. The next stage happened a few years later when, around the age of seven, I began having piano lessons from a Miss Jenny Milroy, who most conveniently lived in Abbotsford Park, just around the corner from our house. From quite early on I was able to take myself to the lessons at her flat without any need of an escort.

Miss Milroy was a gentle lady, though by no means lacking in character. She lived with an elderly mother and a white Cairn terrier, also rather elderly, called Timmy — about the only dog I've ever known who could actually *smile* to order. Piano lessons happened twice a week and I suppose I made reasonable progress, but at this point it was all very light-hearted. I did have a naturally good ear, and could occasionally wow the family's adults by reproducing on the piano hymn tunes and other melodies I'd heard in church or elsewhere, but I was far from being an infant prodigy.

For a long time — in childhood terms — I had yearned to start the cello. Why particularly the cello, I don't know. At this point I doubt if I'd ever heard a cello; I just knew it was a stringed instrument like a violin but much bigger and that it made a much lower sound. Looking back, it seems probable this was something I picked up unconsciously from my mother, who had apparently longed to play a stringed instrument as a child, and almost certainly nursed similar desires for me. But the mere suggestion of my learning another instrument brought heavy disapproval from my father, for whom the dreadful prospect of more music practice in the house was anathema. Considering the extensive size of our house he need hardly have been bothered! But as a result

I had reached the advanced age of ten before my mother was able to get round him about this — as she usually did about most things in the end.

Memory is selective; it's not always the most important things that stand out, but there must have been something extra special about the day of my first cello lesson because I can still, all these decades later, recall so many details about it. The setting was a studio in Castle Terrace, in Edinburgh's old Synod Hall — a room that must have seemed vast to a child, for it was large even in adult eyes. As made plain by a shining brass plate on the door, the studio formed part of **The Waddell School of Music**, which had been founded more than half a century earlier by a Mr William Waddell, father of the two present owners, Maimie and Ruth Waddell. The sisters taught respectively violin and cello, and Maimie also conducted the school's string orchestra.

In the phrase beloved of Victorian novelists, little could anyone have realised at the time that this particular room, with its brown paintwork, its tiny high platform where families of cellos of all sizes roosted side by side, its signed photographs of former pupils, and its lofty windows dominated by a splendid view of Edinburgh Castle, was to play such a significant part in my life during so many years to come. Edinburgh's Synod Hall was demolished long ago, but I still remember everything about that room. In other hands it might have appeared gaunt, but its walls were always colourful with pictures, often including Scottish contemporary paintings; for Maimie Waddell, herself a distinguished painter who exhibited in the Royal Scottish Academy, was a friend and also patron of artists. Pictures by Anne Redpath, William Gillies, Keith Henderson and Penelope Beaton form part of my early recollections. Flowers and flowering plants were always to be seen in various corners. Maybe the huge North-East facing windows did let in a good deal of bracing Edinburgh air along with the magnificent view, but the old-fashioned anthracite stove always provided adequate warmth even in winter.

To this day I could give an exact account of my first cello lesson; and would pay tribute to the excellent counsels I was given about some of the basics of bowing and left-hand technique. From the beginning it was clear that playing the cello was an immensely serious business, and one that would demand hard devoted toil. And my first impression of Ruth Waddell, whom I later came to love dearly, was —

as I complained to my mother — of someone "very strict". Possibly this was in contrast with the gentle Miss Milroy, from whom I was still learning the piano at this point. However, it wasn't long before I had been completely captivated by my new teacher; soon my father was remarking that my conversation seemed to be dominated by a person with the curious name of 'Swaddle'!

As I grew up, Ruth Waddell was to become one of my dearest and most valued friends. She was in many ways a wonderful teacher, capable of kindling in her pupils a love of music and of the cello that would endure for a lifetime. I shall always be grateful to her, knowing that anything I have ever achieved as a cellist, either performer or teacher, I owe to her. Nor does it lessen my gratitude that I've now become aware that certain points about her method were not ideal from the physiological point of view. This grey area had its source, at least partly, in the theories promulgated by the world-famous cellist, Guilhermina Suggia, with whom Ruth Waddell had spent a period of study. Suggia was unquestionably a charismatic personality; she was probably the first woman cellist ever to achieve an international career, but she had some idiosyncratic ideas about cello technique. Being herself of small stature, she was not always aware that what suited her might not suit others of different build. Among the things she advocated was the importance of the 'Straight Bow Arm' and the rigidly angled right-hand and fingers — so tellingly captured in the famous portrait by Augustus John. Ruth Waddell had, it seems, absorbed these somewhat dubious concepts and embodied them in her own teaching, which did occasionally cause some physical problems for her pupils in later life — myself among them. To be fair, it should be stressed that less awareness existed at that time about the paramount importance of basing instrumental teaching on sound physiological principles. Even today the battle has not been entirely won, as I've often been made sadly aware when acting as adjudicator at competition festivals up and down the country; but at least the subject gets far more attention than it did.

In every other respect Ruth Waddell's teaching was admirable; and she was herself a hugely interesting person of wide interests. In addition to her teaching she was also busy as a performer in chamber music and in Edinburgh's Reid Orchestra, of which she was principal cellist for many years. And although her life was dedicated to the teaching she shared with her sister in the Waddell School and its

Ruth Waddell. About 1939/40.

orchestra, Ruth had a splendidly wide range of interests outside music; especially in books, art, theatre, and travel. Unlike her sister she was not herself a painter, but Ruth was both interested in and knowledgeable about art. Obviously this was something that ran in the family: Ruth and Maimie's mother had produced many enchanting pictures in water-colour (rivalling the famous *Diary of an Edwardian Country Lady*), and their grandfather was the well-known Scottish painter Sir Daniel McNee, whose portrait of their grandmother, entitled *The Lady in Grey*, hangs in the Scottish National Gallery.

As well as Ruth's cello lessons, a crucially important influence in my musical development was the Waddell orchestra, which was something of a legend in Edinburgh. The school had over the years produced an impressive number of professional string-players, and its record in teaching was enviably high. But its main glory was the Waddell Junior Orchestra, an ensemble which had developed from the Ladies' Orchestra started by Mr William Waddell in the 19th Century, evolving later into what would now be called a youth orchestra.

At that time, and indeed until some years after World War II, there was not the wealth of youth orchestras at all levels, local and national, that exists today. Nowadays we have all become accustomed to the marvels that these young players can achieve — take for example the National Youth Orchestra's annual appearances at the Proms. But in my childhood the Waddell Junior Orchestra could fairly have been described as unique. Even today it might still be accounted unusual in that, unlike most youth orchestras, it numbered only *string*-players. And although it's impossible to compare standards across a gap of more than sixty years, a tribute paid by the world-famous conductor, Fritz Busch, must surely carry some weight: when brought by his friend Sir Donald Tovey to hear the orchestra perform at some point in the 1930s, he had apparently exclaimed: "In all of Germany, there is nothing like this."

Of course, the relative educational and social merits of string orchestra versus full orchestra can be argued. But for those who play stringed instruments there is something unsurpassable about the quality of sound that can be achieved by a good string ensemble. And the training that was given to us in the Waddell Orchestra was of lifetime value. The Waddell sisters had no use for players whose bows skimmed idly across the surface. The bow had to cling to the strings, drawing forth glorious sound with every inch from heel to tip. We were taught to listen critically to the string tone, and aim for both beauty and strength. We had, too, the rare good fortune of being shown that sounds, as well as being loud or soft, can have an infinite variety of colours.

We learnt to relish the sensation of bows attacking together in the noble opening of a Handel 'Concerto Grosso'. Or, at the other extreme, and using now 'only one hair of the bow', we would try to create a sound so soft as to be almost non-existent — like the faint hum of telegraph wires, Maimie would say.

This particular tone colour could bring a kind of stillness and awe to such music as the opening of Vaughan Williams' *Tallis Fantasia*, or parts of the slow movement in Elgar's *Serenade for Strings*. Maimie called this quality **Magic**. She would sometimes stop us when we had played a phrase, not wrongly but unimaginatively; slowly she would shake her head, saying in dry tones "No Magic". (Which could occasionally be an all-too-apt comment on some of today's aseptically brilliant performers.) And although in telling of the orchestra I seem to be highlighting Maimie Waddell, her sister Ruth had the same knack of being able suddenly, by some turn of phrase or unlikely simile, to open doors whose very existence had been unsuspected.

Most of the young players learnt from Maimie or Ruth Waddell — or from their splendid assistants, Winnie Gavine and Kitty Gregorson, who both did outstanding work. But pupils of other Edinburgh teachers were able to join the orchestra — or to be exact, one of the two orchestras that then existed for younger and older children. These were known familiarly as the 'Big Orchestra' and the 'Baby Orchestra', and between them they covered an age range of about six to twenty. Both rehearsed on Saturday mornings in term-time — the former from nine o'clock to 9.55am, the latter at 10am. I have never been much of a morning person, but the Waddell Orchestra's rehearsals were for many years the highpoint of the week for me. And, since those pupils promoted from the younger to the more advanced group would often continue to work also with the 'Babies', this eventually meant a whole two hours each Saturday of wonderful music-making.

During the winter and spring terms the rehearsals would be mainly devoted to perfecting a programme for the annual concert, which took place early in March for the older orchestra. (In my very early days the 'Babies' had their own special event in December, but this was discontinued when the war began. 1940 was also the only year in my time when no Waddell concert took place.)

People came from all around to attend these concerts, not just from Edinburgh; and even during the war the hall was always filled to capacity, with queues forming to pick up any returned admission-programmes. The performance would usually begin with an

18th-century work, perhaps a Concerto Grosso by Handel, or by the less well-known Charles Avison; but the choice of music always included at least one piece that was a challenge. During my time we tackled in various years such works as the Vaughan Williams *Tallis Fantasia*, the third and the sixth of Bach's *Brandenburg Concertos*, the Mozart *Eine kleine Nachtmusik*, the Grieg *Holberg Suite*, Gustav Holst's *Fugal Concerto* and *St Paul's Suite*, Warlock's *Capriol Suite*, and the Elgar *Serenade for Strings*. In between the orchestral items a hand-picked selection of pupils would perform solos, starting with some of the younger and less-experienced and finishing with those who were already of conservatoire standard. The programme would then come to a rousing end with, perhaps, one of Percy Grainger's light-hearted pieces, or one of the Hebridean suites that Maimie Waddell had herself arranged for the orchestra.

The playing of Hebridean and Scottish music was among the orchestra's most cherished traditions. And we were privileged in being taught the authentic way of rendering Scottish dance tunes, for William Waddell, father of Maimie and Ruth, had learnt in the school of Neil Gow, the celebrated Scottish fiddler. Maimie could impart a lilting rhythm to a Strathspey that gave it a stately character quite unlike the trivial jauntiness it often has. And in her hands the lift of those up-beats in a Reel might have set them dancing in the General Assembly of the Kirk itself.

All these tunes we learnt, not from music but aurally, and our rehearsals always finished with about ten minutes during which we played by ear a splendid variety of traditional songs and dances and were encouraged to add harmonies and descants of our own. The importance of the ear in our training was constantly emphasised, but sight-reading was not neglected. In the summer term, with the spring concert successfully accomplished, we would read through symphonies by Haydn, Mozart and Beethoven, or such works as Mendelssohn's *Hebrides Overture*, or Sibelius' *Valse Triste*. As we were only a string orchestra Ruth Waddell would officiate at the piano (she was a first-rate pianist), supplying with ease all the missing parts and acting as whipper-in for any who might be straying. It was all the greatest fun; and for many of us these sight-reading sessions must have provided our first experience of the great classical symphonies.

Always, in the Waddell orchestra, there was an insistence on the importance of playing anything we tackled to the highest possible standard, with no suggestion that allowances should be made on the grounds of our youth. 'Good enough' was a concept that simply did not exist. We had to aim for perfection, and were expected not only to work hard during our rehearsals but to practise our parts at home. The orchestra carried no passengers, and when it came to the concerts anyone unable to cope with the technical demands of the programme would have temporarily to stand down. Nor did this rigorous attitude ever detract from our enjoyment.

Of course we were human children, and did not always apply ourselves with unremitting seriousness. I remember being reproved on one occasion when, instead of attending to the matter in hand, my desk-partner and I had been comparing the gaps among our back teeth. And many of us would pass the interval between the senior and junior rehearsals in playing 'High Tig', leaping perilously from coal-bunker to bench or chair and back again. Or at other times, until chased away by the hall's caretaker, in playing a version of 'Pooh-sticks', casting our tram-tickets down the stair-well to see which would arrive first. But unquestionably we valued being treated as serious musicians, with the implied compliment that we were capable of achieving a professional standard. I sometimes wonder if there may be a tendency today to demand too little of children? I don't think they appreciate it.

As can be seen, the Waddell School played a huge part in my musical development, but other things were also important. At around the age of twelve I had moved from Miss Milroy to study with one of Edinburgh's most sought-after piano teachers, Miss Edna Lovell, and my piano playing soon began shooting ahead. Playing two instruments was common then among Edinburgh's musical children and was encouraged; and although I would always have thought of the cello as my first study, I did manage to take the LRAM diploma as a pianist; leading ironically to the situation that I am therefore theoretically entitled to teach the piano, whereas — despite years of experience, including at two national conservatoires — I have absolutely no qualification on paper to teach the cello! And it's too late now for anyone to complain.

Miss Lovell is another of those to whom I owe a great debt. She was a person who dedicated her life with an almost unbelievable devotion to her teaching — weekdays and weekends alike, often fitting in pupils for extra lessons even on Sundays. Already in my time she had become a legend, and to the end of her life she was regarded with affection and gratitude among her pupils and former pupils. Looking back (and having learnt much during forty years of marriage to a professional pianist and hearing his students and his ideas on the subject), I can see now that some gaps existed in Miss Lovell's teaching. But regarded as a communicator, she ranks among the best teachers I've ever known. It used to be said of her, and with a grain of truth, that: "Miss Lovell could teach anybody to play anything." Certainly I learnt from her many invaluable things, especially about musical phrasing and about methods of practice. And regarding the latter, much experience in my own teaching has shown me how relatively few young students have the good fortune to be taught anything about practising; so often even the gifted ones appear to think that it implies only 'play it again, Sam', with little idea of why or how.

In addition to all the above activities I also went regularly to a Musicianship Class that had evolved from the old *Chassevent* lessons. Here we learnt harmony, musical analysis and improvisation from a delightful teacher, Miss Avena Norfor, who, in addition to being a good musician, possessed great personal charm. And it was during the improvisation sessions that I discovered, around the age of eleven, I possessed absolute pitch — in other words, the capacity to recognise and name any note without being told what it is. This discovery came about because we used when improvising to work in pairs, at two pianos, with one pupil beginning and the other continuing after an agreed interval. Our teacher would normally have to announce the key for the second player to take over, but one day I found that I didn't need to be told — I just knew.

However, lest anyone be too impressed, I'd point out that absolute pitch — to my mind, anyway — is a somewhat over-rated gift. True, it will help you no end in any form of aural-test exam, or when doing musical dictation, or singing atonal music. But it can cause horrendous problems for instrumentalists when, for example, they arrive to play at a concert and find that the piano has not been tuned to the correct pitch — something that did sometimes happen during my early days of touring round the wilds of Scotland.

It is difficult to describe the extraordinary feeling of disorientation this causes for the performer with absolute pitch. The nearest equivalent, in non-musical terms, might be to imagine making a speech in your mother-tongue but hearing it somehow come out in a foreign language — one with which you are familiar, but are conscious of *not* speaking at the time. Eventually I learnt to cope to some extent, by doing a sort of mental transposition (the grounding in *Chassevent* helped here). But my husband, who had the most exact and acute form of absolute pitch, used to find it almost impossible to make his fingers play a piece in, say, G major, while hearing it actually sounding in G flat! He would even have difficulty in recognising a melody or theme that he knew well, perhaps from a Beethoven Sonata, if it happened to be played or sung in the wrong key.

All round, when the time arrived for me to embark on the next stage of my musical journey, I was fortunate in being pretty well grounded. And, with school finally left behind, it was arranged for me to enrol as a music student at Edinburgh University. This, in my parents' eyes, had the great advantage that, if studying in Edinburgh, I should be able to continue living at home; while, in mine, it meant I could go on having cello lessons with Ruth Waddell and playing in the Waddell Orchestra. Hence it seemed, on both sides, that taking a music degree at Edinburgh University would be the right step.

In those days the university's Music Faculty was still very much the creation of one remarkable man, Sir Donald Francis Tovey, who was Reid Professor of Music in Edinburgh from 1914 until his death in 1940. Tovey had an international reputation, and until the second World War students had been coming to study under him in Edinburgh from all around the globe. This was partly because the curriculum he had devised for the Bachelor of Music degree had special features that were unusual for the time. Not only did it lay emphasis on Tovey's own unique method of musical analysis, but the Edinburgh course was then, to the best of my knowledge, the only B.Mus. course at any British university that contained a *compulsory* practical element. At Edinburgh it was impossible to obtain a music degree, however fluent one's skills in harmony, counterpoint and so on, without being able to perform to at least a certain level. Twice-weekly classes in performance formed part of the course, and score-reading at the piano was compulsory for all students, with a reasonably high standard being demanded in this, although allowances were made for those who weren't first-study pianists.

Edinburgh's music-students also enjoyed many privileges; for thanks to a splendid legacy bestowed on the Music Faculty by its nineteenth-century benefactor, General Reid, a professional orchestra was attached to the department, which rehearsed twice a week in the Music Classroom. Attendance at these rehearsals was an integral part of the curriculum; and this meant that the subject of orchestration did not languish between the covers of learned books but was regularly demonstrated in a practical way. There was also the opportunity for a few of us among the students to join the orchestra as players and to take part in its fortnightly concerts in the Usher Hall — an experience I enormously enjoyed, as well as gaining a lot from it.

However, it has to be said that my first musical interest was then, and has always been, far more practical than academic. I wanted above all to play music, rather than to read, write or talk about it; and although I did in the end manage somehow to produce the three original compositions that were demanded in order to obtain a degree, I never had the smallest desire to be a composer. I'm deeply aware, looking back, that my university years were a formative learning experience, for they taught me much of immense value and shaped my musical ideas in a way that has endured for a lifetime. But the university musical scene is not really mine — despite my mother having spent much time and pains in trying to persuade me that it was.

On a personal level, the time at university did bring me some valued friendships, in particular that with Mary Firth, who is still one of my dear friends today. And those Edinburgh years also brought me into contact with many interesting personalities in the older generation. Among them Dr Mary Grierson, who had been one of Professor Tovey's first students when he arrived in Edinburgh in 1914. It was Mary Grierson, as acting Dean, who held the Music Faculty together during the gap between Tovey's death in 1940 and the appointment of Sidney Newman, his successor, more than a year later. Not only did she give lectures and classes — in harmony, musical history, score-reading, orchestration and formal analysis — she also took charge of conducting the Reid Orchestra for its twice-weekly rehearsals and fortnightly concerts. Today this might not seem so remarkable, but it must be stressed in order to give the right perspective that to see a women conducting an orchestra was most unusual at the time.

Besides, Dr Grierson was further unusual in that she often dressed for the Reid concerts, not in the conventional black but in a bright red jacket and skirt, an outfit that contrasted splendidly with her prematurely white hair. In addition to her academic qualifications and impressive musical knowledge, 'Auntie Mollie', as she was often known to the students, was an accomplished concert pianist, who took part regularly in performances of solo and chamber music. Her musical roots went right back to the giant figures of the nineteenth century, for she had studied during the 1920s with the famous pianist and teacher, Fanny Davies, herself a pupil of Clara Schumann.

On the surface Mary Grierson was brisk and business-like, but she had a heart of gold well-concealed beneath her official manner. I still remember with gratitude her unobtrusive and characteristically kind gesture on the occasion when I arrived, jittering with nerves, to take the score-reading and *viva* examination that formed an important part of the B.Mus. finals. There were no regulations in Edinburgh about wearing formal garb for examinations, and as it was a warm summer day I had turned up in a printed cotton dress, sandals and bare legs, which may explain why the external examiner, Sir Thomas Armstrong — from Oxford University, no less — had remarked audibly to Sidney Newman, the Professor of Music: "Is *this* Miss Moncrieff?" It was a disconcerting start to the exam; but as I diffidently slid into my place at the vast Bösendorfer grand piano, with the three examiners all hovering closely behind me, I suddenly felt the gentle pressure on my shoulders of Mary Grierson's hands, and was much reassured.

Looking back to those days it strikes me as noticeable that musical life in Edinburgh was strongly dominated by women. Nor was this only the result of wartime conditions, for many of the important women in Edinburgh music had already been established well before the war. Tribute has been paid earlier in this chapter to the remarkable work of Ruth and Maimie Waddell, and to that of Edna Lovell. And a host of others come to mind.

There was Peggie Sampson: she was not only a talented cellist who had studied in Paris with the famous teacher, Diran Alexanian, but, on her return to Edinburgh while still only in her mid-twenties, she had been appointed as lecturer in the university Music Faculty. A very good lecturer she was, too; she had an outstandingly good mind, and her classes in counterpoint — although that was never my best or favourite subject — were a model of how things should be done.

In appearance Peggie Sampson was one of those people who could, and should, have been stunning-looking, for she had the most striking deep-set eyes and her facial bone-structure was beautiful.

Unfortunately her hair was always unbecomingly styled and she lacked any dress sense; her clothes would show the most amazingly unsuitable colour-schemes, and it was rumoured she had once appeared at a concert wearing golfing-shoes with her evening dress. After the war she disappeared from Edinburgh, going first to work as a freelance cellist in London — mainly with the Carter String Trio — and later as a lecturer and performer at the University of Manitoba in Canada. But she remains an integral part of my early Edinburgh memories.

Then there was Mona Benson, a colourful personality who enjoyed a wide reputation as recitalist, opera singer and teacher — and not just in Scotland. With her aquiline features, dark flashing eyes, and straight raven-black hair, worn always with a centre parting and in a simple coil at the nape of her neck, her appearance had a certain classical style, which she would emphasise by her dramatic choice of clothes. Her intensely committed singing could never be forgotten by anyone who heard her, and her work as a teacher was greatly admired. At one point in my student days I used to act as pianist for some of her lessons, and learnt a tremendous amount from this.

Another singer of quite a different kind was Joyce Fleming, who, with her pianist colleague Ruth D'Arcy Thomson, brought to 1940s' Edinburgh a refreshingly cosmopolitan breath from Vienna, where they had been living before the second World War. Their flat in Frederick Street became a focal point of musical Edinburgh; and the excellent chamber choir they ran, the 'Student Singers', toured widely and enjoyed much success during the 1940s and '50s.

Neither Ruth nor Joyce was native to Edinburgh, but both were Scottish through and through, although in temperament the two were very different. Ruth, who had a razor-sharp mind and well-defined opinions, could on the surface appear a little introverted; whereas Joyce showed an uninhibited attitude to life that marked her out in 1940s' Scotland. She spoke her mind, too. Once, when I was about nineteen, I arrived at the Frederick Street flat with my hair neatly encased in a hair-net, to be greeted by Joyce with a horrified: "For any sake, Margaret — **not** a hair-net! Do you want to turn into one of Edinburgh's musical spinsters?"

There was, too, the unforgettable Tertia Liebenthal, whose German father, Louis Liebenthal, had settled in Edinburgh during the late nineteenth century. Tertia had quite a wide knowledge of music and she was a dauntlessly enthusiastic amateur violinist, of not more than moderate efficiency but capable of persuading even such renowned artists as Peter Pears to join her in chamber music (as pianist, it should be added, not singer!).

Quite early in the war Tertia, along with certain others (Jean Hunter Cowan and Norna Dalziel among them), had started the long-running series of lunch-hour concerts in the Scottish National Gallery, which — ignoring all other founding members — Tertia always referred to as '*My Concerts*'. Through the years a huge range of performers appeared in the series — including such international stars as Kathleen Ferrier and the afore-mentioned Peter Pears, for Tertia had no inhibitions about approaching any artist, however famous, who happened to be visiting Scotland, perhaps to appear with the Scottish Orchestra (as the RSNO used to be known).

Hospitality of a fairly spartan kind was always available for these visitors, and for others, in the tall gaunt house where she lived in Regent Terrace, overlooking Arthurs Seat and Holyrood Palace. (It was here, in 1952, at one of her musical parties, that I first met my future husband.) Tertia herself was, like the house, tall and rather gaunt in appearance. She had a certain unpredictable side, which could make her at some times your best friend, and at others apparently indifferent to your existence. But she was a genuinely kind person; and her concerts didn't present only the great and famous but offered valuable opportunities to many up-and-coming young Scottish performers, myself among them.

Turning to the orchestral scene: right through my early memories, women were prominent in both the Scottish and the Reid orchestras, with many of them holding responsible positions; and this again was not due simply to the absence of men during the war. The Scottish Orchestra (now Royal Scottish National Orchestra) was actually led for many years by a woman, Jean Rennie; and although the leader of the Reid Orchestra was male — the violinist, John Fairbairn, who was also a lecturer in the university Music Department — the principals of the second violins, violas and cellos were all women. Yet another woman musician who should be mentioned is the cellist, Marie Dare: besides being a composer of some standing — several of her works for cello, and cello ensemble, are still in demand — Marie was the original cellist of the Scottish Piano Trio; and for many years, following Ruth Waddell's retirement, she led the cellos in the Reid Orchestra.

There can be no doubt that I and my Edinburgh contemporaries must have been influenced by growing up in a world where so many women were able to achieve successful careers. It's true that a majority of these women were unmarried, but a few, even in the 1940s, did manage to combine a musical career and marriage. The climate of opinion in musical Edinburgh did not seem to discriminate against women; and, due probably to this, it was quite a shock to me when I arrived in London in the late 1940s to discover the degree of male chauvinist prejudice that existed there in the orchestral world.

In Edinburgh, attitudes had tended if anything to look less kindly on *boys* taking a serious interest in music than on girls — something to which my late husband could bear personal testimony. He had shown remarkable pianistic talent from about the age of four, but he also held a scholarship at an extremely traditional Edinburgh school, the Royal High School; and all through his early years he was forever being told "You'd be far better off outside playing football than spending so much time at that piano!" And probably it was because music was not then a favoured career for men that most of the star talents I remember admiring in my early days were girls. Many from various generations, both before and after mine, went on to have widely successful careers, including the well-known cellist and teacher Joan Dickson, and her sister Hester.

Today, the numerous feminists among my friends have often expressed surprise that I didn't encounter more sexist opposition in my early days. And perhaps it does seem odd that Edinburgh, where ideas were in so many ways old-fashioned, should have been far ahead of the times in producing so many female musicians.

However, before going further, and to round off this part of the memoirs, mention must be made of one musician who had particular and lasting influence in my life, and who was not female: Dr Hans Gál.

I have written elsewhere at some length about Hans Gál, and to sum him up in a few paragraphs is impossible, for he was among the most interesting, complex and remarkable characters I have known. He had come as a refugee to Edinburgh in 1938 on the invitation of the Professor of Music, Sir Donald Tovey, whom he had met on several occasions in Germany and Austria. At that pre-war period Gál had been renowned throughout Europe and beyond, as a musicologist and composer whose works were being widely performed (he was also both pianist and conductor). But, being Jewish, he and his family had been obliged to flee from Vienna following the Nazi annexation of Austria. After an adventurous escape through Switzerland to Britain the Gáls had originally intended to go on to the United States, but thanks to Tovey's invitation Gál had come first to Edinburgh. And here, apart from two short intervals — including some unhappy months of internment during the 1940 British panic about invasion — he was to spend the rest of his long and distinguished musical life.

My own acquaintance with Hans Gál began in about 1942 when, on the recommendation of Dr Mary Grierson, I went to have lessons with him in harmony and counterpoint — or, at least, those subjects were the stated objective of the lessons, but they in fact covered a far wider musical field. And between about 1944 and 1946 I was also lucky enough to attend, along with my mother, the weekly classes that Gál called his *Collegium Musicum* — an experience that opened many musical doors.

These sessions, which demonstrated numerous facets of Gál's talents and personality, always followed a similar pattern. First, at three o'clock, a group of instrumentalists would assemble to rehearse under Gál's direction a work of his choice. This could sometimes be as relatively well-known as Bach's *Suite in B minor for flute and strings* or Schubert's *Trout Quintet*, but was often something unknown to any of us. The time for rehearsal was necessarily limited, and I think the actual standard of performance must have been variable, for the players were mixed in both age and ability. But we all learnt a tremendous amount about getting to the heart of a piece of music as quickly as possible, as well as gaining much invaluable knowledge about points of style and interpretation. We also learnt to be always alert and ready to begin, for Gál was not someone — either as pianist or conductor — who liked to wait for dilatory musicians, being indeed far more likely in his enthusiasm to plunge in regardless, while other players were still trying to sort out their music.

After the rehearsal the listeners would arrive, and performers and audience would then enjoy the splendid tea Hanna Gál always managed to produce despite all the restrictions of food rationing (which of course lasted until about 1954). Next came the actual lecture — for want of a better word — when Gál, seated at the piano, would take players and listeners on a guided tour of the chosen work, pointing out musical and historical features of special interest. Each step was illustrated by musical examples, and underlined with his own inimitable touches of humour. Who but Gál could have demanded special attention to the bass at the opening of a Bach Cantata by saying: "If ever I would be reincarnated, I would like to be a passing seventh in the bass"? (The descending bass at the opening of Bach's *Air in D* — widely known in the version 'Air on the G string' — provides an example of the passing seventh.) Finally there would be a performance of the whole work. And I cannot imagine that anyone who attended those sessions failed to gain life-long benefits from them. How often I've wished that present-day students in our music-colleges could have similar opportunities to acquire what the curriculum hopefully calls 'practical skills' in the preparation and performance of music! But then, there has only been one Hans Gál.

Gál's outward appearance was austere, for the delightful humour and humanity so characteristic of him did not always emerge immediately. So far as I can remember, my first meeting with him in an off-duty situation happened one summer soon after the war, when I was invited, along with my half-nieces Barbara and Petronilla Paton Walsh, to visit the Gál family at St. Abb's Head — a place on Scotland's east coast renowned for its bracing air.

We three were well accustomed to the chilly seas at North Berwick, and were delighted when, after lunch, a swim was proposed. But we were completely astonished when Dr Gál (as I still thought of him then) arrived to join us and went striding into the waves, a figure spare to the point of skinniness in his old-fashioned bathing suit. Few of the adults in our family would have ventured into the sea at this exposed spot! But Gál appeared undaunted by either the cold or the considerable height of the breakers. It turned out that swimming was among his preferred recreations (and it was always to remain so, for, as I learnt many years later, Gál continued until almost into his nineties to swim regularly at Edinburgh's Commonwealth swimming pool).

As the years passed, our relationship gradually changed from that of pupil and eminent teacher to one of warm friendship. And Hans was also to become a much-loved figure, not only in my life but in those of my husband and daughters. The Hans Gál Sonata for Cello and Piano was a favourite work of Alex's and mine, and one of which we gave many performances; including at a Wigmore Hall recital in March 1971, and for a recording now in the Scottish Archives. I also had the honour of playing this sonata, with its simple but deeply expressive slow movement, when the Austrian Institute in London held gala concerts in celebration of Hans Gál's 80th and 90th birthdays, in 1970 and 1980 respectively. On the first occasion the pianist was my husband, but on the second the piano-part was played by the ninety-year-old composer himself. His comment afterwards was typical: "You see, I am modest — so I will say only, I never hope to hear it better played."

A whole chapter could be filled with Hans' pithy and well-turned comments — serious and humorous, and on a variety of subjects, not just on music. Often they were pointed, not to say barbed: when I showed him the three compositions that had successfully if painfully gained me my degree in music, his reaction was a shrug of the shoulders and a dry "Well, *I* would not perform them"; and he once said of a singer: "Oh yes, it is a beautiful voice, but his reactions have the slowness of cattle." He could even appear a little ruthless: when asked if he didn't agree that the rigorous way music students in the Soviet Union (as it was) were made to concentrate on technical work was damaging to their musical development, he scandalised the questioner; replying that, on the contrary, he entirely approved of this strict training, since if any student actually had something musical to say, it gave them the technical means to say it. Adding: "As for the others — if in the process the very little musicality they have is squeezed out, it is no great matter."

On the other hand, Hans could also be generous: I treasure the memory of his saying after a Wigmore Hall recital: "Your Beethoven was glorious." And one remark I particularly recall, perhaps because it was unexpected. This must have been quite late in Hans' life, probably on one of my last visits to the Edinburgh house, where he and Hanna lived in Blacket Place. "The older I get" — and he turned to me with a serene smile — "The more I agree with the Apostle Paul, that love is the only thing that matters."

I like to remember Hans at that moment. And I'll always be grateful to him and to Hanna — who was his mainstay and support during more than sixty years, as well as being a genuinely interesting personality in her own right — for their kindness and friendship.

VIII: Random Wartime Memories

ONCE AGAIN, IT BECOMES NECESSARY HERE to turn back several years. And historical perspective is a strange thing, for today our perception of World War II differs from the understanding that most ordinary people had at the time. With hindsight, and innumerable books, plays and television programmes, it is possible now to see things from a far wider viewpoint. But looking back, I realise that I had at the time — at least in the earlier days — a fairly restricted view of events.

Many things contributed to this. The prospect of war, and its ultimate arrival, had been linked in many civilians' minds with the threat of air raids. But we, who were living in the relative security of Edinburgh, were less directly concerned about this than people living in London or the south coast ports. Edinburgh itself was not considered a likely target for the German bombers (no one had dreamt then of *Baedeker* raids), and the city did not in the event experience many serious air attacks. There were a few — and I remember that the father of a boy I knew was killed in one of them. And on many occasions we went through the classic routine of departing with gas masks to take shelter in the basement. But, most often, when the warning sirens wailed it meant that the German planes, with that unmistakable intermittent hum of their engines, would only be passing over on their way to attack Glasgow.

Oddly enough, though, as I discovered quite recently when doing research for a novel partly set in 1939 Scotland, the area round the Firth of Forth was in fact among the first places in Britain to suffer attack from the air. Several raids were recorded in the autumn of 1939; and I do now vaguely remember our family being rushed home from the North Berwick beach one afternoon in October 1939, when an aerial dog-fight was going on just a few miles out to sea.

In my case, the important reasons for this rather detached attitude lay nearer home. None of the adults in our household was enthusiastic about the war — there was no flag-waving, no patriotic speeches. Understandably, perhaps, bearing in mind that a majority of those surrounding me at home — my parents and their contemporaries — were elderly, and had lived through the first World War, not to mention the Boer War. Undoubtedly both my father and mother accepted that this was a war that had to be fought, but both showed a certain disillusionment about the futility of all wars. And their attitudes towards the conflict were irreconcilably different.

My mother had always been pro-German. She loved the language and had been steeped all her life in German culture. For her, Germany was the land of Goethe and Schiller, Schubert and Schumann — not of Hitler and Goebbels. Besides, she was a living example of how it really is possible to learn too much from experience. Again and again she would revert to the anti-German stories that were circulated during World War I — the tales about how the Germans used to boil down corpses to make soap, and how the Kaiser used to eat babies (I think the latter was also said in the previous century about Napoleon) and other patently ridiculous tales. And because all this had proved to be untrue, my mother was never willing to accept anything said against the Germans, and would dismiss all reports as *Propaganda* — "Well, we all know how it was in the last war."

Nowadays so much has been learnt about the horrors of the concentration camps that, for us today, it seems impossible to accept that there really were intelligent people in Britain during the 1930s who genuinely believed that the reports of atrocities in Germany were "simply propaganda", designed to whip up anti-German feeling — among them my mother.

My father, of course, held completely opposite views. He had been born around the time of the Franco-Prussian war, when a majority of Scottish opinion was anti-German and pro-French; and everything in his background and heredity leaned towards Latin rather than Teutonic culture. He would sometimes hold forth about what Churchill had called "the German menace"; but my mother would simply have dismissed his thoughts and opinions on the subject as coming from someone who was totally prejudiced against the Germans.

In any case, my father was by temperament the complete

pessimist, and always took the gloomiest possible views about the conduct of the war. On the whole, it was better to keep off the subject.

For many ordinary people, who were not actively involved with running the war, the two things that impinged most closely were the blackout and the rationing. The blackout had existed from just before day one; and in our Edinburgh house with its seventeen rooms, it regularly took about twenty minutes to complete the complicated arrangements — a combination of heavily lined curtains, shutters and black paper — that were needed to screen the many large windows. Everyone was extremely blackout-conscious; the air-raid wardens used to patrol the streets, and should the tiniest streak of light be visible from outside, they would ring the doorbell and administer a sharp reproof to the householder. One over-zealous warden is said to have told my mother that if he lay down on our front-door steps, he could just see a light shining through above the door. My mother allegedly replied that she didn't think the German bombers were likely to lie down outside our front door. (But I rather fear that this tale may be apocryphal.)

Rationing was another fact of daily life; and perhaps it isn't always appreciated today that some form of rationing existed in Britain for **almost fifteen years**! — from 1939 to 1954. Hence, although it is always difficult to be sure which are genuine memories, the later years did extend into my adult life. And one thing has become clear to me in watching such TV programmes as *The 1940s House*: no one of later generations can ever truly enter into the life and feelings of those who lived through the actual experiences, because people of the present day are starting from somewhere completely different. For example, I don't think that at the time it struck people of the 1940s as odd, or even particularly tiresome, that coal had to be carried into the house and that the boiler had to be stoked by hand — that was simply the way things were. And take the reactions of the 1990s' TV family to such things as dried eggs: accustomed as they were to an unlimited supply of real eggs, this egg powder seemed to them highly unattractive. But if you are living at a time when the egg ration is often less than one a week, and other foods are in similarly short supply, you don't just have to make the best of a dried egg omelette, you find it positively acceptable. Of course, I was young at the time, but I seem to remember that most of those round me felt the same. With the possible exception of my father . . .

No particular memory remains about the early months of the war; perhaps because, on one level, so little appeared to be happening. The evacuation of Dunkirk in May 1940 is probably the first important memory. But here I find it impossible now to disentangle genuine recollections from the mass of information acquired more recently, and it is particularly difficult in the case of Dunkirk, for it has been the subject of, or background to, so many books and films. It must also be underlined that in wartime news was severely restricted. Nowadays we've all become accustomed to having world events appear almost immediately on our television screens. On September 11 2001 some of us even had the extraordinary experience of witnessing a world disaster thousands of miles away, unfolding before our disbelieving eyes at the moment it actually happened (and by 2003 the day-to-day viewing of wartime events would become commonplace, although paradoxically this often produced an odd feeling of unreality — perhaps the result of watching too many war films?). Things were very different during the second World War, when only scanty, carefully censored reports were available in newspapers or on the wireless, while the newsreels at the cinema were ruthlessly pruned.

However, though I can't now recall exactly how much I knew at the time about Dunkirk, I do for some reason clearly and personally remember the fall of France a few weeks later; and the widespread fears of invasion that followed it, with the uprooting of all the signposts around the country, and the internment of so called 'enemy aliens' — including many who were refugees from the Nazis and who were certainly not pro-German. I remember, too, the considerable amount of feeling against the French that existed then — on the lines that they 'had let us down' by surrendering to the Germans. An irrational tendency to be anti-French remained with me until after I went to live in Paris in 1947, when I gradually learnt that there was quite another side to the matter.

That summer of 1940 marked the first time that we didn't move to North Berwick at the beginning of July. I'm not sure now of the reason; but we were certainly still in Edinburgh on the day that the war really struck home for our family — particularly for my mother. It was 19 August 1940; that morning she and I had been to the library, and we were met at the front door on our return home by my father, a telegram in his hands. It announced that my half-brother Walter Spens had been killed the previous day, during one of the earliest air-raids in the

Battle of Britain. At the time he was attached to the Fleet Air Arm and had been stationed at Ford, near Arundel in Sussex. We never heard any details about the raid — or, at least, I was never told any. But by a specially unkind twist of fate, the nineteenth of August was my mother's birthday.

For me the news was a shock, but there was no overwhelming sense of personal loss. Walter had already been grown up when I was a baby, and for much of my childhood he'd been serving in Malta with the Royal Navy and we had seen little of him. My feelings for him were entirely positive, for he had always shown warmth and affection for the little sister who was so much his junior. But I didn't, in any adult sense, really know him.

For my mother, the loss of her first child while still in his thirties must have been a devastating blow. But in accordance with her character and upbringing, she gave few outward demonstrations of grief. On just one occasion she broke down completely. This was a few days later; we were waiting to hear the News on the wireless, as we did most evenings, and the *Londonderry Air* was being sung in the version known as *Danny Boy*. Suddenly towards the end of the final verse, when the singer reached the words "You'll come and find the grave where I am lying, And kneel and say an *Ave* there for me," my mother burst into a storm of tears, sobbing out that Walter wouldn't have any grave because he was probably all in bits . . . (In fact he did have a grave in the little churchyard at Climping in Sussex; and about thirty years later I was able to visit it with my daughters and we laid flowers there.)

To add to her pain, wartime conditions deprived my mother of even the small comfort of attending Walter's funeral. But there was one strange and wonderfully happy coincidence. When, after that raid on August 18th, the wounded and dying were brought into the nearest hospital, one of the nurses on duty that afternoon was my former nanny, Monica Bond. She had known Walter quite well during the years she lived with our family, and I hope he was able to recognise her. I'm sure her presence would have been a comfort.

From this point on our family did have a more personal involvement with the war. Especially when the bombing of London began in the late summer of 1940; for throughout the various phases of the Blitz, the Paton Walsh family — my half-sister and her children — were living in London. I can imagine that my mother, who was by nature a worrier, must have passed many sleepless nights during this time. The Paton Walshes survived through all the earlier years and the doodle-bug raids and right up until March 1945, but as ill fortune would have it, one of the last V2 rockets of the war hit the end of their garden, partly demolishing the house. No one was killed; but my sister's thirteen-year-old daughter, Petronilla, endured the horrible experience of being trapped for a time in the rubble; and the elder son, Antony, who was eight, suffered permanent damage to one eye.

One extraordinary event does stand out from the early years: this was the dramatic arrival in Scotland by plane of the Nazi leader, Rudoph Hess, on his abortive mission to talk the British into making peace with Germany. On that day in May 1941 it chanced that I was in Glasgow with my mother, taking my cello for some small repair to the workshop of a Mr Smillie, who was well-known at the time. As we walked along the Great West Road on our way back to Queen Street station, the scrawled posters on every newspaper-stand were proclaiming "Hess lands in Scotland". Suddenly the war felt very near. Especially when it turned out that Hess's actual landing place had been not far from Glasgow.

Another personal memory that remains vivid is of an international Girl Guide camp, which took place in the border country near Melrose during the summer of 1943. At the time I was attached to a Cadet Guide Company in Edinburgh; it was this that had led to my connection with the St Patrick's Brownie Pack, described elsewhere, and it now brought me a nomination to attend the camp. Not that I was in any way a specially distinguished member of the Guide movement, being chosen most probably because of my musical abilities, which meant I'd be able to contribute to the sessions of massed singing that were an important feature of the set-up. Perhaps it might also have been thought an advantage, since a majority of the European Guides were Roman Catholics, that I, unlike any of the other Scots, was also a Catholic and would be able to represent Scotland in the R.C. group for prayers, which were always held separately in those days for the different denominations.

The camp had a particularly beautiful site, with the river Tweed running alongside our tents and the Eildon Hills in the background. And it truly was an international affair despite being held in the middle of a world war, with all the attendant restrictions on travel, not to mention food rationing and blackout regulations. How the organisers

International Guide Camp on banks of the Tweed. August 1943.

managed it I don't know, but the groups of teenagers included Polish, Czech, Belgian, French, Dutch, Danish and Norwegian girls, as well as larger contingents from England, Wales, and the host country, Scotland. I don't remember any from Ireland — probably the journey across the sea would have been too dangerous.

Among many happy recollections of that week, a few stand out. One of a polyglot bathing party, when we attempted to swim in the Tweed, and found the current so fast that with maximum effort we could just about stay in the same place. Another: a magical pre-dawn expedition up the Eildons to see the sun rise. And one particular memory which somehow encapsulates everything: that of the nightly Camp Fire sessions, when, in addition to massed singing of well-known items, the programme would include national songs and dances performed by each of the different countries. (In passing, I wonder how, in view of the stringent blackout regulations, we were allowed to have a camp *fire* at all — we were always so strictly enjoined, amongst other things, to keep any torches pointing downwards at night. But of course sunset comes late during Scottish summers — probably darkness hadn't fallen till after we finished.)

The proceedings always ended, as is traditional at Girl Guide Camp Fires, with the singing of "Taps" — but with a difference; for, here, each country in turn sang "Taps" in their own language. An unfading picture remains of the scene, as each small group moved forward to give their rendering, while the others stood silent in the semi-darkness (thinking perhaps of friends or relatives who were far away fighting for the freedom of these same countries). In particular I remember the Norwegian girl, Astrid: tall, striking and typically Scandinavian in looks, she was the sole representative of her nation, and her lone contribution was especially touching. Sad to say, I've long since lost the different versions I collected from all the various groups, and tried to learn in a fit of linguistic fervour. But the images of that week will always endure.

Girl Guides were also central to some of my other important wartime memories. These relate to the residential home for disabled children that the Girl Guide authorities in Edinburgh were responsible for running throughout the war. This enterprise, which was sponsored by the Edinburgh Education Authority but staffed mainly by volunteers, had originally been set up at the outbreak of the war to care for disabled children who were being evacuated from Edinburgh (and after 1945 it was to develop into a permanent 'special school'). Apart from a trained nurse, those on the regular staff were all members of the Guide movement; and Girl Guides of all ages from about sixteen, and from different parts of the country, were encouraged to devote some of their holiday-time to helping with the day-to-day running of the home.

During the war this was located at Earlston in Berwickshire, in a large rambling house with the romantic name of Cowdenknowes. (*The Bonnie Broom o' the Cowdenknowes* is a well known old Scottish air.) The house, part of which dates back to the sixteenth century, is set in extensive grounds, with the garden proper divided from the fields and woods by the River Leader. It is a truly lovely place (today it has become a centre for pony-trekking enthusiasts), and I spent many happy weekends there during term-time as well as longer periods in the holidays, working in various capacities to assist the resident team.

On my earlier visits I was assigned to housework duties; and most of what I've ever learnt about housework is thanks to the stalwart and extremely demanding woman who organised the younger helpers in their cleaning of the enormous house. At other times I worked in the kitchen which provided a first basic training in cooking for numbers, and demonstrated such facts of washing-up life as saucepans needing to be cleaned outside as well as inside — this being something my mother never did, possibly because she had come to domestic chores so late in life.

At Cowdenknowes the atmosphere was always friendly and relaxed; and, solitary as I often was at home, I much enjoyed the company of the helpers, both younger and older. We also used to have the opportunity when off duty to explore the beautiful Border countryside, either on foot or on borrowed bicycles. But undoubtedly the most valuable learning experience came from having personal contact with the disabled children.

There were about twenty of them, both boys and girls, ranging from around nine to eighteen, and they came for the most part from the poorest districts of Edinburgh. Many were victims of polio (still common then), or of spastic paralysis; one suffered from severe arthritis, two from muscular dystrophy (and they were brothers which made it specially sad). Some were wheelchair-bound, others able to move around — even, in a few cases, with a degree of agility despite the hampering callipers they had to wear. But every one of these children showed a most amazing spirit and a cheerful resilience in the face of their problems that was utterly admirable. Above all they demonstrated that children are always children, not made different in any way because of disabilities. The whole thing was a revelation to me, for until my first visit to Cowdenknowes I'd never had any real contact with the physically disabled; and I can recall that up to this point I'd even tended to avert my eyes if I saw a disabled person in the street. Those visits to Cowdenknowes will always bring back affectionate and grateful memories.

Returning to general war recollections: I do, like most people who were alive at the time, have a clear memory of exactly where I was on 6 June 1944, and of hearing the wireless reports that the first D-Day landings in Normandy had been taking place since dawn. (Naturally, though, I wasn't then aware that the sixth of June, thirteen years later, would be my wedding day!) I can also remember at various times hearing some of Winston Chuchill's historic speeches; in particular, the time he concluded by quoting Arthur Hugh Clough's poem about "the tired waves vainly breaking". I can still hear Churchill's characteristic, slightly nasal tones declaiming the final lines: "In front the sun climbs slow, how slowly, But westward, look, the land is bright!" However, as can happen, my memories don't extend to telling me at what point in the war he spoke this, although presumably it was at a stage when things had at last begun moving in the Allies' favour.

An equally strong memory, although in this case not aural but visual, is of the exhibition of French Impressionist painters that was held near the beginning of 1945 in the Scottish National Gallery. (Huge efforts were made following the liberation of France to bring French culture to Britain, in the way of exhibitions, music and theatre.) At that time I had already been captivated by the French Impressionist School, and had reproductions of two Monets and one Cezanne in my bedroom; but not surprisingly I had never before seen any of the actual paintings. In that wartime world, characterised by austerity, not to say drabness, the impact made by the sheer vibrancy of their colour was indescribable; there was one Monet, picturing a cliff-top scene in summer, where it seemed you could almost feel the heat.

Regarding the end of the war, I can't for some odd reason remember anything particular about the celebrations on either V.E. Day in May 1945, or on V.J. Day the following September. I rather think that beacons were lit on top of Edinburgh's Braid and Pentland Hills, perhaps also on Arthur's Seat and the Calton Hill — always a wonderful sight, and one that would have signalled a welcome end to the blackout. But my memories of these victory festivities have become confused with those that marked the two coronations — that of George VI many years earlier, and that of Elizabeth II in 1953. And in the case of V.J. Day, I know that for me, as for many of my generation, rejoicings were eclipsed by the horror of hearing about the two atomic bombs that had been dropped on Japan. It was clear at the time that there could be cogent arguments for dropping *one* atomic bomb, in order to establish for even the most fanatical Japanese that this was the end of the road. But I could never understand why, when this had been made inescapably plain, another bomb had to be used on another city. I still can't.

For most people, the end of hostilities brought mainly overwhelming feelings of relief. Especially for those of us who had relatives in London and other blitzed cities, for it meant the threat of aerial bombardment was over. And now at last it was possible to think about getting on with the ordinary things of life, which for me meant being able to make plans for a course of serious cello studies. Today it feels rather discreditable to think that, with Europe ravaged by war and filled with starving refugees and displaced persons, my main preoccupation was to talk my parents into agreeing that the time had finally arrived for me to leave Edinburgh and begin intensive study of the cello, either in London or somewhere abroad. But it's probable that no one would ever get far in a musical career without a certain degree of self-interest. It's also fair to emphasise yet again that we, at the time, knew less than people do now about the conditions prevailing in post-war Europe.

My parents were still far from happy about the prospect of my taking up the career of professional cellist, but I must have been unusually determined; and my hand was strengthened by the two travelling scholarships I'd been awarded by Edinburgh University — the Andrew Fraser Scholarship and the Bucher Scholarship. The latter was an award that could only be used outside Britain — it had been founded in the days before World War I, when most young Scottish musicians almost automatically went to Germany for their post-graduate studies. But the first named carried no such restrictions; and this helped me to decide that, with conditions abroad still so uncertain, I would do best to use the Andrew Fraser money towards a year in London (all this was of course before the days of student grants). Hence, in the late summer of 1946 I set off from Edinburgh to spend a year studying with Ivor James, who was then one of Britain's most respected cello professors.

In accepting the move, my parents — certainly my mother — may well have decided covertly that, having spread my wings for a year or two, I should be ready to come back and settle down again in Edinburgh. At the time I honestly think this was also my intention, for I had always had a deep love for my native city (on return visits I never fail to marvel at its extraordinary beauty). But things didn't turn out that way. In the end, once having set off for London in 1946, I was never again to live permanently in Edinburgh.

Part Three: New Worlds Beckon

(Overleaf) Me with my hair 'up' — 1944/45.

IX: A Year at Lytton Grove

My choice to study with Ivor James had happened in a roundabout way. Several teachers had been suggested; and at one point Ruth Waddell had been much in favour of my going to spend a year working with Suggia in Portugal. At the time I rather liked that idea, although with hindsight I'm thankful that for various practical reasons it came to nothing. I'd also gone for an interview in London with a certain female cellist, highly recommended, who shall be nameless. But she had worked too hard to convince me that she herself was absolutely the one and only person who could help me (and, dear me, it was plain that I was much in need of help). As a result, by the time I got back to Edinburgh I felt completely disenchanted with women cellists in general, and had made up my mind, not only that I was never going to learn with *her*, but that there was much to be said now for the idea of studying with a male teacher. I already knew a little about Ivor James, for he had adjudicated twice at the Edinburgh Competition Festival when I was competing, and he had made a warmly favourable impression. To ask him for a course of lessons seemed the obvious solution.

The plan of studying in London also had advantages from a practical point of view, since my sister's family, the Paton Walshes, were then living in Putney, where they had moved the previous year after being bombed out of their house in Wandsworth. Their new home was a large detached house in Lytton Grove — a turning off Putney Hill (just a few roads further up the hill than *The Pines*, the villa that had belonged to Algernon Swinburne). And since the house contained an ample number of rooms, this meant I had a ready made home-from-home.

The year I spent at 44 Lytton Grove was a notably happy one for many reasons. Not only was I able at long last to give undivided attention to my cello studies, the year also provided my first real experience of what may be called normal family life, surrounded by lively young people — aged in this instance from around five to eighteen. This was something I'd never really been able to enjoy at home, living as I did with elderly parents and intellectually impaired older brothers, who — though not through any real fault of their own — were regularly the focus of problems and worries. Both Hugh and Philip had many good and lovable qualities, but both also had certain personality traits and behavioural problems which could at times make it difficult for them to be assimilated into ordinary daily life. There had been a couple of years during the war when, for various reasons, both had to be permanently at home; it was a fairly stressful time.

44 Lytton Grove. I originally had the attic room (top right).

When I joined the Paton Walsh household in September 1946, it included four of the five younger members of the family. Barbara, the eldest, had left school the previous July and was studying at a London coaching establishment with the object of gaining a place to read history at Oxford. Veronica — always known as Tigger — and Antony were both at local day schools, and John had not yet started school. The only one absent in term-time was Petronilla, who was then boarding at the convent school in Mayfield, East Sussex, where her mother had been head girl some 25 years earlier. As a result I saw rather less of her during that year, although the close friendship we had built in earlier years always continued.

Meanwhile my relationship with Barbara, who was now nearly eighteen, was to grow steadily with the day-to-day contact; especially during the 1947 summer term, when the room I had been using during the first six months had to be given over to a delightful Swiss girl, Maria — I forget her surname — with whom Barbara was doing an exchange. This meant that I had not only to sleep in Barbara's room but to practise there, while she sat working at her desk only a few yards away. The competition for places at Oxford was particularly hard at that time — far tougher than it had been before the war — because a large number of places were being reserved for ex-service candidates; and it in fact took Barbara three different attempts before she finally was offered a place at Lady Margaret Hall. Undoubtedly it must often have been tiresome for her to hear the endless repetitions and other unprepossessing sounds that are characteristic of instrumental practice, but Barbara accepted it with good will and always said she didn't mind. She and I had our 'spats' from time to time, but enduring links were forged between us.

The year at Lytton Grove also gave me the opportunity to develop a more adult level of friendship with both my half-sister, Patricia, and my brother-in-law, Eddie. As a small child I had admired Patricia greatly but had always felt she seemed a little remote. And it can't have been easy from her viewpoint that, with my being obviously much nearer in age to her children than to herself, people sometimes took her for my mother — which would elicit a quick "Oh no, this is my little sister".

My mother, me, Barbara and Patricia, setting off for a garden party at Buckingham Palace, June 1947.

Then later, as I grew up and began to appreciate the lighter side of her character and her good sense of humour, I quickly became increasingly attached to her. She was an immensely efficient and capable person; and, like my mother, she had risen dauntlessly to the changes brought about by wartime conditions. Before the war her household had always included two resident maids, as well as some form of live-in help with the children; but she had not only taken over the household duties of cooking, shopping and so on, but, in the absence of her husband on active service, had held home and her family of five children together through all the bombardment of London and the final destruction of their house.

In this, Patricia had been wonderfully supported by Meecie — Grace Randall — who remained with the family all through the war. It was only in the summer of 1946 that she had been obliged to leave in order to go and look after her aging mother. She always remained a regular visitor, and often came to stay for long periods and to give invaluable help in various crises; but after this point she wasn't again a permanent member of the household and was greatly missed.

To help a little with bridging the gap, Patricia had decided to invite a Swiss girl from Lucerne, Elisabeth Rey, to come and live with the family for a year as an *au pair*. And Elisabeth remains very much part of my Lytton Grove memories. Among the small things that stand out, I recall that she had brought from Switzerland a tin of Nescafé — now familiar to everyone, but almost unknown in Britain at the time. She and I were much of an age, and, although on the surface Elisabeth appeared very earnest and it took a little time before we got really to know her, she was to become a genuine friend, one with whom the family always kept in touch at intervals. (Long afterwards — it must have been about forty-five years later — when I was holidaying with my husband near Lucerne, Elisabeth and I had a happy reunion; and while Alex, at my suggestion, took a mountain walk, she and I spent a long session together, mulling over shared recollections of the Putney days.)

During the first term I spent at Lytton Grove, Eddie was not with us. He had spent most of the war acting as Provo Marshall in the Military Police, and had served in North Africa and later in Germany. One of his immediately post-war tasks had been to advise on the complete reorganisation of the German prison and justice systems, then during 1946 he was also involved in the historic trials of the Nazi war criminals that took place that autumn in Nuremberg. Shortly afterwards he was demobilised, and in January 1947 he returned to resume his pre-war post as Deputy Governor of Wandsworth Prison.

From my earliest childhood Eddie had always occupied a special place in my affections, to the extent that I had even, around the age of nine, written out and made a formal prayer to God that He would somehow, in some mysterious way, manage to manoeuvre things so that Eddie could become *my* father. However, since I definitely wished to retain my real mother and made this plain, I think such a request would have baffled even the Almighty; and in making it I must have been exceedingly naive. Interestingly, it was not long after this that the cello entered my life, and a few months later I can actually recall making a conscious decision that, all round, it would be best to stay as I was.

Eddie on service with the Control Commision in Germany, 1945/6.

The odd thing is that Eddie in fact shared some of the characteristics that, as a child, I found most off-putting in my own father. He had nearly as explosive a temper, and was possibly even more irritable about small matters. But for some strange reason this did not alienate me in the same way that my father's outbursts had done. Perhaps this happened precisely because Eddie was not in fact my father, and I didn't live permanently with him. Or at least not until that time at Lytton Grove, and by then I was grown up and able to take a more mature view of things. As he explained to me once in an extremely touching conversation we had in the late summer of 1947, the experience of coming back after the war and readjusting to life at home had been exceedingly hard. Like many others returning from active service, he found that in his absence family life had settled into a kind of self-sufficient pattern from which he felt himself excluded. Not surprisingly, there were some difficult moments during that year. But looking back I remember it as a specially happy time; confirming for me that Patricia and Eddie were among the best people in the world.

I also became extremely fond of Tigger, Antony and John, who had been rather too young during the earlier North Berwick days for us to meet on an equal footing, but who now became for me much like younger siblings. We shared many pastimes, both inside and out of doors — a particularly favoured activity being an energetic game that combined elements of dodge-ball with 'French and English'. I don't know what it was called but it had originated with the two Swiss girls; and it was played on a large patch of wasteland opposite the house, where during the war there had been a static water-tank for the firefighters. All through the summer-term these fiercely competitive bouts used to take place pretty well every evening after supper, when there would be a mass rush of all the younger people to finish the washing-up — lots of it, too, with a minimum of eight in the household — and to get out onto the field of battle. But there were also many gentler moments; as when we sat around and giggled joyously together over various radio programmes — I recall particularly Tommy Handley's ITMA and Antony's passion for *Dick Barton — Special Agent*.

Another indelible memory of that year is of the icy winter — a continuous cold spell lasting two and a half months that no one who lived through it could ever forget. The exact day that the big freeze began was 17 January 1947, which was the wedding day of my old and dear friend, Elsie Hamilton-Dalrymple. Barbara and I had attended the celebrations together, and as we returned that evening from the reception the snow was beginning to fall. It continued off and on through several weeks, and a hard frost set in which did not break until late March. Throughout those nine or ten weeks the roof of the house opposite us in Lytton Grove remained invisible under its thick mantle of snow. And the cold struck particularly hard at that time, because all forms of fuel and heating were stringently rationed. The room I was then occupying was on the top floor, just under the snow-encrusted roof; it had only a small gas fire, and due to the low pressure its flame rose barely a couple of inches. The only way I could manage to get my fingers to move at all at the beginning of my practice was to don my wartime siren-suit (what we nowadays call a cat-suit), zip a hot-water-bottle into the front, put on all the jerseys I possessed (clothes were also rationed), and begin by playing at full speed through several continuous passages of semiquavers. The second part of Duport's Study Number 8 in D minor — the bit, familiar to cellists, where all those mountain goats go hopping across diminished sevenths — was specially useful.

During this period there was often no heating at all in the Royal College of Music and similar institutions; and I can't imagine how the professors and students there managed to cope without the benefit of siren-suits and hot-water bottles. Especially the professors; for while the students came and went, *they* had to endure several hours on end.

Due partly to the cold, my work on the cello, which had gone steaming ahead during the first term, now encountered one of those inevitable sticky patches. Things probably weren't helped by my having a bout of flu in the February of 1947; and it wasn't really until the following term that everything started coming together. That summer I began at last to feel the benefit of all the ground-work I'd been doing under Ivor James' guidance; and during this third term everything seemed to blossom and I was able to cover a huge selection of repertoire. It included the Brahms F major Sonata, the Cesar Franck Sonata. the Beethoven Variations in E Flat, the Haydn D major Concerto, the Elgar Concerto and the Manuel De Falla *Suite Espagnole*.

Ivor James, or 'Jimmy' as he was usually known to his friends and pupils, was, in addition to being a fine cellist, an extremely good pianist, well able to play not only the accompaniments for the solos but also the demanding piano parts in the sonatas and other duo works. In this way his lessons, besides providing valuable tuition, gave much enjoyable performing experience. All round Jimmy was an outstanding musician with a wide knowledge, especially in the field of chamber music. As a teacher he did not aim to develop a virtuoso technique in his students, but I am grateful that from him my playing acquired a sound foundation, both musical and technical. And I always remember with affection his quietly humorous comments and his deep resonant speaking voice, both of which used to put me in mind of Winnie-the-Pooh.

Jimmy James was never a teacher to cling on to pupils, and by the middle of the 1947 summer term he was already encouraging me to

In memoriam Barbara Paton Walsh (later Kinch). Killed in car accident in Ireland, May 1992, aged 63.

look around and consider where I should study next. I think he was right to suggest moving on at this point, although at the time I felt sad at the prospect of no longer working with him on a weekly basis (for the next three or four years I did continue to visit him for an occasional lesson). The main question was: where should I aim for? And to study with whom? Europe was now opening up; numerous distinguished cellists from the continent were regularly performing in London. And August 1947 saw the first Edinburgh International Festival, offering a feast of opera, ballet, theatre, orchestral and chamber-music concerts, revealing new worlds for my war-time generation.

From a personal point of view, the most important events of that first Festival were the recitals in the Usher Hall by a specially formed international piano quartet, with Artur Schnabel as the pianist, Josef Szigeti the violinist, and the viola and cello parts in the hands of William Primrose and Pierre Fournier. Their wonderful performances included all of Brahms' Piano Quartets and Piano Trios; and, as every cellist will know, these works offer plenty of opportunities to the cellist. It was the first time that I had heard Fournier, and both his playing and his personality made a deep impression. From that point on I made up my mind to go and study with him, although for various reasons it was to be some while before this became possible. In the mean time, a specially exciting chapter in my life was just round the corner.

X: Scholarships to Paris

THE AUTUMN OF 1947 MARKED THE BEGINNING of a huge adventure, for in October that year I finally achieved my ambition to go and study in Paris. Today, everyone takes visits to the Continent for granted. But at that time, with the second World War barely two years in the past, I had never really been abroad before. A brief trip before the war, when my dearly loved Uncle Fred had taken me in his sailing yacht, *Tamesis*, on a family cruise to ports in Holland and Belgium, hardly counted, eye-opening and enjoyable though it was, for I was then being shepherded in the care of adults; and in any case we had lived entirely on board the yacht. To set off on my own for France, with the prospect of spending at least a year in Paris, was an altogether different matter.

During my year of study in London the funds from the Bucher Scholarship award had been held over, and they now, along with a small amount of savings, provided my entire financial resources until in April 1948 I was lucky enough to win a further award, this time from the Sir James Caird Travelling Scholarships Trust. (The founders of these awards deserve immense gratitude for the way in which, to this day, they open up horizons for young musicians.)

That first journey to Paris must however have been financed by my mother, not my scholarships, for this was the one and only time that I ever travelled first class, and, what's more, in the famous *Golden Arrow*, a train which conveyed the passengers right through from London to Paris, including the transitions on and off the ferry-boat between Dover and Calais (something that was revolutionary at the time). Later I would invariably make the journey in third class (as it was then), and by the line using the Newhaven-Dieppe crossing, which was by far the cheapest route. Although, surprisingly, by the 1950s bargain air fares for students were to become almost as cheap as travel by train and boat.

My first view of Paris couldn't have been bettered by Hollywood: as we approached the *Gare du Nord* the sun was setting, and there on the sky-line, high up on my right and splendidly visible from the train, was the Church of the *Sacré Coeur de Montmartre* — a truly dramatic vista. I've never regretted that it was in autumn, rather than in the more frequently lauded springtime, that I arrived in Paris. To see all those elegant avenues for the first time, lined with trees that were glowing with every conceivable autumn colour, was an unforgettable experience. No one would deny that Paris is also beautiful in the spring, but for me the autumn there is a magical time. And I was exceptionally lucky in finding, almost at the last minute, the particular household that became my home in Paris throughout the entire period of nearly two years that I spent there.

Until the summer of 1947 it had been uncertain for various reasons whether my Paris plans were going to work, and this meant I was rather late in trying to find accommodation. I had applied to several different hostels, including one run by the sister-convent of the Sacred Heart nuns at Craiglockhart, but all were fully booked. And I was becoming rather anxious about the whole project when an Edinburgh friend — the singer, Joyce Fleming (who figures in Chapter VII) — telephoned to say that a lady she knew in Paris, Madame Hélène Schopfer, was looking for a new *pensionnaire*, to replace the young girl who had been staying with her during the previous year.

In two weeks it was all arranged. At the time, though, I had no conception of how fortunate I was going to be. Madame Schopfer was in every way a remarkable person. Her origins, strictly speaking, were not French but American, for her father, an artist, had come from the United States around 1870 to study in Paris, and had then married, taken French nationality and spent the remainder of his life in France. Hélène, who was his only daughter, had grown up in Paris and had been steeped all her life in French culture. She had been sent at five years old to the Franco-American School in Paris, and was not only completely bilingual but spoke English without a trace of accent. At the age of eighteen she had married a Frenchman, Louis Schopfer (the name comes from the region round Alsace), but by the time I met her she had been widowed for several years.

When I first arrived in Paris Madame Schopfer was sixty-nine, though I doubt if anyone would have known it. Her appearance, with her snowy white hair piled up in a bouffant style, sparkling blue eyes, well-rounded but trim figure and unobtrusively smart clothes, was delightful; and her energy would have done credit to a twenty-year-old.

She had one daughter, also named Helène (sadly a younger daughter had died in her twenties), and three grandchildren, Françoise, Hubert and Raymond, who were near enough my age. I believe that for some years she had run a business in the Parisian 'rag trade', but her temperament and interests were musical, intellectual and artistic. She had herself been a good pianist (though hampered, when I knew her, by arthritic hands), and her daughter, Helène Fol, played the piano professionally, frequently acting as accompanist to well-known French artists. Above all Madame Schopfer had what can genuinely be described as a wide circle of friends: they came from a range of backgrounds in the Parisian literary, musical and artistic worlds; and such internationally-known singers as Pierre Bernac and Gérard Souzay were family friends and were regular visitors at her flat. Life as a *pensionnaire* in her household was never dull.

The apartment, where she had lived for a number of years, was on the sixth floor of a late 19th-century building in the *rue de l'Annonciation*, a quaint little street in Passy, running from the *Place de Passy* towards the *rue Raynouard* and the river Seine; the flat itself being situated exactly opposite the Church of *Notre Dame de Passy*. From the balcony, and looking towards the right, there was a splendid view over the house-tops, stretching as far as the *Champs de Mars* and including the upper section of the Eiffel Tower — just the view to make newcomers to Paris aware that they really had arrived.

The flat was not large, but it was remarkably well planned. There was a small entrance hall and a double-sized salon, with glass doors; and although each half was probably only around ten-feet square, the room always seemed quite spacious. At one end of the hall there were two small but quite adequate bedrooms, with the bathroom located between them; the w.c. was off the hall and there was a tiny kitchen at the opposite end of the flat.

For some years Madame Schopfer had shared this flat with an older lady, Madame Fol, who was her daughter's mother-in-law — they called themselves *Les deux Grand'mères*. For financial reasons they needed to take a paying guest; and, since there were only the two bedrooms, one was regularly allocated to a *pensionnaire*, while Madame Fol retained the other and Madame Schopfer slept on a well-disguised divan in the salon.

Madame Fol was quite unlike Madame Schopfer; she was already in her late seventies, and in her case no one would have been likely to question this. She was a small neat woman, barely five foot in height, with a little wrinkled parchmenty face that was dominated by smouldering dark eyes, and features of the type known as nut-cracker. In both manner and appearance she belonged very much to the old school, always dressing in the sober black garments that befitted her widowed status. She was invariably kind and helpful and took endless trouble to be friendly, but she wasn't, perhaps, a specially interesting person. She probably suffered also from being constantly outshone by her far more charismatic fellow-grandmother.

In some ways Madame Fol and Madame Schopfer were a strange team; and, not surprisingly, they quite often clashed, when there would be rapid interchanges of disagreement — too dignified and well-controlled to be called rows, but indicative of a certain level of underlying friction. However, in practical terms the shared arrangement worked well enough; with Madame Fol doing most of the house-work in a slow and stately fashion, while each in turns did the household shopping and Madame Schopfer took charge of the cooking. And an absolutely splendid cook she was!

And not only a splendid cook: Bouboudi — her family nickname which before very long I was permitted to use — was a tirelessly enthusiastic guide to the wonders of Paris. Each afternoon during the first week I spent there, she took me on guided tours of the city, and one day we also visited Versailles — resplendent in glowing autumn colours. It was a wonderful time! In the morning I would practise industriously; then after lunch we would set off to explore the various historic buildings, churches, museums and art galleries. I remember that at the Louvre she completely ran me off my feet despite being so many years my senior! But the most special memory is of my first visit to the *Ile de la Cité* and the Cathedral of Notre Dame, with its amazing facade and those glorious rose windows. Nor do I ever fail nowadays when paying return visits to look for a special plaque Bouboudi pointed out that day: this stands on the south wall of the forecourt and records that here, at this exact place, on (I think) 24 August 1944, an aerial message was received from an aircraft in General Leclerc's advancing army, saying: "*Tenez, bons Parisiens! Nous arrivons.*" At the time, with August 1944 only three years in the past, I found the whole picture this creates very moving. I still do.

Dear Bouboudi! — nothing was too much trouble for her in her efforts to ensure that my first days in Paris were enjoyable, and to make me feel at home — as I very soon did. And this kindness, which far exceeded anything that might normally be expected from a landlady to her *pensionnaire*, was typical of the interest and concern she always showed me throughout the year and a half I lived with her. She was a great lady.

Daily life in Paris quickly settled into a comfortable pattern.

Bouboudi (Mme Helène Schopfer) 1948.

Each morning one or other of the *grand'mères* would bring me breakfast in bed — not purely to indulge me, but in order to allow time for the two of them to get organised, and in particular for Bouboudi to tidy away her bed in the salon and remove any other night-time paraphernalia. I would then be free to make my *toilette*; and while I was in the bathroom my room would be cleaned and the bed made.

During the first year I spent at the *rue de l'Annonciation* there was no hot water in the flat — I think this was quite common in Paris at that time, it being still only two years since the war ended. Today's generation would probably have found this very trying, but I had come from quite spartan conditions in wartime Britain and wasn't particularly bothered. In any case Bouboudi always provided many jugs of hot water, and since the bath itself was available it was easy to have quite a pleasant stand-up wash-cum-bath. Anyone desperate for a 'real bath' could always visit the *Bains Publiques*, which were just round the corner and were extremely clean and well run.

At this time there was also stringent food rationing in France; and, unlike in Britain, foreigners did not receive the same allowance as the natives. We had to queue at the local *Mairie* for what were called *tickets d'isolés*, and these, as far as I remember entitled us only to minimal rations for meat, butter, and cheese. For anything else, visitors were dependent on the good will of their hosts. And how Bouboudi managed it I never knew, but at no point did I ever suffer from the shortages. I do recall, though, that during those first months the jam that came with my breakfast tray was simply horrible! There were two kinds, one pinkish purple and one dark brown. Of the two unpleasant alternatives, the latter was preferable as it tasted vaguely of prunes, whereas the other was reminiscent of mouth-wash.

In passing, it's amusing to note that, whereas the British continued to endure rationing until 1954, the French decided as early as 1948 that enough was enough. By common consent they got together and literally burnt their ration books. And that was the end of that.

The autumn of 1947 was in fact a time of considerable upheaval in France, and that November saw a general strike that lasted for at least three weeks. This affected every single person, for just about everything stopped. Water was available only during certain hours. There was no gas, and no electric power to run the lifts (something you notice if you live on the sixth floor). Hardly any buses, Metros or trains. No dustbins were emptied during the entire period, and the rubbish piled up in the streets. But the hardest thing for me personally was the postal aspect of the strike, for this meant that with no letters either in or out, and no telephones working, communication with home was almost impossible. This could have left me feeling totally isolated, but in two ways I was exceptionally lucky. First, because a family friend who worked in the Foreign Office in London managed to arrange with a colleague at the Quai D'Orsay (the French equivalent) that my letters home would be conveyed in the Diplomatic Bag to London and posted there; and this meant that, although I couldn't hear from my family, at least they could be assured that all was well with me. This certainly helped; but more importantly my relative peace of mind was thanks to Bouboudi's kindness, for by this time I felt so happily settled in my temporary Parisian home.

When originally planning my time in Paris I had hoped to begin lessons with Pierre Fournier as soon as I arrived; but in the event this wasn't possible, because Fournier was engaged that autumn in a six-month concert tour of the United States. I had of course known this in advance and had been advised to work for the first two terms with an elderly French cellist, widely known in his day, called Fernand Pollain. I knew little about Pollain, apart from hearing him strongly recommended by various cellists, including my previous teacher, Ivor James; but Pollain's name would have been familiar to earlier generations, especially in connection with the famous violinist Ysaye, with whom he had performed in trios for many years. Pollain lived at Poissy, about ten miles outside Paris, and I used to travel for my lessons in the suburban train that ran from the Gare St. Lazare; my first journey there marked the first occasion I'd ever seen a *double-decker train* — I don't know if they still have them.

That first lesson began conventionally at half-past-two in the afternoon, and lasted for about an hour and a quarter. But Pollain was such an enthusiast — and such an amazingly generous man — that I was soon being invited to stay for a cup of tea and continue the lesson afterwards. Then by the next term I was frequently asked to come at 11 o'clock in the morning and stay for both lunch and tea, in order that the lesson might be prolonged to about five hours! Madame Pollain was also remarkably hospitable and a character in her own right. Pollain was her second husband, and she had seven grown-up children from her first marriage, and numerous grandchildren, several of them around my age. One of her daughters owned a farm; and it was due to this that lunch in their household was such a lavish affair, with meat and butter and cream all readily available, although for most people food rationing was still tight at this time.

There were perhaps reasons why Pollain liked to have so much time for his lessons. For one thing, there was relatively little of interest going on in his life at this point. For another, he was a great talker, and he liked to recount many anecdotes, often illustrated on his instrument. At this point it was no longer an easy matter for him to play the cello, since he had been hit by a bullet during the liberation of France which had damaged the muscles and tendons in his left shoulder, making it impossible for him to raise his arm to the level of the fingerboard. Undaunted, he had devised a kind of pulley with which his arm could be first hauled into playing position, then allowed to swivel backwards and forwards; and since his fingers and bow-arm still functioned perfectly, it was possible to gain some idea of his former expertise.

He was a lovely man and I learnt much from him, although it was not at all what I had originally wanted to learn. I was painfully aware at the time of lacking certain basics of cello technique, but to any mention of this Pollain would reply "Ma chère Margaret — your technique is all right" — which was plainly untrue. However, I did gain much valuable experience in having to produce a new concerto, sonata or other major work *at least every fortnight.*

Above all I learnt from him the vital importance of putting the music across to the listener — "ze pooblique", as he called it when he attempted to show off his not very extensive English. And Pollain was himself totally shameless in placing the importance of this communication with the listener far above any kind of authenticity — he even went occasionally to the lengths of re-writing certain passages in the classics, in ways that seemed to him more cellistically effective! Quite a change, this, for someone brought up in Edinburgh, where sometimes there is almost too great a reverence for the letter of the law.

As a further indication of his incredible generosity, Pollain all but refused to let me make any payment for these many and lengthy lessons. In the end, and after much argument, he agreed with great reluctance to accept a fee of three hundred francs per lesson. Today that may sound a lot, but at the time, with the exchange rate standing at over 1000 francs to the pound, it was the equivalent of about seven-and-sixpence or *thirty-seven-and-a-half pence*; and even in those days it was completely ridiculous — people of his status were then charging three and four guineas for lessons.

In view of all this kindness I found it impossible to reveal to Pollain that, as from the summer of 1948, it had long ago been arranged for me to begin having lessons with Pierre Fournier. I felt compelled to practise a little deception, by creating for both him and Madame Pollain an impression that, when I went back to Britain for what was in fact only an Easter break, this marked the final end of my studies in Paris. Fortunately, since the Pollains lived not in Paris but in Poissy, I was never found out. And I think it was an entirely justifiable deception.

My return to Britain for that Easter holiday of 1948 was momentous in another way, for I had at this point to come clean about the fact that

I was no longer wearing my hair wound around my head in two sober braids: I had finally taken the drastic step (in my mother's eyes) of having it cut short. To highlight the extreme significance of this, it's necessary to fill in some background. Over many years, and regularly since I was about thirteen, the question of cutting my hair had caused recurring problems between my mother and myself. Hair fashions then were almost the opposite of today: now, long hair is popular for girls and women of all ages, but in the mid-1930s, and certainly by the '40s, relatively few girls had long hair after the age of twelve or thirteen. What's more, no grown-up women at that time would ever have worn long hair loose over the shoulders in public — that kind of hairstyle was for little girls in party dresses (or maybe for courtesans). Even at Craiglockhart, which was hardly the height of fashion, most girls had short hair. But, whenever I suggested that the time had come for me to get rid of my below-waist-length plaits, every sort of objection was raised by my mother. In particular, she would argue that, besides not suiting me, short hair would make me "look just like everyone else" (as if this were not in any case the desired objective for most teenagers).

Protest was useless; I even tried, by way of passive resistance, continuing to wear my hair in two school-girlish plaits throughout my first year at Edinburgh University — anything rather than 'putting it up'. Secretly I'd hoped this might convince my mother that it was absurd for me to keep those plaits. It's true I was younger than many first-year students, but in those days the two pigtails must have looked distinctly out of place on an undergraduate. Anyway, the gesture had no effect: at the end of the year my mother simply hauled me off to the hairdressing department at Jenners — that venerable Edinburgh department store — where the assistant was deputed to create a style with the plaits wound about my head in a sort of coronet. Quite a pleasant fashion in itself, but hopelessly out of date even then.

After that, roughly twice a year, the disputes would break out again. It was particularly galling when my dearly loved half-nieces Barbara and Petronilla Paton Walsh, who both up to this point had had long hair, arrived from London to spend the New Year of 1946 with their hair stylishly cut short. This seemed so unfair! They were younger than me, and *they* were being allowed to follow their choice. But once again, protests were futile.

Today, it's hard to see why on earth I didn't just snatch a pair of scissors and get rid of the offending locks for myself. I don't think that at any age I lacked moral courage, but I was always desperately anxious not to hurt my mother, and she had somehow contrived, as well as painting dismal pictures of how awful I should look with short hair, to give the whole thing a personal slant — even going to the extreme on one occasion of saying: "Well if you must do it, please wait till I'm dead."

In view of all this, it was an astonishing moment when, in March 1948, I mentioned wearily to Bouboudi how much I longed to have my hair cut. For instead of the discouragement I'd come to expect, she said enthusiastically "My dear — I've always wanted to suggest that! You really should think seriously about it." And it so happened that a few nights later her daughter was holding a musical soiree — just the occasion for a new hairstyle. Bouboudi was someone who got things moving quickly: in no time it was arranged for me to visit the highly recommended and excellent *coiffeuse* who looked after her granddaughter's hair, and by the evening of the party the dastardly deed was done.

My hair, released from those constricting plaits, turned out to curl naturally; and the reactions expressed in Paris were entirely favourable, with Bouboudi ecstatic and Monsieur Pollain commenting that the new hairstyle made me look "*Plus jeune fille et moins petite fille*" [more a young girl and less a little girl]. It had, of course, been a deciding factor for me to discover during those first months in Paris that wearing two plaits round the head was a favourite style with small French girls of about six or seven!

All this was most encouraging; but before going home I had somehow to break the news to my mother. The best approach, it seemed, was to exaggerate grossly; so my letter was on the lines of my having done such a terrible thing that I hardly knew how to tell her what it was. And my mother's reaction was entirely typical: her first horrified thought, as she told me later, had been that I must have run off and married a Frenchman . . . And when she discovered that it was *only that I'd had my hair cut off*, she was too overcome with relief to mind very much. (Why didn't I think of that Frenchman before?) She even quite approved of the result; although from time to time she would still produce the old objection that it made me look like everyone else. Well — three cheers for that! And the whole episode marked a first major step on the road to independence.

Nor was it only my hairstyle that had changed when I got back home to Edinburgh that Easter. For one thing, I'd learnt a good deal that was new about food, having become acquainted with such culinary pleasures as *Moules Marinières* and *Ratatouille*, and many delicious ways of cooking vegetables, not to mention developing a taste for yoghurt — now so familiar in Britain but then more or less unknown. Wine, too, had entered my life, for Bouboudi always produced a carafe of *Vin Ordinaire* at the evening meal, to be drunk either on its own or — as preferred by *les grand'mères* — with water.

Identity card photo, Paris 1948.

I had also gained some completely new ideas about clothes. At this stage in the Britain of the late 1940s there was still clothes rationing; coupons had to be produced for all items of clothing, and also for any material purchased for dress-making purposes. The whole attitude was one of austerity, the prime objective having for many years been to save material; hence skirts were cut with little fullness and hemlines fell no lower than the knees. This was also the era of 'Make Do and Mend'; and anyone who was fully grown — as I was by around the age of fourteen — was expected to make their clothes last until they almost fell apart.

At the time I first arrived in Paris, indoctrinated with these Calvinistic ideas, Christian Dior's New Look was beginning to sweep through the Parisian *Maisons de Couture*. And quite early in my visit Bouboudi had somehow wangled an invitation for me to accompany her one afternoon to the *Maison Jean Dessés*, where the new collection was being shown. It was a revelation! These beautiful dresses, with their emphasis on a narrow fitted waist-line, all had enormously full skirts, reaching — even the shortest — to below mid-calf. Plainly they had required untold amounts of material; but without any question the results were wonderfully stylish and elegant.

There were, too, potent influences in my daily life at this point.

Bouboudi was herself a skilled dressmaker and designer, and she devoted much time to making things for her granddaughter, Françoise Fol (a most attractive young woman, then about 24, who at that time was rumoured to have rejected nearly 70 proposals of marriage!). Everything about Françoise was totally *à la mode*, and her clothes exemplified the French word *chic*. She was then working as *vendeuse* in *Maison Franck*, one of the smartest shops in Passy, and this entitled her to a certain discount on clothes. But since her wages were not particularly handsome, relying a good deal on sales commissions, her wardrobe was heavily dependent on the good services of her grandmother. Françoise was a regular visitor to the flat, and the fitting sessions always took place openly in Bouboudi's salon. Quite often I would be asked for an opinion, which was flattering; and although at first I probably retained just the tiniest bit of Scottish disapproval — all this fuss about the length of a skirt, or the fit of a collar — some of Françoise's fervent attitude to clothes and fashion did begin to infect me.

Over the next few months I began to find my sober British garments, with their short straight skirts, less and less acceptable. Not that there was any possibility of making rapid changes; in Britain there was clothes rationing, and in Paris I never had much money to spare. But, when I got home to Edinburgh for that Easter holiday of 1948, I enthused so much to my mother about these glorious 'New Look' dresses that she became determined to see what could be done about renewing my wardrobe. At that time I was extremely slim, 5'8" with a 24" waist, which made me a natural for 'New Look' clothes; and of course the wide flowing skirts were also ideal for a cellist.

Having scraped together some clothing coupons, my mother and I set off to buy material for two summer dresses, which would be made as nearly as possible in the 'New Look' style. We managed also, by letting in broad bands at the waist-line — as I'd often seen Bouboudi doing for Françoise — to lengthen and adapt a couple of my older dresses. And my mother also bought one of the surplus army parachutes that were being advertised at the time, for which no coupons were required. The parachutes were constructed with numerous wedge-shaped panels, and much fiddly work was required to separate these. But the end product was a large amount of best quality white silk; and from this my mother made me three sets of superb pure silk underclothing which were to last me for years to come. Quite a change from Chilprufe vests and Celanese knickers!

However, her greatest dressmaking triumph at this point was the skirt made from some unused curtain material that she had found hiding in a drawer. This pre-war cretonne, in a striking floral print, was transformed into a splendidly full skirt, with soft un-pressed pleats flowing from a wide and closely fitting curved waist-band. Worn with a plain pink linen blouse, for which there had been just enough coupons, it looked unquestionably the height of 1948 fashion.

It was this particular outfit that I chose to wear for my first lesson with Pierre Fournier early in May 1948 — an event I'd awaited with mounting nervous excitement. Playing to any well-known musician for the first time is always a testing experience and Fournier was by then a figure of international renown; I had heard him perform on several occasions at the Edinburgh Festival of 1947. I was terror-stricken at the prospect, and on the actual day of our first session I suffered all the usual nervous symptoms of inability to eat and so on. But I need not have worried: Pierre Fournier was a man of extraordinary charm; he had the great gift of being able to treat a young player as a colleague, not as an inferior; and when we had talked a little and he said "*Alors, quand vous me jouez, je veux que vous vous sentiez tout à fait comme si vous etiez chez vous*" [When you play to me, I want you to feel just as though you were in your own home], it was so clear he really meant this that my nerves miraculously vanished and I was able to play well up to my current best.

That summer I worked with Fournier on a regular basis, with lessons at least once a week. It was a wonderful experience, and I learnt an enormous amount from him on both technical and musical matters. Always Fournier's approach, in teaching as in playing, was straight to the heart of the music. Nothing was ever done for effect; and I recall his actually saying on one occasion "*Plus je deviens vieux*" — he was 43 at the time — "*plus je deviens simple*" [the older I get, the more I value simplicity], which summed things up well. He was also remarkably precise in his manner of organising work: at my first lesson he drew up for me a written plan of technical practice, including the exact timings to be observed for each section. His lessons never over-ran in the way Pollain's had, but we managed during that term, in addition to his strict regime of exercises and of Popper Studies, to cover several major works; including the Boccherini B flat Concerto, the Marin Marais *La Folia* Variations, the Schubert *Arpeggione Sonata*

Pierre Fournier, late 1940s.

and Bach's Suite Number Five in C minor.

    I did work hard — and with good will. But, interestingly, Pierre

Fournier was not among those who advocate endless hours of slogging at one's instrument. He maintained on the contrary that four hours a day of organised, concentrated practice was quite sufficient, and that to do more could be counter-productive and lead to the work becoming slipshod. In fact I seldom managed to complete everything in much under five hours — and sometimes felt guilty about this. But one great benefit from Fournier's organised regime was that it left ample time free for other activities. Such as going to operas (including a first-ever experience of *Pelleas et Melisande*); and to the theatre (I became a regular attender at the *Comédie Francaise*, and particularly remember their production of *Cyrano de Bergerac*); visiting museums and art galleries; simply strolling round Paris with friends, or rowing on the lake in the Bois de Boulogne, which was only ten minutes walk from Bouboudi's flat; not to mention attending a variety of concerts. I recall, too, a ravishingly beautiful *Son et Lumiere* performance at Versailles.

That summer I also had my first experience of playing to a musical audience in Paris; for Bouboudi's 70th birthday happened at the end of June 1948, and a large musical party was held in celebration. This took place at her daughter's flat in the *Chaussée de la Muette* — just up the road from the *rue de l'Annonciation* — where there was a spacious music room with two grand pianos. Many of the audience and the artists (with the exception of myself) were well-known figures on the Parisian musical scene: among them, Pierre Bernac (who sang a group of songs composed by Bouboudi's grandson, Raymond Fol), Gérard Souzay and his sister Genevieve Touraine (also a singer), two well-established pianists, Irene Aitoff and Simone Tilliard (the latter was Bernac's regular accompanist at his master-classes), and various composers who were prominent at the time, among them Henri Sauget.

To be invited to perform in this company was hugely flattering; but it was an awe-inspiring occasion. I well remember being unable to eat a morsel of the superb buffet supper that took place before the musical programme; but I have absolutely no recollections about my own playing of a Sonata by the Italian composer, Tessarini, in which I was accompanied by Bouboudi's daughter, Helène Fol — a first-class pianist. However, things must have gone reasonably well, for afterwards people were extremely complimentary — and complimentary in a way that French people are *not*, in my experience, unless they really mean it. In particular I valued a comment from Bouboudi's stepbrother, a learned doctor and a passionately committed amateur musician, that the playing in the fast movements had been not "*la virtuosité inane*" [empty virtuosity], but full of life and colour.

A couple of weeks after Bouboudi's party the time came for me to return home for the summer vacation. I had my last lessons for the time being with Pierre Fournier, and began organising my departure; in particular, gathering together the many things accumulated during the past nine months ready for despatch to Britain by registered luggage. Then, unexpectedly, with only a few days to go, I was astonished and far from pleased to hear that a certain young man from Edinburgh had arrived in Paris and was clamouring to see me. This was someone I had met at a dance in Edinburgh during the Easter holiday, who had taken a violent header and had pursued me with dreary persistence all through my time at home. Not that there was anything actively wrong with him; he simply wasn't my type — very earnest and altogether a total bore. I'd tried desperately to indicate my lack of interest but had clearly failed, for one evening that July, when I was sitting in the salon after dinner chatting to *les deux grand'mères*, a message came from the concierge's lodge that this same young man had not only arrived in Paris without any advance notice, but was there downstairs at the front door, with a request to come up and visit us.

Well, there are advantages in living on the sixth floor. While the old-fashioned lift was in transit, I had time to put Bouboudi sufficiently in the picture for her to come to my rescue. I hurriedly shot off to lurk in my bedroom, leaving her to deal with the situation, which she entered into with the mischievous enthusiasm of a Despina or Suzanna. When the poor young man arrived at the door she welcomed him politely into the salon and, pretending that she didn't speak English (Bouboudi, of all people!), she explained in slow careful French that I was out, and that I was in fact very frequently out, and that it would be best for him to telephone me in the morning to see if I was free at any time. What Madame Fol made of all this pantomime I can't imagine; but in her case, and perhaps fortunately, it was true that she spoke almost no English.

In the morning, when he duly phoned, I had made my plans. Somehow, for his sake as well as mine, I had to indicate that his quest was fruitless; but I had no idea how to handle the situation directly. So, having declined his pressing invitations to go out for a meal, I informed him that the only possibility that day was the hour between noon and one o'clock when, if he cared to accompany me, I had to visit some of the local shops to purchase a goodbye present for Madame Fol. Even at the time I felt almost sorry for the wretched man as he trailed after me in and out of the many draper's shops in Passy, while I experienced quite extraordinary problems in finding some stockings of the right colour, quality and size — Madame Fol's feet were in fact unusually small, which provided an excuse for rejecting pair after pair of those presented before moving on to another shop. Finally, having at last purchased two pairs — in two different shops — I bade him a friendly goodbye outside our flat, and wished him an enjoyable stay in France. It was a classic case of being cruel to be kind. And it worked: a few months later we heard that he was engaged and would be marrying early in the coming year.

For me, Paris was now beginning to feel almost like a second home. My spoken French, after the best part of an academic year, was fluent, even colloquial; and under Bouboudi's guidance I was getting acquainted with a range of French literature. I remember in particular a very moving novel about French Resistance prisoners in a concentration camp, *Le Silence de la Mer* by Roger Vercors; and my first reading of Alain-Fournier's *Le Grande Meaulnes*; as well as launching enthusiastically into Romain Rolland's monumental saga of *Jean Christophe*, and enjoying it although I don't think I ever reached further than volume four of the ten.

It had been an added bonus that at the time I began studying with Pierre Fournier his English had not yet reached the excellent standard it did later, and hence that he preferred to speak French during my lessons. He spoke the language with the kind of special affection that French people often show for their mother tongue, and with such style that it was a constant pleasure to listen.

I now had in prospect a nine-month absence from France; for first came the long summer holiday, and then in the autumn Fournier was departing for an extended tour of the Americas and would be away until April 1949. This made it sensible for me to spend the winter in London, having occasional lessons from my former teacher, Ivor James, and, most importantly, in trying to make some contacts in the music profession (always a difficult matter at first for those who like myself have not attended one of the main music colleges, and hence are not known to other musicians).

However, the sad farewells to Paris were lightened by the prospect of a visit to Brittany which had been arranged earlier in the summer. At this time Bouboudi and her daughter, Hélène Fol, owned a picture-book small cottage at Tréouguy, a minute hamlet in Finistère — the far western corner of Brittany — and they had invited me and my sixteen-year-old half-niece, Petronilla Paton Walsh, to spend part of August with them. (Barbara, at this point, was on an exchange visit to Italy.)

Brittany was an adventure in many ways. For one thing, the journey from London was not the relatively easy matter it would be today but took us rather more than twenty-four hours. This may seem incredible to those who are used to car-ferries, frequent air services and most recently the Channel Tunnel, but at that time public transport had not yet recovered from the problems caused by World War II.

We set off from London about 8 o'clock in the morning, from the long vanished Air Terminal in Kensington High Street, whence a bus took us to the old airport of Croydon (London Heathrow was not yet up and running). For both of us this was our first experience of air travel and I think we were terrified, although I, as the older member of the party, felt obliged to preserve a calm exterior. By today's standards the plane was tiny, less than 20 seats, and it took us to the historic city of Caen in Normandy, which I suppose was the only airport lying vaguely on our route that was currently operational.

Caen itself was something of a shock, for, although we were both used to seeing bomb-sites in London, here so little rebuilding had been completed since the 1944 invasion of Normandy that the impression was of an entire city in ruins. The only building of any size that remained was the impressive church of the *Abbaye aux Hommes*. It, too, had suffered damage, but it provided a welcome refuge during the many hours we had to spend in Caen, before continuing our journey by an evening train to Rennes. Presumably we must have explored, and must have found somewhere to eat, but the chief memory that remains is of the quite horrendous 'Hole-in-the-Floor' that was the only loo available — another first experience.

Having arrived in Rennes about 11pm, we caught a midnight train to Quimper, which we didn't reach until 8 o'clock the next morning. No sleepers or couchettes, either. And there was more to come: first, a journey by bus from Quimper to Pont-l'Abbé, the nearest place of any size to 'La Folie de Tréouguy', our hosts' cottage, where we finally arived by taxi at around 10.30am. Never had a bath and a couple of hours in bed seemed more welcome.

As well as 'La Folie' itself, which was a tiny cottage with just three-up and two-down, a kind of studio had been built at the end of the charming little garden. This, in addition to tables, chairs, bookshelves and so on, contained two comfortable divans, and there was an en suite shower-room with w.c. and hot-and-cold. The studio also boasted a serviceable upright piano. This well-designed little building provided comfortable sleeping-quarters for Petronilla and myself, and we took our meals in the cottage with Bouboudi and her daughter — who, like her mother, was a splendid cook.

This was my first real opportunity to become closely acquainted with Hélène Fol, for contact with her in Paris, although agreeable, had always been brief. Now I quickly realised what an

Petronilla in school uniform, aged about 16.

interesting and characterful woman she was; and not just an excellent pianist, which I already knew, but a cultivated all-round musician, as well as having many interests outside music. Her name in the family was *Biche* — a nickname that initially can sound odd to those whose mother tongue is English, but one that's often affectionately bestowed on little girls in France. Becoming friends with Biche was one of the highlights of a wonderful holiday; in many ways she was rather a downright person, and she did not perhaps have quite the same remarkable charm as her mother, but she possessed a delightfully sardonic sense of humour.

Both Petronilla and I fell in love with Brittany, its countryside and its people, many of whom at that time were still wearing their beautiful national costumes every day, not just for festivals. Our friends didn't possess a car, we but we nevertheless managed to see most of that corner of Brittany. To explore the immediate neighbourhood we went sometimes on foot, sometimes on bicycles. (Petronilla showed a disconcerting inabilty to remain on the right-hand side of the road, but fortunately there was little traffic in those days.) Then for expeditions further afield, when we were often accompanied by Bouboudi and Biche — both excellent tour-guides — we used the buses. These must have covered almost everywhere in the region; and among the many memorable places we visited were the fascinating walled town of Concarneau, the painters' paradise at Audierne, the picturesque fishing port of Douarnenez, and the starkly impressive coast of the Pointe du Raz. We also enjoyed a happy afternoon swimming from a vast and deserted Atlantic beach at Loctudy. We spent more than we should have on Quimper pottery, consumed a disgraceful quantity of cream cakes (an unusual luxury then for British visitors), and developed an addiction to Breton *crepes* which remains with me to this day (as does some of the pottery). Everywhere we admired the little churches and the touching *Calvaires* that line the country roadsides. Altogether, it was an unforgettable ten days.

From Brittany we slowly made our way home, travelling this time via Paris — a twelve-hour journey from Quimper — thence by train and steamer back to London, where we caught the sleeper train to

The studio in the garden of 'La Folie de Tréouguy'.

Scotland, our final goal being to join the annual family gathering in North Berwick.

I can't now remember much about the North Berwick part of that holiday. Life must have followed its usual pleasant patterns. But the second Edinburgh International Festival, which began in the third week of August, brought me a highly prestigious professional engagement — one of my earliest. This was to join the renowned Boyd Neel String Orchestra in a performance at one of the Freemasons Hall morning concerts, when their programme included Richard Strauss' *Metamorphosen*. This beautiful work is written for an ensemble of 23 solo string parts; and since the Boyd Neel numbered only 21 regular members, they had sought for two young players who lived in Edinburgh to take part in the performance. Someone had recommended me and a viola player, Brenda Buchanan — another former member of the Waddell Orchestra. Of course it happened that Brenda, like me, was no longer actually living in Edinburgh, but we both still had family to stay with in the city, and hence the orchestra did not need to pay for us to be brought up from London!

It was a wonderful experience; and in the course of time it brought me various other engagements with the orchestra; including in March 1949 a memorable performance on Radio 3 of Fauré's *Requiem*. This was directed by the redoubtable Nadia Boulanger, who was then a international figure, attracting musicians from all around the globe to study with her in Paris. Many well-known composers from Britain, America and all over Europe were among her former pupils; and she was a world authority on French music who had personally known Gabriel Fauré (originally she was his pupil and later became a colleague). As a conductor and trainer she was brisk and even a little intimidating — quite different from Boyd Neel, whose approach was in general friendly and relaxed. With Mademoiselle Boulanger everything had to be executed with the most utter precision, in exactly the way she wanted, and her comments were dry and to the point. But an impression came across of such musical stature and breadth of knowledge that to work with her, though it could be frightening, was both stimulating and inspiring.

In all I must have done about half a dozen engagements with the Boyd Neel Orchestra. And this led to my learning one salutary lesson in connection with the Inland Revenue! For later that year, when they sent me a form enquiring about my income, I replied in perfectly good faith that I was still studying and financed only by scholarships. Back came a notice demanding to know why I had not declared a number of engagements with the Boyd Neel Orchestra, on dates as given . . . Fortunately when I wrote from Paris, to apologise and explain that I had genuinely forgotten about those concerts, they believed me. But from that point onwards it made me aware that, in any profession, Big Brother is indeed watching one's financial doings.

Probably the most memorable thing for me about the winter of 1948/49 was the number of 'Pea-Soupers', also known as 'London Particulars' that took place during November and December. These were a new experience, as there had been none during the winter I'd spent in Putney two years previously; and although I'd met fogs and sea mist often enough in Scotland, those belonged to quite a different category. All this was happening some years before the Clean Air Act; and in those days, when a real pea-souper enwrapped London, the old saying about not being able to see your hand in front of your face was very nearly true. Most certainly it was impossible to see the kerb as you walked along the pavement, let alone to see the other side of the road, which made crossing over a hazardous business. During that winter I was living in Hammersmith, which is well served by underground trains — the only form of transport that works at all in 'smog' conditions — but even getting from the house to the station was difficult. It could only be accomplished by hugging the wall at the side of the pavement, and uttering a prayer before the occasional and inevitable road crossing.

    By May 1949 I was back in Paris, happily installed once more with *les deux grand'mères*, amd resuming regular lessons with Pierre Fournier. That summer Fournier gave a number of important concerts in Paris, including performances of all six Bach Suites for unaccompanied cello, and a recital with Françis Poulenc in which they gave the first performance of Poulenc's recently composed Sonata for Cello and Piano. This took place, as did a majority of solo and chamber music recitals at the time, at the Salle Gaveau in the *rue Singer*; a hall that's always linked in my memories with red plush and gilt paint, and a vivid recollection of the long queues that always formed outside the artists' room after the concerts, with most of the audience lining up to congratulate the performers — a ritual Bouboudi called "*Faire la Sacristie*".

That June in Paris saw a heat wave, with temperatures well in the thirties (over 90 degrees fahrenheit) that lasted for several weeks; and in order to practise the cello without danger of melting, I had first to close the shutters in my room and throw the windows open wide, then to remove all my garments apart from a bra and pants. I also regularly went swimming at the Piscine Molitor; and here on various occasions I would act as escort to Pierre Fournier's eleven-year-old son and only child, Jean-Pierre, for during this term my standing with the Fourniers had grown to become rather more that of a family friend than just a student. Undoubtedly I was at this point a little in love with Pierre Fournier, who was a most attractive and charming man. But then, as expressed with Gallic realism by a twenty-year-old French girl I knew at the time, "*C'est normal d'etre amoureuse de son professeur*" [It's normal for a girl to be in love with her professor]. And, in support of this, I recall that during that summer I happened by coincidence to be reading *Music Study in Germany*, Amy Fay's fascinating account of life as an American piano student in Germany during the mid-19th century, which colourfully describes the adoring train of female pupils that always surrounded *her* master, the great Franz Liszt. Nevertheless, looking back, I can honestly say that during the actual lessons with Fournier my attention was focussed exclusively on the cello — perhaps indicating a significant degree of dedication.

I also always got on well with Fournier's wife, Lyda, who was herself a character astonishing enough, with her brilliantly blonde hair (not natural, she informed me) and stunningly fashionable clothes, to have come from the pages of a highly coloured novel. She was not French but Russian, and possessed one of those cavernous Slavonic voices, as well as a wicked sense of humour and a knack for passing barbed comments that made her definitely a better friend than enemy. I remember her describing one rather colourless female cellist whom she particularly disliked as "*Un vrai type de Marguérite de Faust — enceinte*" [type-cast for a pregnant Marguérite in *Faust*]. And she made the amusing complaint about their cleaning lady that "*Elle ne fait meme pas promener la poussière*" [She doesn't even take the dust for a walk].

Lyda's personal history had been eventful: she had originally been married to the world-famous cellist Piatigorsky, with whom she had come at some point to live in Paris. Here, in the mid-1930s, she had divorced him to marry Fournier; and it was always said that, having first put Piatigorsky on the world map as a cellist, she then proceeded to do the same for Fournier. In every way a redoubtable personality, Lyda had no reticence about making her views known, anywhere and at any time. Sitting between her and Pierre during a film about Brahms and the Schumanns, Robert and Clara, was quite an experience. During one scene, when the young Brahms was nobly resisting his incipient passion for Clara, a dramatically stage-whispered comment reached me: "*Ce n'était pas du tout comme ça entre Fournier et Piatigorsky, je vous assure*" [I don't mind telling you things weren't like that between Fournier and Piatigorsky]. For some reason Lyda always seemed to approve of me — perhaps because, unlike some of Pierre's many young female adorers, I took the trouble to show genuine interest in her and in Jean-Pierre. I even was given an invitation to stay after one lesson and have dinner with the family — an event that gave great excitement to *les grand'mères*, and caused Bouboudi to exercise her dressmaking skills in altering one of my dresses that, to her critical eye, was too short in the waist for me.

All round it was a happy term, with the patterns of life established in the previous year being followed for the most part. But it came to a dramatic end in mid-July, when a telegram arrived summoning me to return immediately to Edinburgh, because my father, whose health had been deteriorating all summer, had taken a turn for the worse and was now seriously ill. The journey back marked my second experience of air travel — this time not to Croydon, but to Northolt. And some account of my father's death has already been given in an earlier chapter.

That summer of 1949 was to be my last extended stay in Paris. But during the next three years I made regular visits. The time in July 1950 included a new experience, when a charming young man — English but bilingual — who was working in Paris took me to a night-club housed somewhere in the depths of a left-bank cellar. He warned me that the songs performed by the cabaret artist would be distinctly on the rude side; and certainly the approximately half that I understood would confirm this. Then the following year there was a memorable moment during the *Quartorze Juillet* celebrations when, in the course of the traditional dancing in the street, the column I was in came suddenly face to face with another that was being led by a flautist from Edinburgh, someone I'd known well but hadn't seen for at least six years (he had often played in Hans Gál's *Collegium Musicum* sessions). And in June 1952 the Director of the British Council in Paris, Dr (later Sir) Harry Harvey Wood, arranged a recital for me and a long-standing friend from Edinburgh, the pianist Mary Firth. For this we had of course to include some contemporary British music in our programme, and we chose the Alan Rawsthorne Sonata for Cello and Piano, which was still fairly new at the time and was a first performance in Paris, as well as a Sonata by Handel who just about qualified as British. The other major work was the Sonata in B flat by Dohnanyi which was a favourite of ours at the time.

After that I didn't see Paris again until 1973 when I was invited by a singer colleague, Roxane Houston, to take part in an Anglo-French concert at the *Cercle Interallié* — a most elegant room with ceilings covered in elaborate paintings — that was being held in celebration of Britain's new membership of the European Union. Unfortunately my husband was not free to take part, but by coincidence the pianist engaged turned out to be a former pupil of his, Peter Jacobs. And Alex and I did eventually manage to see Paris together several times. On a couple of occasions we treated ourselves to a short package holiday. Then, one year we were invited to act as escorts for three students from the Royal Academy of Music who had been chosen to give a recital at the Conservatoire. By then Bouboudi was no longer alive (she would have been well over 100), but we were able to visit Biche who was still living in the flat at *8 bis Chaussée de la Muette*, and afterwards to walk together from there to the *rue de l'Annonciation* where Bouboudi's flat had been. That brought back many happy memories of those years in Paris that had been so important in my early life.

XI: Theatrical Interlude

Nowadays, some children's greatest ambition is to become a pop star. In a similar vein, the children of my early days would often yearn to go on the stage or into films. And although I had already decided by about the age of thirteen to make music my career, before that I frequently longed to be an actress. Not that I had any experience of the theatre. But an important event in my Edinburgh childhood was the annual season of J.M. Barrie's *Peter Pan* at the Lyceum Theatre; and going to this, like attending the pantomime at Christmas, was a yearly ritual in our family. *Peter Pan* always held a special magic for me; and when I was about nine I was given a copy of it — a copy, that is, of the original play, not the story-book version. This book with its pale blue covers became my constant companion, and during the next few years I learnt most of the title role by heart, and used to give performances of it to an imaginary audience.

Throughout my earliest years, and probably even until I was as old as eleven, one of my favourite ploys was pretending to be someone else. The identities I assumed would vary from characters in books to those among my friends whom I currently admired — or envied. I even remember at one point, aged about seven, trying to impersonate my aunt's cocker spaniel, who seemed to live a rather delightful existence. And I was fascinated to learn quite recently, when watching a TV interview with the actress Susannah Yorke, that she too had played this particular game as a child. It was specially interesting that in her case this had led her not only into acting but later into writing novels. As she put it: "When you're an actor you can usually play only one role; as a writer you get to play all the roles."

During my younger days, any experience of real-life acting was restricted to school plays; these happened fairly regularly and were always enormously important in my life. Acting at that time provided a major emotional outlet. I can still remember, in the course of a play about early Christian martyrs in Spain, declaiming some dramatic lines to the effect 'Eternity is long and life is short'; and, at the other extreme, particularly enjoying a comic sketch in French where I played the leading character, a lady who behaved with a disgraceful lack of self-control when visiting the dentist. I always entered heart and soul into these events; at times perhaps with rather too much enthusiasm, for when we performed the death scene from *Julius Caesar*, the girl playing the title role — who was a good friend — complained about the vehemence with which I stabbed her.

Then, two quite different kinds of theatrical experience were added during the war years. The first, a performance in the Lyceum, one of Edinburgh's two main theatres, that was staged by an international Roman Catholic women's organisation known as *The Grail* (still flourishing today in various parts of the world). A feature of their work is the presentation of large-scale religious pageants (notably, a number were held in the thirties at London's Royal Albert Hall). These make much use of choral-speaking, rather in the classical Greek style, and of 'Rhythmical Interpretation' — a kind of mime that incorporates dance-movement and singing and owes its origin to a Dutch woman, a founder-member of the organisation, with the splendidly colourful name of Baroness Yvonne Bosch von Drakenstein. Through personal contacts I had become involved with this production, as had my long-standing friend Elsie Hamilton-Dalrymple. Together we strove to acquire the particular and quite complicated skills needed to take part in, among other things, the Interpretation of *Rorate Caeli Desuper* — the Advent antiphon — sung in its plainchant setting. (Quite recently, after more than half a century, we found we could still go through the entire routine — movement, Latin words and music.)

Today I can't help wondering what Edinburgh made of such a decidedly *Papist* affair; but at the time my special interest was in treading the boards of that same Lyceum theatre where, not so many years earlier, I'd been watching entranced as Peter Pan and Wendy flitted through the windows of the Darling family's nursery. And it probably did me no harm to learn then, quite early on, that the backstage premises of a theatre are often far from glamorous.

It must have been about a year later, sometime during the winter of

1943/44, that Mrs Rosalind Kennedy, whose daughter Katherine was a fairly recent friend, invited me to take part in a large-scale charity performance in the form of a non-stop revue that she was presenting at Edinburgh's Lauriston Hall. Katherine and I had originally become friends through musical contacts — she was a cello pupil of Ruth Waddell's and played in the Waddell Orchestra, as well as having piano lessons from my teacher, Edna Lovell. She was a most delightful girl, who was destined from around the age of sixteen to captivate large numbers of Edinburgh's young men; and she was clearly the darling of her mother — a dynamic lady with a formidable personality. Katherine's mother had both organising ability and experience in theatrical productions, and taking part in her show was demanding, for she knew to the last detail exactly what she wanted. Members of the cast were mainly inexperienced, and they varied in age from students in their early twenties to quite young schoolchildren, but everything ran like clockwork. It was also great fun. I learnt much later that Mrs Kennedy had the reputation of being an aloof and even rather frightening character; and certainly she spoke her mind, but she was always extremely kind to me, and to most friends of her younger daughter, whom she plainly adored. (Her relationships with her son, Ludovic Kennedy, who became well-known as a writer, politician and broadcaster, and with her elder daughter, Morar, were apparently less happy.)

Even when launched into serious cello studies I continued to hanker for opportunities to act, so when I found myself living in London between 1946 and '47, I volunteered to take part in what was known as 'The Old Girls' Play' at St. Mary's, Ascot. (My not very distinguished time at the school was sufficient to qualify me for this.) The play chosen for that particular year was Oscar Wilde's *The Importance of Being Ernest*. It was being produced by an 'Old Girl' with some experience of the theatre, Polly McIrvine (who later married the well-known TV and radio personality Frank Muir); and it struck Polly as an amusing idea to cast me — Margaret *Moncrieff* — in the role of Algernon **Moncrieff** (in those days the Old Girls' play was always performed by an all-female cast), and this was a part that gave me plenty of scope.

The rehearsals were enormous fun, and certain phrases from the play became part of daily life in the family household at Putney where I was living at the time. Not just that ever notorious query of Lady

Bracknell's, "A — HANDBAG . . . ?", but such other gems as "To lose *two* parents looks like carelessness", "The idea is grotesque and irreligious", or "I am thankful to say that I have never even *seen* a spade", along with many others.

The play eventually had two performances during March 1947, one at Ascot and one at the sister convent in Hampstead. All round, being part of this enterprise was a most rewarding experience, and I remember with satisfaction that, when a review appeared later in the St. Mary's school magazine, it included my name among three of the cast who had shown "outstanding acting ability". And before anybody points out that this was *only* a school magazine, I'd like to add with some smugness that the other two mentioned were both at RADA!

However, it should be clearly stated at this point, in deference to my many friends in the professional theatre, that a career on the stage was never seriously in question for me. Apart from anything, at five feet eight inches I might well have been too tall for a female; and in any case the demands of music were always far too strong. Later on, though, I did actually get some first-hand experience of the real-life theatre when in August 1953 I was asked to join a group of four players in providing incidental and interval music at the St. James's Theatre — a splendid old building in Pall Mall that, sadly, no longer exists today but at that time belonged to and was run on behalf of Laurence Olivier (who, along with Vivien Leigh, attended one of the post-performance parties). This was a splendid job; for, apart from anything, it provided something quite unusual in a freelance musician's life — a regular weekly pay packet. It also left the players free to do other work in the daytime, and even, by engaging an approved deputy, to go off elsewhere from time to time and take part in the odd solo or chamber music concert. I managed, among other engagements, to fit in a recital at Edinburgh University (when my duo partner, Mary Firth, was a good friend from earlier days), and a performance of the Dvorak Concerto in Chelsea Town Hall.

Altogether the St James's Theatre engagement lasted nine months, and, for the first of the three productions in which we took part, we provided not only interval music, but also had to come on stage during the last act and play softly in the wings. This meant extra pay — bumping up our wage packet to a starry total of twelve whole pounds a week — a fair amount of money in 1953 terms.

This first play was *Anastasia* — an account of the attempt to prove the identity of a young woman who was claimed by certain interested parties to be the Grand Duchess Anastasia, the youngest daughter of Tsar Nicholas the Second. (It preceded by some years the film of the same name with Ingrid Bergman in the title role.) And because we were on stage each evening we came to know many of the cast, who used to gather round while we played — the men in particular being intrigued to see a girl playing the cello (I was the only female in the quartet). There used to be much silent joking and repartee, but one night we musicians got into dreadful trouble — and not surprisingly. It happened because after nearly three months I suddenly felt so bored with the soupy Russian folk song we had to play night after night that, on an wicked impulse, I began changing my sober pizzicato bass-part into a sort of tango, and the other members of the quartet then followed suit. As a result the actors, who were supposed to be rendering a particularly nostalgic scene, were in danger of corpsing all over the place, and we got into the most awful row with the stage director, Tony Pelley — not that anyone could blame him. I cringe to remember it, but I don't think any of us realised at the time what an appalling thing we were doing.

We weren't given the sack, but survived for a further five and a half months to provide interval music for two more plays: the first, *Pygmalion* with Kay Hammond and John Clements; the second a play whose title I've now forgotten, with Googie Withers and John McCallum. There were no further productions. And, after that, it was only the occasional invitation from singer friends — among them the Scottish tenor, Duncan Robertson — to visit dress rehearsals at Glyndebourne that brought me anywhere near the footlights.

However, I did have a brief spell in movie-land which should perhaps be included here. This came about in the summer of 1971, when I was unexpectedly asked to take part in recording the music for Ken Russell's film of *The Boy Friend*. For this, the orchestra was rather unusually constituted in that, while there was a full contingent of wind and brass, the string section consisted of only two violins, a double bass and myself on the cello. And during the sessions I learnt a good deal about the extent to which things can be faked in recordings. On this occasion, in order to balance the inequality of numbers between the string section and the others, we string-players were positioned in a separate part of the studio, with a huge, ceiling-high screen separating us from the wind and brass. This all but cut off the sound from the other players, and meant, not only that we had no problem in hearing ourselves but that the volume produced by the strings could be separately and immensely boosted in the recording. I remember being amazed, when they played the first 'takes', to hear that the four of us sounded almost like the strings of the Vienna Philharmonic!

It was also fascinating to see how much care must go into synchronizing music and action. Each bit of music has to be, first exactly timed to a fraction of a second, and then recorded while the relevant section of film is being shown on monitors. A particularly difficult sequence involved the accompaniment to a tap-dance performed by one of the actors while descending a staircase. And of course all the vocal numbers had to be recorded with the singers, to be later woven into the sound-track, which meant rubbing shoulders with 'Twiggy' and the other stars involved, not to mention with Peter Maxwell Davies, who had arranged the musical score, and with the director, Mr Ken Russell, himself. From a personal point of view this engagement happened at a specially fortunate time, as it coincided with my husband's setting off on a protracted tour of the Far East and kept me fully occupied at the moment of his departure. Not that it really softened the separation, but it did help to provide a distraction!

Certain ties with the theatre always continued, for the neighbourhood where our family was living from 1961 onwards was popular with the theatrical profession and included a large number of actors and their families. One friend during the early years was Sylvia Syms; her children were much of an age with ours, and since they attended the same nursery school and dancing class we used to share a car-ferry. And when our younger daughter, Alison, was about four, it happened that Sylvia was playing the title role in the annual London production of *Peter Pan*. Naturally we all trooped off to see a performance, which everyone greatly enjoyed, but there were some problems for the youngest member of the party. Alison had always known Sylvia under her married name of Mrs Edney, and she obviously had difficulty in sorting out the real from the fictional. To the point that, as we left after the play, she inquired — in all seriousness — "Will Mrs Edney fly home from the theatre tonight?"

A handful of other things from times past, both distant and more recent, belong to this chapter. Going back first to 1957: at some point that summer, soon after Alex and I were married, he was engaged to provide musical settings for the songs in a new play, *The Queen and the Welshman*, by Rosemary Anne Sissons. This was at the request of Teddy Burnham, a well-known producer for whom Alex had provided the music in a previous production. (Alex in fact had a very considerable gift for composition, although later the pressure of work in other directions gave him little time to develop it). The play, which was based on the story of Henry the Fifth's widow Katherine and her marriage after Henry's death to Owen Tudor, had first a tour in the provinces and later a short run in the London West End. It was notable mainly for providing Edward Woodward, then a relatively little known actor, with one of his first major roles.

Moving forward to 1994: that year marked the centenary of the school-story writer Elinor Brent-Dyer, and I, as her biographer, was asked to appear in a video that was being made to celebrate the occasion by Ju Gosling, under the title *The Chalet School Revisited*. It involved my narrating on camera an eight-minute account of Brent-Dyer's life and achievement, which was divided into and filmed in four two-minute slots; and I remember being astonished to find how much time and trouble went to the filming of a mere two-minute sequence. This was something I'd known in theory about film-making, but hadn't experienced personally before, not even during the *Boy Friend* sessions. At the time I had barely recovered from a bout of summer flu and, being still a little under the weather, I found the whole thing absolutely exhausting — especially the endless repetitions that were needed. It was a huge effort to keep the concentration focused; and thereafter I would certainly never have nursed the faintest ambition to act in films!

A final mention now, to complete this theatrical interlude, although it concerns neither me, personally, nor Alex but our elder daughter, Catriona. She at the age of not quite sixteen decided to try for one of the smaller roles in *Romeo and Juliet*, which had been chosen that year as their joint production by Latymer Upper School and her school, Godolphin and Latimer. And Catriona is perhaps the only person who ever attended an audition for the relatively small part of Lady Capulet only to be offered the leading role of Juliet, for which she hadn't dreamt of applying. It's also amusing to recall that, while Romeo was played in this production by a certain *Jamie* Grant, his now famous younger brother *Hugh* Grant was only one of the minor characters.

Part Four: Meeting of the Worlds

(Overleaf) Outside Baileys Hotel, South Kensington, where our wedding reception was held on Thursday 6 June 1957.

XII: Alex

AT THE BEGINNING OF THESE MEMOIRS, it was stated that one of my primary objectives in writing them was to give a picture of the social upheaval that has taken place during my lifetime, as well as to underline the widely different backgrounds of my husband and myself. And by this point some general impression must have emerged of my family circumstances and upbringing. Now, I'd like to try and capture something of the very different world from which Alex came.

    He and I first became acquainted at the beginning of 1955; properly acquainted, that is, for we had met once or twice at musical parties, and he in fact always claimed that right back in 1945 we had together helped to push a grand piano across the platform during one of the Edinburgh Competition Festivals! "How did you meet your husband?" is a question I was often asked after he and I had performed together at a concert. To this I used to enjoy replying, quite truthfully, that it was "Through the L.C.C" — or London County Council, as the organisation in charge of London was called at that time.

    This happened because a piano trio to which I'd belonged since 1952 was suddenly in January 1955 left without a third player, when our pianist, David Tod Boyd (son of the renowned violinist, Isolde Menges), accepted an appointment as *repetiteur* with the Carl Rosa Opera Company. David's new position meant that he would be spending most of his time on tour with the company, which ruled out further concerts with our trio. But at exactly this point the L.C.C., in the form of the Inner London Education Authority, offered the trio three days of work doing concerts for their schools. Plainly, with a paid job being offered, we were not going to reveal that we were now without a pianist, so the violinist, Jackie Bower, and I immediately set about

155

The trio with Jackie Bower, which brought about our original meeting.

looking for a suitable substitute. Someone mentioned a young Scottish pianist, Alexander Kelly, who had made his London debut the previous year at the Royal Festival Hall under Sir Thomas Beecham, and we decided to see if he would be interested. We already knew Alex's name and he was of course a fellow Scot — Jackie Bower, like me, came from Edinburgh, where we had both been in the Waddell Orchestra; and there proved to be a further link in that all three of us had held awards from the Sir James Caird Trust.

Alex agreed to give things a go; and that first batch of school concerts proved so enjoyable that, when the trio was offered other bookings, it seemed the obvious thing to continue as a group. At this juncture the 1956 Mozart bi-centenary was on the horizon; and we were lucky enough to be invited to perform all the Mozart piano trios (along with other works) in a series of five concerts for the Northampton Music Club — a project that naturally involved meeting regularly for rehearsals. I also, in January 1956, had to find a pianist for a London recital, and it seemed good sense to ask Alex to join me for this. One way and another, then, we were spending a lot of time in each other's company. But although by the summer of 1956 I would certainly have thought of him as a most congenial friend, the idea of any closer relationship never crossed my mind. Apart from anything else, I was somewhat involved at the time in various unsatisfactory love affairs. But before describing how matters were eventually resolved, I want now to go back more than twenty-five years, in order to consider Alex's origins and background.

As a person, Alex was no more inclined than I am to share intimate secrets with outsiders, or even with friends. Until the night when we became as near as we ever did to 'being engaged' — perhaps 'reaching an understanding' would describe it better — I had known almost nothing about his family background and home. I knew that he had grown up in Edinburgh, had attended the Royal High School, and, after winning a major award from the Sir James Caird Trust, had gone on to study with Harold Craxton at the Royal Academy of Music in London, but little else.

The bare bones of his personal story were first revealed to me on 21 December 1956, during an evening we spent at a crowded pub in Marylebone Lane that no longer exists. Gradually, in the succeeding days, he told me more — as much in fact as he himself knew at the time. But it was to be many years before some of the details emerged; and to this day some are still unknown.

Alex had grown up in the family of James and Mary Kelly, and their two daughters, Mary and Isa, who were his elders by respectively 21 and 16 years. In the early days the family had lived in a small cottage at Gilmerton, a village just outside Edinburgh. Then, at some point in 1934, they had moved to a new bungalow, part of a development on the main Gilmerton Road into the city. The little house, which was named 'Marina' (presumably it dated from the year of Princess Marina's marriage to the Duke of Kent), had been built for the Kellys by their son-in-law, Bob Fleming, who at that time ran his own small building firm in Edinburgh. And for the next twelve years, right up to the autumn of 1946, this solidly built stone bungalow, set in a neat, square garden, was to be Alex's home.

But James and Mary Kelly were not his natural parents: Alex had been adopted by the Kellys at an early age. This, however, had always been wrapped in secrecy, and was something that he himself had only discovered at the age of sixteen, when he had to produce a birth certificate in connection with his scholarship application. A dreadfully traumatic experience . . . he could recall just sitting at the table, the adoption certificate in his hands and the tears pouring down his face. In fact, it was only as recently as the late 1980s that we were able to piece together some account of his earliest years.

Alex had always remembered a young woman, with very dark hair and eyes — "a little brown creature", he sometimes called her — who used to visit him in his early days at the Kelly family home. After a while she disappeared, but for many reasons it seemed possible to him in later life that she could have been his mother. And because he even remembered her name I was able eventually to confirm this, and to trace Alex's original birth certificate. From this and other researches, and conversations that became possible later with his adopted sisters, Mary and Isa, it emerged that Alex's natural mother was named Annie Lugton, aged about 24. She was the daughter of an East Lothian ploughman whose family lived on a farm near East Linton (a village about 25 miles outside Edinburgh, roughly half-way between Dunbar and Haddington).

This much is fact. But the identity of Alex's father can only be a matter for speculation, since no name is given on the birth certificate. However, at the time in question Annie Lugton was a domestic servant in the house of a widower — he had better be identified here only as 'Mr M'. And, although there's no actual proof to be found, it is surely significant that 'Mr M' not only paid the fees at the children's home where Alex was originally placed, and the fostering fees when he was first with the Kelly family, he also offered to make a financial settlement in Alex's favour when, later, the question arose of formal adoption. (This offer was rejected by Mary Kelly, Alex's adopted mother, on the grounds that: "None of the others brought any money with them when they came into our family, and neither does he have to bring any.") Now, does a man do all this, just for the illegitimate child of his cook-housekeeper? To me, it seems unlikely. Moreover Alex could recall that as a small boy he had more than once been taken to play the piano to 'Mr M'. It would all fit . . .

Once the adoption formalities were completed, Annie Lugton disappeared from Alex's life. And I've always regretted that, although I did in the 1990s finally manage to trace her, it was too late — she had died earlier that year. I would so much have liked to meet her and to thank her; and I often wonder if she knew about Alex's progress and his successful musical career. There were frequently notices of his concerts in various Scottish newspapers; and at the time of our wedding there was a lot of publicity, including a full-page article in a now defunct Scottish tabloid, *The Bulletin*. She could well have seen this; and my daughters and I occasionally speculate about an unidentified gift among the wedding presents Alex and I were sent. This was a large hexagonal bowl in blue pyrex, with six matching smaller bowls, and it came from a well-known firm in Edinburgh. As there was no card with it I telephoned the shop to ask the name of the sender; only to be told that there was no way of knowing, as the buyer had not paid by cheque but in cash. No one else ever claimed to be the donor; so was this, just possibly, Annie Lugton's gift to her unknown son?

Alex at about seven.

At least it was possible over the years to show a measure of gratitude to Alex's adopted family, who, despite the inevitable ups and downs of family life, were in general very supportive to him. Above all, he always retained a great affection and respect for his adopted mother. There seems to have been a bond between them from the beginning; and a charming story is told that, when Mary Kelly was being taken round the children's home to choose which child they would foster, a little boy with a pointed face, huge brown eyes and dark curly hair, held out his arms to her as she passed the pram where he was sitting. And that settled it . . .

Many years later Alex was to describe his adopted mother in this poem (written in the 1970s/80s?) :

>My Mother
>My mother, a small fierce woman,
>Was all of five-foot nothing,
>With the biggest heart in all the countryside,
>And a temper that flared
>Like a burning haystack in the
>Hottest, driest summer.

> She took in her dead brother-in-law's son
> (His dad had been killed in the War),
> From time to time she took in her
> Half-sister's bairns, when their
> Dad in one of his bad turns had
> Drunk away nearly half the furniture.
> She took in her niece's girl
> (Got on her by some randy unknown student)
> And she even took in me.
> Neither beggar nor tramp ever went empty from her door.
>
> But when she was in one of her takings,
> Strong men crossed to the other side of the road
> And the family took to their heels.

Sadly, by the time I first met her in 1957, Mary Kelly was already failing in health and I was never really able to know her. However, she did live to see our elder daughter, Catriona, as a baby; making this comment once on the strong likeness at that time between the baby and Alex: "Well, there's no doubt who *your* father is" — a remark that seemed a trifle unexpected in the circumstances!

With Alex's adopted father I didn't have even this minimal contact, since by this point he was not only bed-ridden but had lost his memory. James Kelly was then well in his eighties, which means he must have been born in the 1870s. He had been a miner, which placed him a fair way up the social scale in working-class terms; and his weekly wage of four pounds a week was considered in the 1930s to be relatively handsome. Like many men from the old-fashioned Scottish working class, he had a great respect for learning and for books — being probably an example of the stereotype that used to be described as *likely to grudge a child sixpence to buy sweets but happy to hand out the price of a book that cost many times more.*

The Kelly family were clearly not well-off; but when it became plain that their adopted child was both intelligent and gifted, a considerable effort was made to give him some of the right opportunities. And by co-incidence it happened that Alex's older sister, Mary, gave piano lessons, and hence that the piano entered Alex's life right from his earliest days in the Kelly household. Very soon — certainly by the age of four — the little boy was clamouring (Alex himself used the word "screaming") to be taught the piano, and it was immediately clear that he had talent. That he also had huge determination was demonstrated when, at the age of six, he suffered a broken femur and had to have his left leg encased in plaster from the waist to the ground. This, normally, would have made piano playing almost impossible; but Alex insisted that he should be laid flat on his face on a table in front of the keyboard, and from this position he somehow continued to play.

By the time he went to the village school, aged five, Alex had learnt several party pieces; and it happened that these included a Waltz that the head teacher herself performed one afternoon at the end of lessons. Afterwards a small voice was heard saying "I can play it better than that" — a remark that some teachers might have found unpalatably cocky. But this kindly young woman had not only taken it in good part, but had been interested enough to ask Alex for a performance. To her great credit, she was even ready to agree that the child was absolutely right! And she decided to speak on Alex's behalf to Dr Herbert Wiseman, who was then Head of Music for the Edinburgh Education Authority and an important figure on the Scottish educational scene. (He was also, later on, to be a significant influence in both Alex's and my careers.) At first, her requests that Dr Wiseman should visit her school in Gilmerton in order to hear this talented little boy were brushed aside: Dr Wiseman, she was briskly informed, was forever being asked to come and hear talented children perform, and more often than not it all turned out to be a terrible fuss about nothing. But eventually the great man was persuaded to turn up; and in the event he was genuinely impressed with Alex's gifts.

From then on Herbert Wiseman, who used to be affectionately nicknamed the 'Father of Scotland's Musical Bairns', was to be a kind of guardian angel to Alex, keeping a constant eye on him and monitoring his progress. In due course he pronounced that the time had come for Alex to have lessons from someone accustomed to teaching advanced pupils. He recommended a Mr Walker Cameron, who was then well-known among Edinburgh's piano teachers; and from this point Alex was to work with Donald Walker Cameron until, in September 1946, he went to study at the Royal Academy of Music in London. Not only that: Donald also grew to become a friend; and he and his wife, Myna Cameron, always continued to take a close interest in Alex, both as a musician and a person, and to give any support and help that they could.

At the Royal Academy of Music, Alex's student days could fairly be described as a catalogue of successes — although it's unlikely that he himself would have allowed me to say so. Certainly he must have won every prize and scholarship available to piano students at that time — as testified by the Boards of Honour that used in former days to decorate the main staircase and first landing at the Academy, many of which carried his name in one year or another. He also became renowned for performances of various large-scale works; in particular Beethoven's *Diabelli Variations* and *Hammerklavier Sonata*, Hindemith's *Ludus Tonalis* (probably a first ever performance at the RAM). and both the *Handel Variations* and *Paganini Variations* (Books I and II) of Brahms.

In addition to studying piano with Harold Craxton, he also had lessons in composition from Lennox Berkley and organ lessons from Douglas Hawkridge. (On one occasion in the late 1960s, when we were on a concert tour in Scotland and visited a stately home where there was a chamber organ, I remember being astonished, never previously having heard Alex play the organ, when he sat down and gave a most competent performance of a Bach Chorale Prelude.)

In all, Alex spent five years at the RAM, although his studies were interrupted between 1949 and 1951 by the then compulsory period of National Service. During this he was posted for most of a year with the occupation forces in Germany, working in the Army Education Corps. Here his duties involved a variety of tasks: they ranged from giving piano lessons to the Colonel's wife and musical appreciation classes, to teaching general subjects and working in basic literacy and numeracy skills with young soldiers, some of whom had never learnt to read or write. This teaching experience, so he always maintained, was to help him greatly in later life; even if the general teaching did involve some hectic swatting in mathematics — never Alex's favourite or best subject.

By 1953 he had embarked on a freelance career, combining solo engagements, ensemble work, and accompanying singers. His particular bent for chamber music developed early, and among the artists with whom he gave numerous successful concerts at this time were the well-known Scottish cellist, Joan Dickson, and the clarinettist Georgina Dobree, who had been a fellow pupil at the RAM and with whom he now formed an ongoing musical partnership. Another fellow student with whom he collaborated on a regular basis was Jean

Harvey — well known both as pianist and violinist — who would later form a piano trio with Alex and me.

He also contrived to fit in a certain amount of teaching; and this included Saturdays in the Royal Academy of Music Junior Department, where the rate of pay, to the best of my recollections, was then ten shillings an hour — viz. 50 pence! (In fairness, it must be stated that this amount was worth considerably more in those days, and that it was in any case the standard rate.) In addition to all this, Alex was invited to form a two-piano duo with a rather older colleague, Miles Coverdale — another former Craxton pupil. And it was with this duo that he made his official London debut in 1954, performing a concerto for two pianos by Johann Christian Bach with the Royal Philharmonic Orchestra under Sir Thomas Beecham.

This summary, then, provides some picture of the young Scottish pianist, Alexander Kelly, who in January 1955 agreed to join two other Scots — the violinist Jackie Bower and cellist Margaret Moncrieff — in a piano trio.

Alex on National Service in Germany, 1950/51.

XIII: Two Worlds Meet

ALEX USED OFTEN TO SAY THAT REHEARSING and performing with ensembles was an excellent training for marriage, because concert conditions tended to bring out the worst in people! And to some extent I think he was right. Certainly neither of us entered marriage without some knowledge of each other's faults and failings. For us, things were very different from the way they had been in my mother's time, when — as expressed in an old saying she often quoted — no matter how well you *thought* you knew a man, you always *married* someone else. But probably Alex and I were lucky in having things happen in the order they did — in other words, in having a warm friendship and a happy musical partnership before any closer relationship developed.

I've no idea at what point exactly Alex's feelings began to change; and, as already indicated, I was incredibly slow to see what was going on. Perhaps one reason could have been that he was younger than me, and perhaps I was still sufficiently influenced by my background and upbringing to assume unconsciously that this ruled out the idea of a serious relationship. However that may be, at this point Alex was in my eyes a valued and most congenial friend with whom I shared many interests, and not just in music. He was in fact someone who stood out as being exceptionally knowledgeable in many fields, widely read, and with an informed appreciation of the visual arts. He was highly entertaining, we always laughed a lot and he was excellent company. Into the bargain, he got on well with my mother and with other members of my family. But I was completely taken aback when, one afternoon in November 1956, he suddenly began making declarations that suggested something quite different.

In later years we often smiled together over this incident, which we

Meeting of the Worlds

always referred to as 'Buckingham Palace Road' — that being the place where we were standing at the time. I remember it was a Tuesday; and that that morning our trio had been giving another of the LCC school concerts; after which Alex had accompanied me home to my mother's flat in South Kensington, where we had a late lunch. In the afternoon I was due (wearing my other hat as piano-accompanist) to rehearse with two singers who lived in a top flat in Buckingham Palace Road. And I was rather puzzled when, after lunch, Alex insisted on coming with me on the journey to Victoria — which he pronounced to be on his way home.

Publicity photo of Alex in about 1955.

Since he at that time lived in Ealing, which is in exactly the opposite direction, I did find this a little strange. He further insisted on escorting me all the way from Victoria Station to the downstairs entrance of my friends' flat. Here, on the corner of Buckingham Palace Road, he proceeded — not to make himself clear, indeed far from it, but to indicate a very serious change in his feelings for me. I can still picture him at that corner, pouring forth a stream of words, with the bright red of a pillar-box in the background. Completely dazed, I made my way up four flights of stairs to my friends' flat, where I remember collapsing on a chair and trying to explain that I *thought* I had just heard a proposal . . . And of course it wasn't only the unexpectedness of it all: at that stage I was in a state of complete confusion, semi-involved emotionally with two different men — one of them married. Which made it seem hardly an ideal moment for more complications . . .

During the ensuing weeks things did gradually become clearer, although I can't now remember exactly how long it took. At one point we held hands together through a performance at Sadlers Wells of the opera *Martha* (which contains the well-known air *The Last Rose of*

Summer). But the deciding event was probably a concert we gave with the trio at a stately home in Suffolk early that December. Here, after the dinner which followed the recital, both the violinist and I were separately propositioned by our extremely eccentric host (we checked the details together later on). First he took each of us dancing in turn — and dancing, by the way, to classical music, none of your dance music rubbish. Then, during these somewhat complicated manoeuvres, he expressed an urgent desire to take photos of us in the nude, and spent much time explaining that it was entirely ridiculous for anyone to feel prejudiced about such a natural thing . . .

Into the bargain I also had to cope that evening with fending off the advances of another man whose fancy was turned more directly to thoughts of bed; his particular chat line being to extol the beauties of the Carolingean ceiling in his bedroom — an interesting variant on the usual. And I think it was the contrast with Alex's considerate, gentle and truly personal treatment that helped me to see matters in a new light. It struck me so forcibly that, although he, Alex, was the only one there who really did care about me as a person, *he* was not pestering me or making a nuisance of himself. Even if he did occasionally mention in rather plaintive tones that the room *he* had been allocated was very cold and bleak . . .

Scottish legal tradition embodies a Latin phrase that my father sometimes quoted, to the effect that *the law stops at the threshold of the nuptial chamber*. And maybe it wouldn't harm some of today's needlessly explicit books, TV and films if the underlying principle of reticence was occasionally observed. Suffice it to say here that when Alex and I returned to London the next afternoon, having had a long, serious discussion during the train journey, we had advanced a fair way along the road to understanding. It was only a fortnight or so later that we spent that evening in the Marylebone Lane pub, described earlier, which marked the beginning of an unofficial engagement and long-term commitment.

At this early stage we told no one. There seemed little prospect at the time of our being able to marry in the very near future — not much money and nowhere to live. Besides, we had seen too many engagements foundering in the wake of endless enquiries such as "Now, when are you two getting married?" In particular, the violinist in our trio, Jackie Bower, had been engaged on and off — always to the same man, though with interludes — for literally seven years; and even being in the background of that was quite taxing. So we decided that until we could set a definite date for our wedding the news would not be made public.

Naturally enough, as the weeks went by we did begin to share the good tidings with a few of our close relatives and friends. Among them, of course, my mother and Alex's adopted family. And it's at this point that things developed so differently from the way that they might have done had all this happened thirty years earlier. For in those pre-war days, or perhaps at any time while my father was still alive, it is safe to say that the most appalling crisis would have developed had I announced my intention of marrying the adopted son of a mining family, and one who was moreover the fatherless illegitimate child of a maid-servant.

Of course, at the time of our marriage I'd reached an age when, even in the old days, I could have gone my own way, but the repercussions then would have been horrendous. In 1957, things were blessedly different. And although at an early stage my mother had apparently confided to a friend that this "wasn't what she would have chosen at one time", she was in fact extremely fond of Alex and always gave us her entire support, keeping any misgivings to herself.

Nevertheless, I'm glad we none of us knew at that point about a dreadful problem that had arisen when some busybody asked my godmother, Miss Isabel Maxwell, whether she thought Lady Moncrieff was aware that her daughter was, as kindly expressed, "marrying a foundling". Now my godmother was a well-known and respected inhabitant of North Berwick who came from a county family; she was a thoroughly good and conscientious woman, and (as we learnt later) she was so worried about this report that she decided to consult a Father James Christie, one of the Jesuit priests at Lauriston Church in Edinburgh, to get his opinion as to whether it was her duty to inform my mother. To Father Christie's credit, his advice was that she should say nothing.

Anyway, the Moncrieff and McClelland ancestors should not feel too smug and superior in the hereafter, because some of the objections that did arise to our marriage came from the other side, although these were not social but religious. For Alex's adopted family were Plymouth Brethren, and to them the idea of anyone connected with their family marrying a Roman Catholic was extremely disturbing. By this point Alex's mother was of course too old and frail to travel to

London for the wedding, but his elder sister and her husband actually declined to attend. (I feel able to mention this now, because in later years our relationship became extremely cordial and affectionate and they were always notably kind to our children.) Nor were they the only people in Edinburgh to express both disapproval and foreboding to Alex about the dangerous step he was taking in joining his life with a Catholic. And to think that this was happening in **1957**, not 1917 . . .

Our own main anxieties about getting married were financial. We were both just about getting by at this point, but neither of us was making a lot of money — I, if anything, was earning rather more than Alex, and this didn't help, either, as he had old-fashioned ideas on the subject of 'kept' husbands. Then, quite unexpectedly, in April 1957 Alex was offered a twenty-week engagement to act as resident pianist, in a group that provided music through the summer months at the Delaware Pavilion in Bexhill-on-Sea. The salary was sixteen pounds a week; and the prospect of that kind of money on a regular basis seemed incredible riches to us at that time. Alex had no hesitation in accepting the job. And in less than four weeks all the arrangements for the wedding had been made: the church and the reception booked, the announcements sent off to the papers, the guest lists completed and the invitations sent out, the wedding rings bought, and my wedding dress well on the way to being finished (the glorious brocade material was a generous gift from my cousin Noel Moncrieff).

We also had to find ourselves somewhere to live in Bexhill, and this, with the summer season about to begin, could have been difficult, but here once again we were lucky. At first we spent part of a day going round the Bexhill house-agents with no success. There wasn't much on offer, and most of it was anyway too expensive. Things could have seemed a little bleak, but a woman who worked in one of the agencies waylaid us outside their office, and whispered to us that she knew unofficially of a small flat to let at the top of one of the other houses in the road where she lived. She gave us the address of the landlord; we called to see him, and in no time everything was settled.

The flat, consisting of two reasonably sized and adequately furnished attic rooms, a bathroom and tiny kitchenette, was on the top floor of a pleasant house, within easy walking distance of both the Delaware Pavilion on the sea front where Alex would be working and the station — something that was important to us in those days since we had no car. The rent, at three guineas a week, was extremely reasonable; and provided we would agree to begin paying this straight away, the flat would be immediately reserved for us until the middle of October. By this point it was less than three weeks to our wedding day, and we gladly agreed to the arrangement.

Both of us were busy musically right up to the day before the wedding, partly with teaching commitments and partly with a most important concert on Sunday the second of June. For that day was the exact centenary of Elgar's birth in 1857; and the Northampton Music Club, where our trio had been making regular appearances during the past two seasons, was celebrating the occasion with a gala concert of Elgar's music, at which they had invited us to take part in performances of the String Quartet and the Piano Quintet. The Music Club committee had hoped that Elgar's daughter, Mrs Carice Elgar Blake, would be able to attend the concert; and although — not surprisingly in view of the centenary's national importance — she had not been available to do so, Mrs Blake did come to a repeat performance we gave of the programme later that year. She spent some time after the concert talking about the first movement of the Piano Quintet, with its curiously elusive character, which she said was partly inspired by the strange, even eerie atmosphere of the Sussex landscape round Findhorn where Elgar was living at the time.

The wedding itself took place at the Catholic Church of Our Lady of Victories in Kensington — not then situated in its present handsome building off Kensington High Street, but temporarily housed round the corner at the Congregational Church in Allen Street, the original church having been destroyed during the Blitz. By mutual agreement between Alex and me, the proceedings were kept as simple as possible. Nearly 200 people attended — despite the wedding's being held on a Thursday, rather than at the more usual weekend — but there was no formal sermon during the marriage service, and no long-winded speeches at the reception. Alex did conform to tradition in wearing Morning-Dress, complete with grey top-hat; but he and his Best Man, Andrew Downie, travelled most of their journey to the church in Andrew's bubble-car, although they did feel it more suitable to park this undignified little vehicle a few streets away and to make their actual arrival in a taxi.

I have the happiest memories of that day. Apart, that is, from one dreadful moment when first reaching the church escorted by my cousin, Uncle Fred's son Roland Adams, who was giving me away. For the instant I saw Barbara, my Matron of Honour, waiting on the steps with her bouquet of yellow roses, I realised I'd somehow managed to forget my own flowers — a glorious sheaf of my two special favourites, dark red roses and lily-of-the-valley. And if the time of waiting while the flowers were fetched was uncomfortable for me, it was a hundred times more so for poor Alex, helplessly marooned in the front bench to await the bride in full view of all. The delay also caused problems for the organist, who was not actually a professional and had by this time used up his entire repertoire, with resultant panic. From outside on the church steps I didn't hear this, but it seems the unfortunate man was reduced to attempting a Bach fugue he'd found lying in the organ loft, which rather overstretched his capacities, and brought silent groans from the many musicians in the congregation, notably Alex's former professor, Harold Craxton, who was sitting in a prominent position with his wife and family.

Depending on how you look at it, Alex and I had either a bare two days of honeymoon, or an extended period of four and a half months. His engagement as Bexhill's sea-side pianist began with a day of rehearsals on Saturday the 8th of June; and since the previous weekend had been taken up with the Elgar Centenary concert, we had decided to hold our wedding on Thursday the sixth and to go straight down afterwards to the little flat in Bexhill. This then became our home until the middle of October. And, both at the time and since, I've felt glad that things turned out as they did, for it seemed a much more natural way to begin married life than the conventional sojourn in hotels.

From the musical point of view Alex's job was something of a mixed bag. The resident ensemble consisted of five players: the first violin, who was also the boss and organiser, a second violin who doubled on the accordion, a cellist, a double-bass player and Alex as pianist. The band's repertoire belonged to what might be called the 'Palm Court' category: mainly light classics, and selections from opera and from all the best known musicals of the 20th and late-19th centuries. Alex was also frequently starred playing potted versions of popular piano concertos — Grieg, Liszt, Rachmaninoff and so on, as well as in regular performances of the *Warsaw Concerto*. Even today, 45 years on, the romantic D flat variation from Rachmaninoff's *Paganini Rhapsody* can still carry me back to that sea-side bandstand in Bexhill.

The work schedule wasn't heavy, even including rehearsals. But it did spread over a lot of time, because the duties involved playing every day for an hour and a half in the afternoons and two hours each evening, with the exception of Friday evening and Saturday afternoon which were left free. Then on Sunday evenings there was always a 'Gala Concert', held not on the out-of-doors bandstand but inside the Pavillion. For these grand occasions the resident quintet would be augmented by around seven or eight players from London, and well known singers from Covent Garden or Sadlers Wells (the ENO hadn't then started) would appear with the 'orchestra' as soloists.

There was usually a longish interval between the Sunday afternoon rehearsal and the concert, and Alex and I, who were the only people to have any kind of base in Bexhill, used greatly to enjoy being able to invite the soloists to fill the gap by coming to relax and have a meal at our flat. One visitor I particularly remember was Josephine Veasey, then near the beginning of her distinguished operatic career; she happily made herself at home and threw off her shoes — something rather less usual for a first-time guest in those days than it might be now.

Being able to entertain people was among the great assets of having our own flat. And, throughout the four-and-a-half month period we spent in Bexhill, relays of friends and relatives would visit us; some just for a meal, others to stay for shorter or longer times. Guests belonging to the younger age groups were given camp beds or lilos in the sitting-room; but when my mother came, or older friends, the charming elderly lady who lived in the lower part of the house would kindly offer the use of one of her bedrooms — a gesture of goodwill that was much appreciated.

Bexhill is not in itself a particularly enthralling place; there is an old church of some interest, and some pleasant corners near it in that older part of the town; but once you have explored this quarter, and walked a few times along the coast in either direction, little else is on offer. However, the town did at least have a repertory theatre in those days; and we were able, as well as visiting several of their productions on Alex's free evenings, to make friends with some of the company — one of whom was delighted to take over our flat when we finally

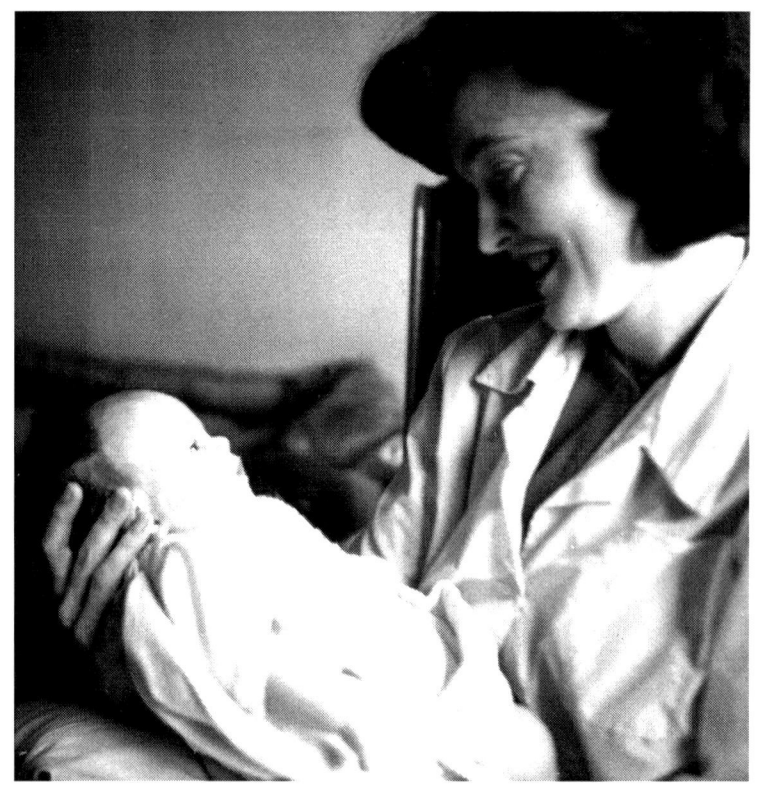

Me with Catriona aged six weeks, November 1959.

returned to London at the end of the season.

When that moment arrived, we were more than ready to resume our normal professional life in London. It had been a wonderfully happy time; and I had much enjoyed the final fortnight, when the regular cellist had to depart for family reasons and I was asked to deputise for him. But the charms of playing light music selections, on an increasingly chilly outdoor bandstand, do tend to diminish as October progresses. On the other hand, saying goodbye to the Bexhill flat was a wrench. It had been our first home. It's true we were fortunate in being able at this point to rent the lower half of a maisonette in Cornwall Gardens, South Kensington, of which my mother owned a short lease, but it was to be well over three years before we at last lived somewhere that was really our own.

That in fact didn't happen until March 1961, when after much frustrating experience of house-hunting we finally were able to move into the house in Barnes that was to be our permanent home from then onwards. (The twenty-first of March 2003 marked for me 42 years of living here in Barnes; more than half my life, and far longer than I've ever spent anywhere else, even including my original Edinburgh home; I had actually lived at eight different London addresses during one twelve-year period.)

Some important things in life seem to come about almost by chance, among them our purchase of this house. For it just chanced in the winter of 1960 that my half-sister, Patricia, and her husband were invited to a Sunday morning drinks party with friends of theirs who lived in Barnes. Here they were introduced to a Mrs Diana Tomlins who lived a few houses further down the road; and when Patricia mentioned that her sister had been looking without success for a house in Barnes, Diana Tomlins immediately suggested that I should come and talk to the owner of the house opposite to hers, as she knew he was about to put it on the market, and might be happy to bypass the house agents for a quick sale. Some busy telephoning then took place; and a few days later I set off for Barnes in a succession of buses, taking our fourteen-month old daughter, Catriona, in her push-chair — we didn't yet own a car.

Barnes, on the south side of Hammersmith Bridge, nestles in a sheltered loop of the Thames; originally the land here was an alluvial river-deposit, making the soil splendidly fertile, and in former days much of the district was covered by orchards which supplied the fruit-markets in Hammersmith. It has always been an attractive spot, with its riverside walks, extensive common, village green and pond; but in 1960 Barnes was far from being the incredibly sought-after neighbourhood it is today. House prices were still reasonable; and the residents included a considerable number of struggling musicians, actors, poets and artists. Now, in the 21st century, things are very different.

Our present house also looked very different on that cold December afternoon from the bright friendly house it was gradually to become. The owner, Mr Thum (pronounced **Tum**) had been living there since long before the second World War, and had been on his own during the past ten or more years. His taste in house decoration may have been practical, but it was decidedly sombre: all the doors, skirting boards and dadoes in the hall and on the upper landing were painted **black**; as were the banisters, the dado and the treads on the staircase. Then, in the downstairs rooms, the paint-work — and there was a lot of it — varied from dark Vandyck brown to a shade that my husband tastefully named 'palest diarrhoea', while things upstairs were similar.

It didn't help that the living-room part of the kitchen had only a narrow window in one corner, not looking out into the garden, but into a rickety sort of glassed-in lean-to that Mr Thum had himself erected beside the kitchen (the house was full of his amateurish, not to say 'Heath Robinson' efforts at DIY, all of which had eventually to be dismantled). The actual kitchen was minute — just a small peninsula attached to the back of the house, and its only window also looked into Mr Thum's lean-to. There was another glass extension, politely referred to as a conservatory, at the end of the main sitting-room, which effectively blocked such light as was admitted by the windows with their dreary brown paint. The general effect was of a very dark house — something I particularly dislike. Nevertheless, Alex and I had by this time become almost desperate after house-hunting fruitlessly for more than a year in various parts of London. We were longing to find somewhere of our own, and in any case my mother's lease of the maisonette in Cornwall Gardens had only a few months left to run, after which the terms of the new lease were likely to be prohibitive. One way and another, before I set out that afternoon Alex and I had agreed that if this Barnes house was even remotely possible I should go ahead and make an offer on the spot.

We little knew at the time how extraordinarily lucky we were going to be. But even at the start it was clear that Mr Thum's house, despite the depressing decor, had several promising features. Most important of all, although only semi-detached it provided the one essential requirement: a fair-sized room on the outer side, sufficiently remote from the neighbours to be usable as a music room. Yet more fortunate: due to the fact that the house is built at a bend in the road, it and its next-door neighbour stand at quite a wide angle, which provides a far greater distance between the two houses than is usual in this and similar roads.

It also means, as we soon discovered, that ours and the next-door gardens, being fan-shaped rather than narrow rectangles, are far larger than any others in the vicinity — something that our daughters and their friends greatly enjoyed, even if everything did become rather wild and overgrown. And it was pleasant to find that, because so much of the land had been orchards in the past, our garden, like many of those in Barnes, was well stocked with fruit trees. At that time there were apple, pear and plum trees, as well as gooseberry and black-currant bushes, some of which still survive today. (We won't mention the brambles that tend to rampage at the back — at least the fruit is delicious.)

The Barnes house in about 1977.

Indoors, another obvious bonus was a second bathroom, on the ground-floor off the kitchen. True, it was at that time just a grotty wartime conversion from the original coal-cellar, but its mere existence was an asset for me in combining kitchen-work and child-care on one floor. The house also provided an adequate number of rooms, and was in a pleasant neighbourhood. There was even a garage — admittedly it was somewhat tumbledown, and as yet we had no car, but having a garage at all was a plus point. To make an offer seemed the obvious thing. And Mr Thum was particularly kind to us, in that he not only accepted the offer straight away, but actually allowed us a slightly lower price than he had originally intended to ask from the house agents, on the grounds that it saved having to pay a commission.

Before moving in, we decided to spend some of my legacy from Aunt Georgina on having a proper window made in the living-room part of the kitchen, and to do some basic decorating. Above all, to replace the black paint-work of the hall and staircase with white and yellow (the latter was our small daughter's favourite colour at the time). This cheered things up amazingly; and in the course of the next ten or eleven years we were able gradually to make many more radical improvements. First (when friends of ours set up a local building firm) to extend the whole back of the house; an operation that was scheduled to take four months, and in the event lasted more than twice that time. It made the winter of 1964-65 a supremely uncomfortable experience: the entire back wall had to be removed, and during more than seven weeks only scaffolding and sheets of heavy industrial porothene protected us from the wind and rain; workmen were perpetually under foot, rubble sometimes fell into the soup as we sat huddled together eating in a corner of the hall, and for at least a month the entire family had to share one room, with camp beds lined up in rows.

But in the end it was all worthwhile. The extension gave us a large open-plan kitchen-living-room and a spacious sitting-room on the ground floor, both well provided with windows; upstairs there was a much bigger bedroom for Alex and me, as well as a new music-room, nicely situated on the outside of the house. Then later on, in 1972, we were able to have the attic converted into a two-room flat, which though not strictly self-contained has its own bathroom and cooking facilities. I often wonder what Mr Thum would have made of it all.

The years since coming to Barnes have been full of incident — a time that has been intensely happy, and always rewarding even if occasionally stressful. For me, the problems of balancing the

Alison and Catriona aged about 10 and 12.

Alex in the 1980s.

demands of motherhood with the life of a professional cellist were sometimes formidable. But I hope that our children never lost out. I think they never doubted that, while many things in life were important to Alex and me, our love for them and for each other always came first. And on the subject of working mothers, I was once much encouraged by hearing a comment made by my elder daughter. She was then around thirty, of decidedly feminist leanings, and when asked at a job-interview about the possible conflict between academic and family life, had responded: "One of the things I admire most about my own upbringing was being shown, quite early, that there were certain times when my mother was **not** available." That was comforting. (But, in passing, it's impossible not to wonder what **man** at an interview — even today — is ever asked the same question?)

Perhaps a flavour of the hurly-burly of daily life in our Barnes home is conveyed in the following poem that Alex wrote, probably in the early 1980s.

Hurried Letter.

On your last visit,
Life here, as ever, was hectic,
The telephone rang and rang.
People came and went.

Nevertheless there was the old
Familiar fierce affection that always was.

What was, still is,
What used to be remains,
What was shared is still there,
Always.

These forty years have seen the development of our professional lives, in performing and teaching; and, for both of us, the opening of new worlds in the field of literature — for me as a writer, and for Alex in poetry. The time has seen the childhood of our daughters, their growing-up and the unfolding of their successful careers — one as a professional cellist, the other as Reader in Russian at New College Oxford; more recently, the arrivals of our grandchildren.

Then, in October 1996, came the brutal shock of Alex's sudden and unexpected death at the age of only 67. A blessedly quick and peaceful death for him; but leaving for us a gap that can never be filled.

And I shall not attempt to chronicle the happenings of the past forty and more years in detail; but will aim in the final section, *Living in Three Worlds*, to survey a broad time-span, divided under four headings.

First: *World of Music* (Performing and Teaching)

Next: *Brief Thoughts on Friendship*

Third: *Kellys Cottage* (an account of family holidays)

Finally: *World of Words*.

Part Five: Living in Three Worlds

(Overleaf) Alex and me in Venice, 1990s.

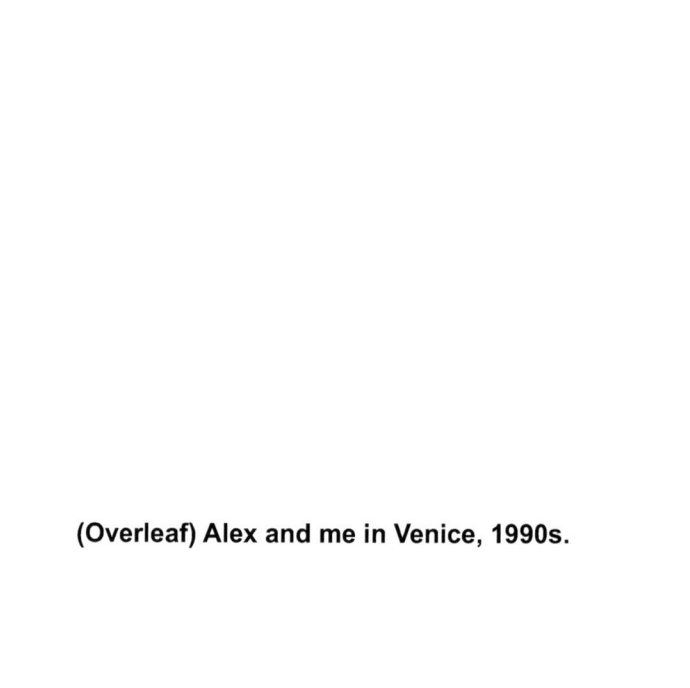

XIV: World Of Music

EVERY YEAR, CONCERT PROMOTERS AND AGENTS receive mountains of publicity material from performers, both aspiring and established. These leaflets will vary from the basic one-sided flyer to the lavishly produced and photographically illustrated four-page brochure. But all will contain a flattering description of the artists concerned, along with would-be impressive accounts of their careers to date, and a selection of carefully vetted extracts from newspaper criticisms of their concert appearances. And, sad to say, a majority of these productions will finish up in the wastepaper basket, many of them unread. Little wonder, perhaps, for it must be faced that the publicity brochure is not a medium distinguished for its literary interest, and the account of one performer's appearances around Britain and Europe – or in the USA, Canada or wherever – will read much like another.

With these thoughts in mind it would seem wise to avoid giving a blow-by-blow account either of my concert career or of my husband's. It must be taken for granted that, in the standard phraseology of the brochure, we both did the usual quota of "touring widely in the British Isles" – in our case covering between us literally from Cornwall to the Outer Hebrides and from the Channel Islands and the Kent coast to Orkney and Shetland; and that we also took part in "numerous London recitals" and gave "regular broadcasts of solo and chamber music" with various different ensembles. We were lucky, too, in getting a number of concerto opportunities, and owe a lot in this field to the late Harry Legge and his splendid Rehearsal Orchestra for providing both of us with much valuable experience.

Instead of chronicling things in order, this section will aim to pick out concerts that were important for various reasons; also some of the occasions where unexpected or amusing things happened.

For instance, I wonder how many cellists have had to descend a ladder in order to reach the platform, as once happened to me when I was doing a charity concert in Edinburgh? This was held in a cinema where there was no proper stage, only a ledge about six feet deep in front of the screen, with just enough room for the performers and an upright piano. No one had warned me that the only access was through a door at least eight feet up, and I only learnt of this at the moment the door was thrown open and I saw a yawning space in front of me, with a metal ladder leading downwards. Well, luckily I was young at the time and had a better head for heights than I do nowadays. I simply handed my cello down to the pianist who was waiting below, gathered up the long full skirts of my evening dress, and descended as gracefully as possible.

Then there was the occasion when Alex and I and two colleagues were on an Arts Council tour which took us to the far west of Scotland. We arrived in a place that had better remain anonymous, and on going to reconnoitre at the village hall we were unable to find a piano anywhere, though we searched with increasing desperation in all the inter-connecting rooms that surrounded the main hall. A disconcerting prospect, this, since every item in the programme involved the piano. Eventually the organiser arrived and did manage to unearth a piano from a locked cupboard under the stage. But that wasn't the end of our problems. For the moment Alex started to play, it became obvious that this instrument was more out of tune than any piano any of us had ever met. Things were more or less all right in the lower register, but as the notes got higher the pitch got flatter and flatter. With the result that, if an ascending scale was played in, say, D major, it finished up approximately in D flat. The cacophony when trying to combine the registers can hardly be described. We did consider cancelling the concert, but were reluctant to disappoint the music club members in this remote place. So, on the principle that the show must go on, we somehow contrived to get through the programme, with Alex playing the piano as quietly as possible – indeed with uncharacteristic reticence. But afterwards, when we mentioned politely but firmly to the lady who was the local organiser, that the piano really was dreadfully out of tune and needed the most urgent attention, we were surprised at her frosty reactions. Until, that is, someone whispered to us that it was she, personally, who had been responsible for the tuning . . . !

Of course, certain people do seem to act as a focus for comic incidents; one such being our old and dear friend William Bennett, almost always known as Wibb (his initials are WIBB). Wibb is both a superb artist, who has achieved international renown as a flautist, and a sparky, decidedly original character. Very seldom did a concert-tour in which he was involved fail to produce some amusing – or occasionally hair-raising — moments. There was the time when he had entertained a school audience with a totally fictitious account of the piccolo solo he was about to perform, which he used to enjoy pretending was an imitation of the song and habitat of the lesser spotted hedge-warbler (a bird unknown to ornithologists). Each time he told the story it acquired further and more unlikely details, but no one to date had ever queried him. However, at the end of this particular concert he was publicly thanked by a dead-pan headmistress who explained: "As a keen bird-watcher myself I was especially interested in this piece . . ." Then there was the occasion during a concert held in the theatre at Bryanston in Dorset, when Alex and I were waiting in the wings to begin the second half and Wibb seemed completely to have vanished. Frantic searches were in vain. But at the last moment he was discovered rapidly descending a ladder from the flies where, invisible to all below, he had spent the interval making a tour of discovery. Another time, as we made an early morning train journey across north-west Scotland, Wibb astounded the other occupants of our carriage by producing from what appeared to be his music-case a small cooking stove, on which he proceeded to make coffee and an entire cooked breakfast. And there is a picture that always stays in my memory, of Wibb standing literally on his head, motionless in one corner of a hotel dining-room, to the obvious disapproval of the rather prim young waitress.

Touring round provincial music clubs can not only give performers a repertoire of amusing anecdotes; it may also, over the years, provide a cameo of changing social conditions. For example, during my very first extended tour for the Arts Council in Scotland – now over fifty years ago – it was impossible at any of the relatively modest hotels where we stayed to get any kind of evening meal other than High Tea; and since this without exception meant bacon and eggs, which was also the standard breakfast menu, we did find after a fortnight that the charms of this excellent dish had waned considerably. Today, in fact even by the mid-1960s, the same hotels would be offering a dinner menu with possibly three different choices. There would also in the present day be plenty of en-suite bedrooms, which at that time were unknown in smaller British hotels.

However, hitches are not confined to provincial music clubs; they can and do occur at concerts in London. Once, when our piano trio with Jean Harvey was playing at the Austrian Institute in South Kensington, a sudden power cut wrapped all that part of London in darkness. Fortunately this happened during the interval, which gave time for candles to be found; but there weren't a great many of these, and the only way of arranging them meant that Jean and I had to sit with our backs to each other and to Alex at the piano. We were thankful that the work we were due to perform – Schubert's Trio in B flat – was one we knew well. And during the performance we made an interesting discovery: despite being unable to see each other, we had no problems in co-ordinating things. Suggesting that the secret of ensemble playing lies, not so much in eye contact, nor even just in listening, but in a kind of indefinable 'radar sense' that comes to exist between players who work and perform a lot together.

Appearances in London are always important, and during a long career I took part in five Wigmore Hall recitals; the first as early as March 1950, at a stage when I was still officially studying part-time, but was invited by Ibbs and Tillett, then one of Britain's foremost concert agencies, to play in a series of lunchtime concerts they were promoting at the Wigmore to introduce young artists. Ironically, the notice I received next day from Martin Cooper, then top music-critic of *The Daily Telegraph*, was one of the best I ever had, stating unequivocally that: "*Margaret Moncrieff's fine tone and rhythm and good sense of style marked her out as an accomplished cellist.*" And yet I was unquestionably a far less good performer at the time than I became later, when the best of my notices would sometimes contain at least one less eulogistic comment.

My husband had the same experience. His first solo recital at the Wigmore Hall in March 1960 brought splendid crits from both *Times* and *Telegraph*, and a long notice in the *Guardian* that was headlined *The Promise of Greatness* — a height never quite reached again. Which suggests that music critics, consciously or otherwise, often take a slightly different attitude to young and less established performers.

As well as the Wigmore Hall recitals, at three of which Alex also played, I must have taken part in concerts at all the standard London

Alex and me after a recital at the RBA Galleries, talking to the artist Charlotte Halliday and her brother Stephen. November 1958.

venues — including the less well known R.B.A. Galleries, Leighton House, and Cowdray Hall (no longer in existence), as well as in the

Purcell Room, Queen Elizabeth Hall and Royal Festival Hall. The last named was specially significant; for the occasion was a recital by the internationally famous French singer, Gérard Souzay, at which I and the flautist William Bennett were engaged to play the flute and cello obligato parts in Ravel's *Chansons Madécasses*. This gave us only a minor role in Souzay's concert, but one that was nevertheless highly prestigious. And on a personal level this concert stands out in my memories, as I was three months pregnant at the time with our younger daughter, Alison. Today she is herself a professional cellist, and I sometimes think of this as her first important concert appearance.

A theme of pregnancy seems to run through a number of my concert memories at this time, for with both our babies I managed to continue playing until a very short time before their births. It so happens that the cellist's seated position can be perfectly comfortable for a pregnant women, besides making her condition relatively inconspicuous. At one concert, when our first child, Catriona, was at least seven months on the way, a member of the audience who came up to talk afterwards announced with satisfaction as she eyed me, "Yes, I *thought* you were expecting" — making clear that this had plainly been a matter of doubt! And with our second baby, Alison, I was in fact performing in public only two weeks before she was born; although this wasn't quite as intended but resulted from Alison's having decided to arrive two weeks early.

With our elder daughter there had been a rather longer gap, with nearly six weeks between my last concert at the end of August 1959 and her birth on 6th October. That year, 1959, had in fact been a specially busy one musically for both Alex and me. Beginning right back in the January, when he had given a performance of Brahms' Piano Concerto in B flat with the Hendon Symphony Orchestra, for which I'd been invited to play the cello solo part in the slow movement. Our schedule had included an extended Arts Council tour in Scotland during February, several broadcasts, chamber music recitals with various ensembles, and two gruelling recording sessions in August.

The latter both ran for five and a half hours continuously and took place during a heat wave — an experience that would have been fairly exhausting even for a cellist who wasn't nearly seven months pregnant at the time. The recordings were organised by a company that has now ceased to exist, called *Delysé*; and they involved the piano trio accompaniments to what are often incorrectly known as Beethoven's Scottish Songs. To be more precise, Beethoven made around 150 folk-song arrangements that are by no means all Scottish, but come from every part of the British Isles. The songs are set for a vocal quartet of soprano, alto, tenor and bass, combined in a variety of solos and different ensembles; and Beethoven provides for the accompanying piano trio a role that is not merely supporting, but includes some striking introductions and interludes.

Almost immediately after the recording sessions we had to set off for Edinburgh, to take part in a series of recitals that were being held during the 1959 International Festival to inaugurate the newly rescued St. Cecilia's Hall in Niddry Street. This attractive little 18th-century concert room, with its elegant cupola and its many historical associations, is now attached to the Music Faculty at Edinburgh University; but prior to 1959 it had for many years been used as a dance hall, before falling into a semi-ruined state. The building had come into the ownership of an extremely eccentric lady, Miss Magdalen Cairns, who had been interested enough in the history of the hall to spend time and money in having it restored; and my husband had somehow managed to arrange with Miss Cairns for an ensemble to which we both belonged, the New Recital Group, to present six afternoon programmes during the 1959 festival in celebration of the hall's reopening as a concert venue.

For these concerts we were joined by the violinist Joan Spencer, flautist William Bennett, singers Eilidh McNab and Duncan Robertson, pianist Margaret Norman, and harpsichord player Ruth Dyson. And one of the programmes was devoted to music that could have been, and probably was, played during the hall's original 18th-century days; including some of the arrangements of Scottish folk songs made by both Haydn and Beethoven at the request of the eighteenth century Edinburgh publisher, George Thomson.

This particular concert had attracted a lot of advance publicity and interest; but on the actual afternoon it very nearly didn't happen, when the temperamental owner of the hall (who had possibly over-indulged at lunchtime) suddenly and for no obvious reason threw a tantrum and refused to unlock the doors of the hall. The audience was due in less than half an hour, and when gentle reasoning had achieved nothing we were all getting extremely worried. Perhaps it was a rush of pregnancy hormones, or maybe the generations of lawyers in my ancestry came to the rescue, but I found myself informing her that she was under binding legal contract to admit the public, and that either she handed over the key immediately, or I would go straight to the Sheriff Court — which was just across the road — and get them to deal with the matter. Fortunately this threat (which could doubtfully have been carried out) did the trick, for Miss Cairns had a deep respect for the Sheriff. And despite this inauspicious beginning the concert proved most successful, with a full house, and afterwards an excellent revue from Frank Howes, then chief music critic of the *Times*.

After the festival I had originally been booked to play the Brahms Double Concerto in late October, but had been obliged to turn down the engagement when it became plain the date would be too soon after the baby's arrival; and that autumn I had also to pull out of a Wigmore Hall recital which included the first performance of Cyril Scott's Trio for flute, cello and piano. Here, my part — in an ensemble called the Lyric Trio with William Bennett and Margaret Norman — was taken by the well known cellist Antonia Butler (who would later become a close family friend and the wonderful first cello teacher of our daughter Alison). But I had always been determined that neither pregnancy nor motherhood should stop me playing the cello. No matter that during many months of both pregnancies I suffered horrendously from what is often misleadingly called 'morning sickness' — in my case, the morning being the one part of the day when I wasn't affected — I did somehow manage to keep going. And it helped to keep my name before the public that, due to the miracles of radio, on the evening of sixth October, that same day when Catriona had arrived at six in the morning, a recording of flute trios in which I'd taken part earlier was headlined in the *Radio Times*, much to the amusement of those who were visiting me and the baby in hospital at the time.

Throughout our performing careers both Alex and I concentrated largely on chamber music. Partly on practical grounds: there are, even in national terms, few pianists or cellists in a position to devote their musical lives only to solo-playing. But, for both of us, it was also a matter of choice. And among our most rewarding experiences in this field were our piano trio with Jean Harvey as violinist, the flute trio with William Bennett, and the piano quartet with Tony Howard, violin, and Harry Legge on viola — all four of these players being notably charac-

August 1974: The Mazzanti Piano Quartet rehearsing in Edinburgh for broadcast. Left to right: Harry Legge, Tony Howard, me, Alex.

terful and entertaining people.

In the early days I also had to decide, as a young string-player, whether or not to aim for an orchestral position. Players on contract in the major British symphony orchestras enjoy a degree of financial security that, practically speaking, cannot be achieved by chamber musicians. But playing in a symphony orchestra is a pretty full-time job, leaving little leisure and energy for other musical activities; and in the 1950s and '60s the many smaller, part-time orchestras that today can offer young players a kind of half-way house did not yet exist.

Even today, most string players have to choose either the relative financial security of a permanent orchestral job or the ups and downs and constant uncertainty of a chamber music career. There can be a theoretical possibility of bolstering financial matters by doing some freelance orchestral work. But this demands instant availability, and — as I soon found — anyone who turns down offers more than once or twice will not be asked again. However, I did during the 1950s have a number of engagements with the London Chamber Orchestra, which was conducted then by the late Anthony Bernard, to whom I'd been given a personal introduction; and these included several BBC

Alex with Princess Alexandra after a concert at the former Arts Council rooms in St. James's Square. Late 1960s.

programmes, of which two stand out in my memory. In the first, the orchestra provided Bizet's incidental music to *L'Arlésienne*, which was recorded live during the actual radio presentation of Daudet's play — memorable for an outstanding performance in one of the leading roles by the distinguished actress Gladys Young, with her unmistakable voice. There was a moment, following a tragic suicide near the end of the play, when she spoke the lines: "Look down there, soldier! And then tell me no one ever died for love," that always stays with me. The other was a programme of contemporary music, about which I remember nothing except the performance of a wordless melody that was sung by a very young and, as yet, almost unknown Janet Baker.

For pianists, the problems were similar, but even more difficult in that they had no real equivalent to orchestral jobs. In their case, bread-and-butter engagements consisted of, for example, playing as accompanist for singing teachers, or working with ballet companies or choral societies. A few pianists would aim to join an opera company as repetiteur, but this usually involved a more long-term commitment, with consequent loss of freedom.

Alex certainly did his share of working as a 'hack pianist'; and he soon also became involved in teaching, for which he had quite remarkable gifts. As early as 1960 he was offered two days teaching at the Royal Academy of Music; and this gave a certain amount of financial stability to our lives, although at that time conservatoire teachers did not have regular salaries, but were paid piecemeal on an hourly basis. Any lessons missed, through illness or whatever cause, were not paid for — sick pay and pensions being mythical creatures then unknown in conservatoire life. Nor was there was any security of tenure, for in theory any appointment could usually be terminated at twenty-four hours notice.

Nowadays it is hard to believe that this situation continued until the 1980s, when at last the system was dragged into the present day and things put on a proper financial basis. In the mean time, Alex had become one of the most sought-after piano professors at the RAM, where following the reforms that took place in the '80s, he was to be the first Head of Keyboard Studies, a position he held from 1984 to 1992.

My own experience of music college teaching — in my case mainly at the Royal College of Music — had also begun back in the 1960s, although for many years I worked only as a deputy teacher, as I was reluctant to take on a regular commitment while our daughters were still of school age. This applied particularly to joining the Junior Department of the RCM, where I had first acted as a deputy in 1963 and greatly enjoyed the work. The problem being, that to teach regularly here would have meant giving up every Saturday in term time, and this I was unwilling to do. It wasn't until 1979, when our younger daughter left school, that I felt able to accept a regular appointment in the RCM Junior Department; and by then I had already been deputising for some years in the Senior RCM, where in due course I was invited to join the cello faculty.

In the mean time I also, between September 1980 and July 1990, was the principal visiting cello teacher at Wells Cathedral Specialist Music School in Somerset. This involved leaving home at the (to me) hideously early hour of 6.45 a.m., driving to Paddington and catching a train to Bath, followed by a 45-minute taxi ride to Wells; fitting in seven or eight hours teaching before making the whole journey in reverse, to arrive home about 11 o'clock at night. A most exhausting schedule, but the work was hugely rewarding; and over the years it brought me into contact with some quite remarkable young cellistic talents. For me it was as much a learning as a teaching experience.

In particular, I learnt much about the matter of performance nerves. And by nerves I don't mean the kind of pre-performance jitters that can often fill with agony the time before a concert, nor the rush of adrenalin that many experience just after going on the platform. If properly handled, these symptoms can even help a player, by giving what's known as performing edge. But some musicians can experience continuing feelings of self-doubt that cause them to be incessantly aware of every negative aspect of their playing. For such people, any little mistake — and performers at every level do make them! — will seem huge, dwarfing all other aspects of their playing. And it was in listening to the regular concert appearances of my students, both at Wells and later at the RCM and the RNCM, that I became aware of the complete irrationality of this attitude. It struck me so forcibly, while regularly sitting in the audience and acting as listener rather than performer, that, with the very rarest exceptions, audiences are there to enjoy the music; and that, far from lying in wait for the performer to stumble, the listeners simply want everything to go well. Of course things can be different at music competitions; but, even on these occasions, not everyone present is hoping that disaster will strike the other competitors.

During this same ten-year period I also had an engagement to spend the Thursday of each week playing for schools in Hertfordshire — a job that came my way through the good offices of an old friend, Ann Blake, who played the violin in the group. All round, it was a most enjoyable assignment. It also left me, after having visited schools of every level throughout the county, with the conviction that a school's success owes little to its buildings and facilities, or lack of them, but everything to the quality of its teaching staff — above all, that of the headmaster or headmistress.

A surprise appointment followed three years after I left Wells, when in 1993 I was invited to act as visiting tutor at the Royal Northern College of Music in Manchester. This was completely unexpected, for by rights I was then past the official retiring age. But, as I recall saying at the time to the Head of Strings, Rodney Slatford, "If you're daft enough to invite me at my age, I'm daft enough to say Yes." Nor did I ever regret it. The three-year connection I had with the RNCM was immensely worthwhile. I particularly like the Royal Northern's system of dividing the hour-and-a-half of time allotted to each student into two parts: one hour being an individual one-to-one lesson, plus half-an-hour that is pooled in a joint open session along with all one's other pupils. In this way every student gets the benefit, not only of individual attention, but also of regular opportunities to play in front of others.

Returning to the performing side of our careers, I'm aware of having failed to cover many important events, including the two extensive concert tours Alex and I made in 1971. The first of these, in June, took us to Romania and Bulgaria; and for both of us this was our first experience of visiting Eastern Europe. At that time both countries were very much behind the Iron Curtain and shared many of the same conditions; but the impressions we were given differed widely, due to our different status in the two places. During our visit to Romania we stayed at the British Embassy in Bucharest; and although as guests of the Ambassador we enjoyed certain privileges, including being driven round in the Embassy limousine, we were continually aware of being foreigners in a police state and the objects of bureaucratic suspicion. We were warned by the Ambassador that all the rooms in the Embassy were bugged — something he mentioned in a completely matter-of-fact way that was particularly chilling; and the wife of the Embassy's Military Attaché told us that she and her husband could never discuss any private matters at home except by writing notes to each other.

Not that the ordinary people — any we were able to meet — were other than delightfully friendly, for the Romanians tend to prefer the Western nations to their Eastern neighbours. But our treatment at the customs in Bucharest Airport, for example, was frighteningly brusque and peremptory; with commands of "Stand here!", "Open this!", "Wait there!", barked out with machine-gun ferocity. This contrasted amazingly with our reception in Bulgaria. For here we were the official protegés of an organisation known as The Committee for Cultural Relations, and hence directly under the protection of the Bulgarian government.

That fortnight we spent in Bulgaria taught us just what privilege can mean in a supposedly classless society where everyone is meant to be equal. Everywhere we went, it was plain that our escorts needed only to mention the Committee for all doors to be opened. A restaurant that was apparently full when we arrived would somehow turn out to have the best table still available. Seats would be found for us at the opera, to see a performance that had been sold out many weeks before. And when we arrived at Sofia Airport for our return journey, we were simply waved through the customs without even being asked to open our luggage.

On the other hand, the Bulgarian people in general seemed rather more wary of the British than the Romanians had been. As a nation they have always leaned more to the East than to the West, and regard the Russians as their deliverers from what they often call their 'Turkish Yoke'. However, we were fortunate in having personal contacts, for during a recent two-year period an extremely talented Bulgarian student, Toshko Stoyanov, had been a pupil of Alex's at the Academy. And when we first arrived in Sofia we were surprised and delighted to find that the Committee had arranged for Toshko to be one of our official guides on our tour. We were even allowed to spend an informal evening at home with him and his extended family, which on a personal level was one of the highlights of our visit.

Other special memories from this time include the Whit-Sunday High Mass in Bucharest's Roman Catholic Cathedral (a fairly high proportion of Romanians are Roman Catholics), at which the choir sang Schubert's Mass in E flat, accompanied by full orchestra and in the entire uncut version. This had its parallel in Bulgaria, when we were taken to a Saturday evening service at the Alexander Nevsky Basilica in Sofia, where the Orthodox liturgy was presented by a magnificent choir consisting almost entirely of singers from the Bulgarian State Opera. Then there was our tour through the famous Valley of the Roses, and the cherry orchards of which Bulgaria is rightly proud, with an opportunity to pick unlimited quantities of gorgeous cherries courtesy of the Bulgarian government. And specially memorable was the drive up the Shipka Pass, where from a spectacular height of nearly three thousand feet we could view, across the mountainside, the vast yet impressively simple memorial, dedicated to the Fallen in the 1878 War of Liberation.

Something shared by the audiences in both Romania and Bulgaria was the extraordinary intensity with which they listened to music. This quality seems to be characteristic of people who are living under harsh conditions — apparently performers in Britain often found a similar response when giving concerts during the last war. Certainly the atmosphere at the recital in Sofia which ended our visit was unforgettable. The set-up was not ideal: the hall, which belonged to the Union of Cultural Workers, was drab and uncompromising in appearance; it had a rather dead acoustic and a piano long past its best. And we were both feeling exhausted after days of attending official gatherings during which there had been no opportunity to practise. (The Bulgarians are partial to holding formal receptions at nine in the morning, at which guests are served, not with coffee but with *Pliska* — plum brandy — and slabs of chocolate.) I doubt if it was really a very good recital, but the response was touching. And the basket of roses we were given at the end of the programme was of a quite unbelievable size: when placed between us on the platform it practically hid the grand piano.

Our second overseas tour in 1971 was totally different in character. Alex had departed only a few weeks after our return from Bulgaria, to undertake four and a half months of examining in the Far East for the Associated Board; beginning in Malaysia and then going on to Hong Kong. In addition to his busy schedule of examining, he had undertaken a number of recitals, in both solo and chamber music. There was plenty of demand for concerts and we decided that I would join him in Hong Kong towards the end of his visit, with the idea of getting some cello and piano engagements together, and afterwards making part of the return journey into a holiday, visiting different places along the route.

Musical memories that stand out include our broadcast recital from Hong Kong; not specially of our own performances of Beethoven and Faure, but of being taken to hear the rehearsal of a Chinese opera that was being held in the next-door studio. A decidedly strange experience; not that the Chinese music of that time was particularly *avant garde*, being oddly rather Hebridean in character, due to much use of the pentatonic mode, but we found the favoured pitch for female voices in opera to be almost painfully high and shrill; making it difficult at times to preserve an expression of polite interest.

Another memory that remains — so often, it's the trivial things that stay with one — is of a moment in Penang, in an open air setting, when I was playing the Prelude to Bach's First Suite for unaccompanied cello, and saw inexorably moving towards me across the floor the most enormous spider to ever have come my way — it looked bigger than the palm of my hand. Most fortunately something deflected it before it actually reached me . . .

We had been particularly fortunate throughout our Far East travels, in that Alex, having already visited all the places where we stayed, had managed in the course of his tour to make friends all along the route (making friends was among his special gifts). This gave us a wider range of acquaintance than is possible for many tourists; it meant, for instance, that in Hong Kong we were able to meet not just the British residents but several of the Chinese families. We were even able to visit some of their homes, which is relatively unusual for Western visitors. For me, it was a specially interesting experience to be asked to give a cello lesson to a young Chinese lad — a talented fifteen-year-old, who happily played Prokofieff and Lalo to me at one end of the family living room, while at the other end his parents, along with his siblings and a handful of visitors, carried on with things in an easy unobtrusive way that proclaimed this was all part of normal family life.

Alex and me in Penang, with Oh Eng Sin, Principal of the Penang Ballet School, 1971.

Once the musical part of our tour was completed, we were able to use the journey home as an opportunity to visit Bangkok, Iran and Istanbul, which all lay more or less on our route back to London. It was a memorable holiday; and I feel particularly grateful for that once-in-a-lifetime chance of including pre-revolutionary Iran in our itinerary. We were there for less than three days, during which we stayed mainly in Tehran; but, by using internal air-flights, we managed also to see the vast and impressive ruins of Persepolis — golden in the autumn sunshine — and the beautiful cities of Shiraz and Isfahan. Of all the wonderful places we visited on that trip I think the last-named would rank as the most unforgettable. Isfahan has an incredible situation more than 6,000 feet up among the mountains, with endless views over the curiously dust-coloured plains. The city is filled with glorious mosques, courtyard gardens and fountains, and the air has a special quality that brings some understanding of the adjective 'wine-sweet', that was beloved of the ancient Greeks. After that, even Istanbul — the last point on our tour — though fascinating, seemed less extraordinary. Although we were hugely impressed by Santa Sophia and the Blue Mosque (in that order), and the dramatic views from the ramparts across the Bosphorous.

A quite different side of our performing activities should be mentioned next: the Christmas concerts at Stevenson House, near Haddington in East Lothian. Over the years, between the early 1960s and the mid to late '70s, Alex and I must have taken part in sixteen or more of these very special Christmas celebrations; and, although it's now nearly 25 years since the last occasion, even today Christmas-time always rekindles memories.

The Dunlops who owned Stevenson were in many ways unusual people to come from a well-off, country-house background. The late Jack Dunlop, who was the head of the family, had not been content simply to enjoy the leisured life of a country gentleman, but had trained for and become expert in two professions — medicine and accountancy, in both of which he practised. He also had an extensive and well-informed interest in music and the arts; and it was his hobby to run Stevenson House as not only a family residence but what might almost be called an arts centre.

The main house, which is of 16th-century origin, is set in delightful grounds beside the River Tyne (the Scottish Tyne, that is); and Jack had transformed various out-buildings into homes for different members of his family. Among them was his sister, Isobel Dunlop, who lived in a charming house converted from the old stable-block. It was through Isobel that our connection with Stevenson, usually known affectionately as 'Stevie', came about. She, although a woman of independent means, was a dedicated, hard-working musician, who at one point had even been described as "among Scotland's leading composers", and she had been tireless in promoting the cause of music in Scotland, in particular that of her fellow contemporary Scottish composers. She had also been the financial patron and mainstay of a most successful vocal quartet, the Saltire Singers; and originally it was with this group that the custom of "Stevie's" annual

Christmas concerts had begun.

The traditions were already well established by the 1960s when Alex and I first took part. The setting was the large drawing-room, which was capable of holding an audience of seventy or more. Here there was always a ceiling-high and beautifully decorated Christmas tree — with real candles, not fairy-lights — standing in the bay window, leaving just enough room for the grand piano and the five performers. There were two singers: the tenor, Duncan Robertson, and, during all but the final years, the soprano Nancy Creighton (in the last two performances her place was taken by Carolyn Coxon); and three instrumentalists — Alex, me, and the violinist Daphne Godson (a fellow pupil of mine in the Waddell Orchestra during the 1940s, and later a fellow student of Alex's at the Royal Academy of Music).

The group of musicians would always assemble at Stevenson at least a couple of days before the actual concert, in order both to rehearse and to enjoy the splendid hospitality offered by the Dunlop family. We would work relatively hard in the mornings and late afternoons, having perhaps profited from country walks after a delicious lunch; then, in the evenings we would settle down to a feast of good food and wine, for all the Dunlop women (Isobel, her sister Jean, and Jack's wife, Betty) were superb cooks who delighted in producing gourmet meals, while Jack took pride in his cellar.

But the inner core of these occasions was the concert itself, and for all those taking part it came to encapsulate the whole spirit of Christmas. Each year the proceedings followed a similar pattern. First, all the drawing-room lights were extinguished, and Alex and I (neither pianos nor cellos being notably mobile) would slip into our places in the darkened room to wait with the audience. Then, following the sound of twelve chimes from the old ship's bell hanging in the hall, the joyful carol 'Ding Dong merrily on high' would be heard in the far distance, gradually getting nearer as the singers, accompanied by the violinist and bearing lighted candles, slowly advanced into the room to take their places.

The lights were then switched on, and the first half of the programme would proceed like a normal chamber-music concert, with each artist performing items that might or might not have Christmas connections. In this respect the singers had a wider and more obvious choice available than the instrumentalists; although we found, for instance, that such music as the Rondo Finale from Mozart's first

Piano Trio in G major always fitted in well, the theme having almost the character of a Christmas carol.

It was only after the interval, during which the audience was refreshed with coffee, mulled wine or whatever, that the music became specifically related to Christmas. This second half of the evening always consisted of 'The Christmas Story', a work that Isobel Dunlop had in part composed and in part arranged. The text came from one of the Chester Mystery Plays, and was narrated in dramatic recitative-style by the singers with colourful piano accompaniment; and these sections were interspersed with a variety of carols. Most were set for one or other, or both, of the solo singers, accompanied only by violin and cello; but in about four of the best-known the audience was encouraged to join enthusiastically, while Alex at the piano was revelling in ever more extravagant accompaniments, and Daphne and I provided exultant descants. The final carol for the audience was always 'Hark the Herald Angels sing'; and as the strains died away the piano would begin weaving a gently rocking accompaniment that gradually led into the German carol 'Stille Nacht, heilige Nacht'. And at this point the lights were once again extinguished and the singers, carrying their candles, would process slowly out of the darkened drawing-room, and far away along the network of corridors, with the final lines becoming only just audible from the distance.

The magic never failed to work. The Dunlops were very special people; and taking part in these Christmas concerts was for Alex and me a particularly happy experience, and one in which our daughters were lucky enough to be invited to join from about the ages of ten and twelve.

A final word now on Alex's work in teaching, and recalling in particular his thirty-six year's connection with the Royal Academy of Music. Today it is remarkable to see the number of Alex's students who have become well-known in the music profession. Many as performers, in solo or ensemble music, or as accompanists or repetiteurs; others have branched out into broadcasting and television; one is a renowned piano technician, who travels the country giving advice on rebuilding pianos; another is the editor of a well-known music periodical, and another runs a most successful music shop in London; yet another works in concert promotion; and another has become an enthusiastic County Music Organiser. Many are now themselves successful and dedicated teachers, and not only in this country: the conservatoire staff in Seville includes one, and pupils of Alex's are prominent in, among other places, Singapore, Hong Kong, Korea, New Zealand and the USA.

Yet more important, perhaps, is the number of these students who over the years became far more than just pupils. Alex had an extraordinary capacity for making friends with his students, and for taking a genuine interest in them as people that was always caring but never intrusive. As a result, his pupils became very much part of family life. Throughout the years a steady stream of aspiring pianists, at all stages, poured through our kitchen to drink cups of coffee or join the family meals; or sometimes just to sit and chat while the time fixed for their lesson disappeared across the horizon — Alex never having been a teacher who watched the clock.

It so happened that a fairly high proportion of Alex's students were male; and, for our daughters in their growing-up years, this probably helped to counterbalance the 75% female make-up of our immediate family circle, and the fact that they attended an all girls school (Godolphin & Latimer in Hammersmith — in those days it was still an LEA school).

A vast number of these pupils, both male and female, became good friends — far too many for me to be able to name them. But two should be mentioned, since they actually shared our home for a while. The first, David Crabtree, originally came to stay for a weekend and in the event remained for two years. The other, Anthony Williams, spent a similar time with us (in his case by previous arrangement), living in the small flat at the top of our house. Both David and Anthony were part of the extended family in a very special way; and for Alex and me they became much like the sons we never had.

Alex was also regarded with enormous affection by colleagues and friends, both musical and otherwise. The remarkable numbers, both men and women and of all ages, who openly shed tears at his funeral, following his sudden and untimely death in October 1996, gave striking testimony to this. And in the months afterwards a touching, almost overwhelming flood of letters reached us from around the globe. Even today the post will occasionally bring an appreciative card or letter from someone who didn't hear the news at the time.

In addition, during recent years many recitals — including one in Singapore and two at the Royal Academy of Music — as well as broadcasts and CD recordings, have been dedicated to Alex's memory by friends and former pupils. Two of the latter have named their sons after him. No danger that Alex will be forgotten.

Alex in about 1993.

XV: Interlude for Brief Thoughts on Friendship

SAINT AELDRED, THE TWELFTH-CENTURY ABBOT of Rievaulx Abbey in Yorkshire, once wrote that the "joys of friendship can surpass all other human joys" — a sentiment with which anyone who's been blessed with good friends would agree. This is not to question the supreme joys of a happy marriage, but friendship also plays an important role in marriage; and, significantly, many happy couples, married and otherwise, would describe their partner as their best friend.

During these memoirs some of my friends and colleagues have appeared, but for the most part only briefly. Now, before going further, I'd like to record something more detailed of these friends, and ideally of many others; the problem being, where to start? Each phase of life can bring new friendships; some will endure, others, for various reasons, will not. And a yet more difficult question arises: who should be included?

In my long ago Girl Guide days we used to sing a four-part round to this rhyme: *Make new friends, But keep the old, The one is silver, The other gold*. The words embody the kind of platitude that can be sung mindlessly in childhood. But it recently came home to me how extraordinarily fortunate I've been in the matter of 'old friends', when a sixteen-year-old student expressed her amazement on hearing that I'd just been visiting a friend I'd known since I was six years old. She was still more astonished to learn that this was by no means my only 'old friend' — that there were in fact six others, all of whom I've known for at least fifty years, and some for more than seventy.

Here, then, are sketches of those people who've remained my friends since the very early days. Nor does it in any way lessen the value I place on my many wonderful newer friendships, if I name here only this particular group. First on the list comes Elsie Gibbs, née Hamilton-Dalrymple, who shared so many parts of my early North Berwick and Edinburgh days, and whose eldest daughter is my godchild. Elsie, with her huge, deep-set eyes, exuberant hair and intense enthusiasm for life, isn't in fact the *oldest* of my friends in years, but she is unquestionably the longest-standing — I literally can't recall a time when I didn't know her. Despite some long gaps we've always remained close, for the instant we meet the years just vanish.

Next comes Gracie Dods, now King: I must have been about six, and she only a little older, when we first met in the *Chassevent* Music Class. Her approach has always been stimulatingly no-nonsense, but also full of humanity and a delightful humour, for Gracie is someone who hugely enjoys the funny side of things. After a varied and successful career in the theatre, which included taking part in two much acclaimed productions at the Edinburgh International Festival — *The Thrie Estates* and *The Gentle Shepherd* — she married a Presbyterian minister (he had been working as an extra in *The Thrie Estates*). Having accompanied him to many different parts of Scotland, and spending some years in Jamaica, she lives nowadays in Perth and teaches piano to a wide age-range of pupils. I'm much in her debt for help with various writing ventures; she is both deeply critical and generously appreciative.

(In strict chronological order, the next — had life not happened later to send us on separate paths — would have been Jean Shelley. Her mother, Claudia Shelley, was important in my early years, and Jean herself figures in the chapter on 'Schools'. But unfortunately she and I lost touch after we grew up, which rules her out of what may be called the '**half-century-plus**' category.)

Prue Wilson comes next. Today, Sister Prue Wilson, a nun who has held many responsible positions in her order, the Society of the Sacred Heart. Prue was the only fellow pupil at Craiglockhart with whom I was able to form a real friendship, and we have been friends ever since. She is a person of quite remarkable insight and gifts; as widely recognised in the year 2001, which marked her Golden Jubilee as a nun, when impressive numbers of people came from all around the country to join in the celebrations. To me and my family Prue has always been the traditional tower of strength, ceaselessly caring and interested — as well as being enormous fun.

A few years later came Mary Firth. Since my student days, Mary has been both a dear friend and a valued musical colleague and concert partner. Her support, affection and understanding have been unfailing; and, besides possessing a deeply serious quality, she has a splendid capacity to enjoy a good gossip and giggle. (I'm also indebted to her late husband, Dr George Firth, for much valuable career advice and encouragement.)

Silvia Beamish, always known to family and close friends as Sassy, comes next. We first met in 1946, when she was a first-year student of singing at the Royal College of Music (she was to become widely successful as both singer and teacher), and we quickly established a bond. I also spent from October 1951 to December 1952 living as a lodger in her parents' South Kensington house, just off Gloucester Road. Sassy has been another wonderfully supportive friend — I've lost count of the number of occasions she has come to the rescue in various crises. We've also, through the years, enjoyed some hilarious times and many shared musical experiences, particularly when I had the good fortune to act as her piano-accompanist for concerts or auditions — something that was always most rewarding. Nowadays Sassy lives in the USA, but we still remain closely in touch.

Next, I'll name Frances Richards, née Somervell (granddaughter of the composer Sir Arthur Somervell). Frances was also a paying-guest in the Beamish household between 1951 and '52, and I spent the next three years living with her at the house in Phillimore Gardens belonging to her father, Hubert Somervell. She is the youngest of this group, having been not quite fifteen when I first knew her. Our friendship blossomed as she grew up and has now lasted more than the half-century. Among the seven, Frances is today the only one who lives in London — in fact, less than fifteen minutes walk from me; and she is yet another of those quite invaluable friends who have stood by me through the various ups and downs of life, as well as sharing many lighter moments.

The last to be named, the cellist Amaryllis Fleming, should in chronological terms have come before Frances, since our friendship began three years earlier, in 1948. But, sadly, Amaryllis died in August 1999, at the relatively early age of 73. We had by then been friends continuously for 51 years — ever since her visit to Paris in the summer of 1948, when I was living there at Madame Schopfer's. The illegitimate daughter of Augustus John, Amaryllis was a highly colourful personality, immensely striking in appearance, and widely thought of as a *femme fatale* — which undoubtedly she was. But this was only part of the story; for the publicity that surrounded her often overlooked the fact that, in addition to her stunning appearance and her musical and cellistic talents, Amaryllis was also an outstandingly intelligent and all-round cultivated woman; one, moreover, possessed of a fantastic sense of humour. Alex and I enjoyed many delightful winter holidays with her in Venice; and these, in addition to the cultural delights, offered what could be described as a laugh a minute.

Indeed, if I were to search for one thing shared by all these seven dear friends — as well as by so many of the newer ones — it would be summed up in the word *laughter*.

XVI: Kellys Cottage

THE FIRST EVER REAL HOLIDAY FOR THE KELLY FAMILY was a ten-day trip to Majorca in the winter of 1963-64. At this point I had come into a small amount of money from my mother's estate, and it seemed a good idea to whisk everyone away from the London winter to spend a few days by the Mediterranean. Majorca in December 1963 was still relatively unspoilt; and our visit proved a highly enjoyable time, made specially pleasant by the delightful reception accorded everywhere by the Spanish to our two small daughters — than aged two and four. Everywhere we went people would break into beaming smiles at the sight of *Las niñas* — something that didn't always happen in Britain. Of course, there could have been a hitch in the middle of our stay when Catriona, our elder daughter, was suddenly stricken by what was clearly, to me, a severe attack of mumps — an illness that had been going the rounds in her nursery school before Christmas. The thought of possible quarantine complications was worrying. But the charming Spanish doctor who was summoned by the hotel assured us that Catriona was suffering only from *tonsillitis*; and since she made an amazingly speedy recovery, and was playing on the beach about twenty-four hours later, this didn't spoil the holiday. (Throughout childhood this was to be Catriona's pattern with illnesses: one day of feeling extremely poorly, with a high temperature, and even in the case of measles a period of delirium, then back more or less to normal the following day.) It was odd, though, that a couple of weeks after our return to London both our younger daughter Alison and I came down, not with tonsillitis but with *mumps* . . .

At around this period we were lucky in often being able to visit a house in Kent owned by my half-sister, Patricia, and her husband, who generously allowed members of the extended family to use the house in turns. It was situated on the Kent coast at Littlestone-on-Sea; a seaside resort that is not in itself an outstandingly interesting place, but the locality has many advantages for family holidays, and three in particular. First, there are numerous sandy beaches within walking distance; second, the Dymchurch-Hythe miniature railway has a station at New Romney — just up the road from where the house was situated; third, the Romney Marshes with their wealth of lovely old churches lie just behind Littlestone.

From a very early age our daughters loved to visit these churches; and they were fascinated to discover in Newchurch the grave of Edith Nesbit, whose stories they were already enjoying. They also, during one Easter visit, were enchanted by the literally hundreds of tiny lambs to be seen in fields all over the Marsh; and on one occasion we actually saw a lamb being born and just staggering to its feet. That particular visit also brings back memories of a beautiful 'Easter garden' in the church at Rye. It was the first example any of us had seen, this charming custom not being generally observed in the churches we frequented at home.

There were also our family visits during the 1970s to the Austrian Tirol, which will be described in the final chapter. Then, in the late 1980s and into the mid-90s, Alex and I spent some memorable winter holidays in Venice with our very dear friend and colleague, the cellist Amaryllis Fleming (who sadly died in 1999). Amaryllis was not only knowledgeable about Venice, where she had lived for a time, but an endlessly entertaining companion. A highlight was possibly our visit one February during Carnival, which is a magical season in Venice, with vast numbers parading the streets in gorgeous traditional costumes and masks, making it seem that time has stood still.

However, undoubtedly our family's most life-changing holiday experience happened in 1967. It all came about when a couple of lines in the small ads column of the *New Statesman* happened to catch my eye; they stated simply: "Primitive cottage in west of Ireland available for holiday lets. Sleeps six. No mod cons. Glorious views. Six and a half guineas a week."

Now that sum, even in 1967, was not a lot of money; and I was sufficiently intrigued by the advertisement to write immediately to the box number given. I sent a list of queries and enclosed an addressed envelope but — probably from experience of living abroad — thought it better to send the postage stamps separately. For some reason this greatly appealed to the advertiser, and she placed our application ahead of the many others she received. With the result that it was quickly arranged for us to rent the cottage for three weeks from late August to mid-September. (At that time the children were at the local convent school, where the winter term didn't begin until around the 20th of September.)

My husband wasn't able to accompany us on the outward journey as he was working at the Edinburgh Festival, and only free to join us for the second and third weeks. So on about August 23rd I set off in our red Triumph Herald estate car with two small girls aged five and seven, and an astonishing variety of baggage packed into every crevice of the car. We had been warned to take sleeping bags, towels and so on, as well as certain household items, including such things as coffee which at that time was far more expensive in Ireland than at home.

The first stage of what was to prove an epic journey, worth describing in detail, involved the two-hundred-mile drive to Liverpool, where we caught the night ferry to Dublin. And the ferry in those days was not the relatively smart affair it is today, but a rather grotty ancient steamer, on to which the cars had to be loaded by crane — a horrid business to watch, with the car dangling precariously high in the air. We did have a cabin of sorts, but it was pretty unattractive, and one of my daughters caught a flea — which she kindly passed round to the rest of us.

The following morning we had to disembark at about 6am, and then to wait in a large bleak building of the cattle-shed variety, while the cars were unloaded. Altogether a not very promising start, and we embarked rather soberly on the next stage of our journey. First we had to cross Dublin, and it was when we reached the other side of the city that things began to improve. We hadn't yet had any breakfast — no food on the boat in those days — and when, just outside Dublin, we came to a small establishment grandly called the West County Hotel, I decided to stop and see what they could offer us.

From that moment the magic of Ireland started to work. The Irish have some of the same capacity as the Spanish for welcoming children, and we were immediately made to feel at home. (In later years a visit to this unpretentious little hotel became a traditional part of our outward journeys.)

The cottage we were renting was on the far side of County Mayo, in Achill Island — which is indeed an island, though joined on to the mainland since the late nineteenth century by a causeway-bridge. From Dublin it entails a journey of more than 200 miles, but we had been given plenty of directions and finding the way was no problem. By early afternoon we'd reached the small Mayo town of Claremorris, which I knew to be within about fifty miles of our destination, so we stopped for a quick lunch. We were making good time. Not a care in the world.

First we drove along a secluded country road which my instructions had described as both a scenic and relatively quick way to reach Castlebar, the next main town on our route. Then suddenly, a couple of miles along this lonely road, the car spluttered to a halt. The cause was soon plain: we had run out of petrol. From more than thirty years on, I have to pay homage to the perfectly calm way my children accepted things and were undaunted by our situation, marooned as we were in a solitary wood in the midst of unknown Irish countryside. In any case, we were to be in luck. Quite soon a small van came along towards us, and when I begged the driver's assistance he assured me there was no problem: he was on his way to Claremorris, where he would ask his friend at the local garage to come out and bring us a can of petrol. As he drove off, he leaned from his window and remarked conversationally: "And you can call him Paddy Reilly."

Duly rescued by Paddy Reilly, who arrived after a remarkably short interval, we proceeded on our way and were coming within sight of the island when, the weather having been sunny and fine all day, it now began to rain with the kind of determination that was so admirable in Bruce's spider. The further we went the harder it rained, and by the time we crossed the bridge onto the island it was doing what my mother used to call raining both ways.

Finding our route was still easy enough: Mrs Boydell, the leaser of the cottage, had sent a sketch map; and after about five miles we were actually able to make out *our* cottage through the driving rain, nestling in the distance on the side of Slievemore mountain. We had been told to call first and collect the keys at the house of a Major De Vere White, who lived in a road lower down the mountain. His cottage was easily found; and clad in mackintoshes we stood outside in the relentless downpour, hopefully ringing his door bell.

No reply. We tried again, with no success. Perhaps he might have gone up to our cottage? We clambered into the car, turned back along the road and took the turning Mrs Boydell's map had indicated. It led us up an increasingly narrow and bone-shaking road, past two impressive graveyards and a large white cottage surrounded by hydrangea bushes, to the small dwelling that hopefully was to be ours for the next three weeks. But here, too, there was no sign of Major De Vere White.

Back then to his cottage. Still no reply. And by this time it was past five o'clock; we were all getting wetter and wetter and I had two tired hungry children on my hands. Fortunately Mrs Boydell had mentioned a small hotel, the Amethyst, in the nearby village of Keel; so abandoning the Major, we set off for Keel to try and find a room for the night.

At first no luck here, either: all the rooms in the hotel were booked. But now for the first time we met Mrs Thea Boyd, the proprietor of the Amethyst, and were straight away plunged into one of the intriguingly varied aspects of life in Achill Island. Mrs Boyd was clearly a woman of personality; not quite the expected owner of a small hotel in the far west of Ireland but, as we learned later, a graduate of Trinity College Dublin, a cultivated woman with artistic tastes, and the sister of a well-known Irish painter, Dorothy Blackham. Her appearance was imposing: tall and well-built, with short, very straight grey hair and piercing blue eyes, she was a person who rarely smiled. My daughters tell me that on that first occasion she even seemed to them a little intimidating, but she couldn't have been more gracious and helpful. First, she made the welcome suggestion that we should have a meal before looking any further. Then, while we were eating she must have made some enquiries, for quite soon one of the young waitresses came up to our table saying that her mother could put us up for the night, if that was any help.

Most thankfully I accepted the offer. Mrs Gallagher's cottage turned out to be quite near; and, although the only facilities were provided by an earth closet at the back of the cottage, the bedroom was clean and comfortable and the welcome friendly. The breakfast was of generous proportions — even if the children rather baulked at having boiled milk with the cornflakes; and the bed and breakfast charge for all three of us was a mere three guineas.

The following morning we returned to the Amethyst with a view to making telephone contact with Major De Vere White. This had been Mrs Boyd's own suggestion the previous evening; and I found it both amusing and slightly puzzling that, while she immediately set about getting the operator to call the Major's number for us (no automatic telephones at that time in Achill), she made it clear in a stately way that I would then have to take over the call — "The Major doesn't speak to *me* you know. I'm one of a long list." (A complicated history lay behind this, as we were to discover in due course.)

This time the Major was at home, and it was speedily arranged that we should now go straight up to our cottage where he would await us with the keys. And thus began our second experience within a day of meeting one of the outsize personalities of Achill Island. To describe Major Newport De Vere White as a character would be vastly to understate things. He was a quite remarkable man with a remarkable history, of which we gradually came to know a little — it included a number of years in a Japanese prisoner-of-war camp. As far as that first meeting was concerned, the main impression he gave was one of extreme annoyance — not by any means with us, but with his friend, Mrs Boydell, who had made the grave error of not informing him about the time of our arrival, simply taking for granted that he would be at home. (We would rapidly learn that Major De Vere White was not a person to be lightly taken for granted.) So outraged was he about our having been kept out of the cottage, that he took it upon himself to write to Mrs Boydell insisting that she repay us the three guineas charged by Mrs Gallacher! What else he said to her I don't know, but sure enough, a few days later we received a postal order.

The Major unquestionably came from the Irish upper class, but his appearance belied this. Except on state occasions he always wore an ancient check shirt with the sleeves rolled up, rather dilapidated brown corduroys, heavy-duty Wellington boots and — both inside and out — a shabby, dark-green beret. In the course of time he was to become a real friend to all the family, but we didn't see much of him that morning: he simply introduced us to things at the cottage — not a lengthy business — and, having invited us to call upon him at any time for assistance if we needed it, he departed leaving us to investigate our temporary home.

And not only that: for now, with the sun shining, we were hit by the quite astonishing beauty of the scenery and could begin to appreciate the idyllic situation of this 'primitive cottage'. True, it had no electricity, no piped water (though plenty was available in the nearby stream); no sanitation, no proper cooker. Just two rooms about fourteen feet

Kellys Cottage as it is today, after the former shed was rebuilt.

square, sparsely furnished, with a large open fireplace in the living room, and a lean-to shed with an Elsan at one side, while the shell of a ruined cottage lay beyond that. But the view in front of us stretched down over the mountainside and across an inland loch to a curving beach more than two miles wide, flanked on the left by dramatic eight-hundred-feet cliffs extending into the far distance — next stop, Canada. Behind us loomed the impressive Slievemore mountain — over two thousand feet high. Other mountain landscapes, carpeted in heather, lay to right and left. Everywhere fuchsia bushes in riotous red bloom were growing wild, and the banks of the lovely little stream, that ran through a miniature gorge beside the cottage, were lined with orange mombretia. From that moment we fell in love with the place. And today, thirty-five years on, we have not changed our minds.

In the 1960s and '70s, life in that obscure corner of Achill Island was only just beginning to catch up with modern times. Our cottage lay well off the beaten track on an unmade road, with just two other cottages, one above, one below us; and both those dwellings, which were occupied by local families, were then nearly as primitive as ours. At that time our neighbours were still ploughing their fields by hand, and the main method of transport was by donkey-cart. Mechanical appliances were rare, the land was usually unfenced, and the donkeys and cows used to roam freely across the mountainside. For London children it was an enchanting new world; and our daughters at five and seven were able for the first time in their lives to wander around at will and to explore the surrounding territory on their own. The cottage property embraced three acres of land, and the children would disappear together up the mountainside for long stretches of time — although we did take the precaution of providing them with loud whistles so that they could quickly summon help if needed. We also kept a whistle to summon them! (Years later we were told that this had caused much amusement to one neighbour, who was heard telling a visitor: "They used to **whistle** for them, like little dog-eens.")

My husband was eventually able to join us at the end of August; and with him we discovered many parts of the island and learnt something of its amazing landscapes. For the children, the beaches were naturally of special interest: to see wide and completely unspoilt stretches of sand, with only a sprinkling of people, was a new experience for children hitherto accustomed only to the English south coast. And more than half a dozen splendid examples lay within a short drive from the cottage; some surrounded by massive cliffs, others punctuated by rocky pools and headlands. We also enjoyed swimming in the crystalline Atlantic sea, with its endlessly varying spectrum of colours. Or rather, the two girls and I did; and on one or two fine days even Alex, who was a non-swimmer, used to don bathing-trunks and sport with the children in the shallow waters. The two-mile-wide expanse of Keel Strand — the beach viewed from our cottage — was specially good for this, as the gentle slope of the sand makes it possible to walk in for a considerable distance without getting more than knee-deep, while at the same time the breakers, which are usually of a considerable size at Keel even in calm weather, help to add a touch of excitement.

It was a wonderful time. Although, on a rather less idyllic level, it should be mentioned that the midges in Achill Island were then of a ferocity only equalled by those in certain parts of the Scottish Highlands. In 1967 I had not yet taken to wearing trousers regularly, as I do most of the time nowadays, and that summer my legs from heel to hip were just about one continuous midge-bite. Thanks be for modern, efficient insect-repellents.

During the holiday a genuine friendship began to grow between us and Major De Vere White. Not that we had failed to notice that he was

On the beach at Keel, Achill Island, 1974.

a person with whom one had to exercise caution, for it was quickly apparent that he could take offence rather easily. Before long it emerged that, during his years in Achill, he had managed to fall out with a fairly high proportion of the local inhabitants. The causes varied; but the end was always similar — to quote his own oft-repeated phrase: "After that, things were never the same again." (Later, there was to be a happy change in this.)

It made us no less careful that the Major's attitude to us suggested he had taken a great liking to our family. This became clear when he was spending an evening with us towards the end of our visit. We had been expressing regrets at having to leave the cottage when he suddenly asked: "Well, why don't you buy it?" And he revealed that this cottage did not in fact belong to our landlady Mrs Boydell, but was leased to her by the actual owner, a Mr McNamara in the village of Pollagh, who was about to put it on the market. The price, inclusive of several acres of mountainside, was £500 — and that wasn't a lot even at the time.

So keen was Major De Vere White for us to acquire the property that he volunteered both to assist with all the necessary legal business and to act as on-going caretaker for the cottage during our absences. It was a tempting prospect. But Alex was inclined to be chary of the enterprise, and we left Achill without having taken an affirmative decision in the matter, with the children weeping disconsolately as we drove off across the mountainside.

After we got home I thought long and hard. At the time I was doing a stint of teaching at the Colchester Technical College which was relatively well paid. My bank manager assured me that I had enough in hand to purchase the cottage and pay the legal fees. So, having decided to make this a surprise for Alex and the family, I entered into secret correspondence with Michael De Vere White (except with relatives, he never used his official given name of Newport, preferring to be known by his army nickname of Michael). And it was arranged that he would send his letters care of a friend who lived a few doors down the road from us, from where I would then collect them.

With Michael to handle the Irish end of the negotiations, there were no real problems. Even though the legal business actually took almost two years to complete, things were sufficiently advanced after only about six weeks for me to share the wonderful secret with Alex and the family. Nor was there any question about their enthusiastically joyful response.

From the following summer onwards we began to make regular visits to the cottage, occasionally managing an Easter break as well as a more extended time in August and September. In due course we accepted an offer under the Rural Electrification Scheme to connect us free of charge to the main electricity supply — we had only to pay for the actual wiring of the cottage. We purchased a small gas-ring and grill to be used with the easily available Kosangas cylinders; also a decent Elsan; and we gradually acquired some chairs and tables. But the cottage was to retain its essentially primitive character right up until the 1990s. At that point my elder daughter and her husband took it over, and devoted time, money, and hard work to having full facilities laid on and the old shed rebuilt to provide a new room with bed-gallery. The result is that the cottage now boasts two en-suite bedrooms! — although from the outside it still retains its original character.

By the summer of 1973 we had been visiting Achill Island regularly for six years; we were being kindly accepted by the local people; or as well accepted as 'blow-ins' ever are in a small island community —

and it does help to have the surname Kelly! We had become regular visitors to the Amethyst Hotel, where we would have lunch most days, and were now on excellent terms with Thea Boyd, the characterful proprietor. And Michael De Vere White had become a much valued family friend. Not only did he — by his own request — continue to look after the cottage for us during the many months we were absent, he always spring-cleaned it scrupulously before our arrival, laid a fire in readiness, and placed jam-jars filled with flowers around the two rooms. On a couple of occasions he completely renewed the whitewash on the exterior walls. He would also supply us with various items in the way of crockery and cooking utensils, and always insisted on lending a small double-bed which exactly fitted a recess beside the fireplace in the living room, and meant that Alex and I, unlike the children, did not have to sleep on camp beds or lilos. (I once made the error of asking whether we couldn't contribute to his expenses on our behalf, to be brusquely assured "My good offices are not for reward of any kind" . . .)

During our visits Michael was a regular guest at the cottage, always accompanied by his beloved black poodle, Baloo, and in the earlier years by Butch, his equally beloved bulldog. He also would often entertain us at home and treat us to the wholemeal bread and scones that he enjoyed making. His cottage was less primitive than ours, in that it had both electricity and a bathroom, and some good furniture; but it was fairly basic, and was always almost overrun with animals — not to mention smelling strongly of the meat he used to boil up for them. One way and another, we didn't find it too surprising to learn that the lady to whom he had briefly been married (in St Margaret's Westminster, no less) had found life in his cottage not to her taste: she had apparently objected strongly to having dogs sleeping on the bed.

No one could have denied that the Major was eccentric. But his background was impeccable: the De Vere Whites are a well-known Anglo-Irish family from County Limerick; and, while in himself Michael was Irish to the bone, he had had a public school education in England and had then gone on, first to study at Wye College of Agriculture in Kent, then to work on a rubber-plantation in Malaya (as it then was known). This would have been sometime before World War II; we never knew his exact age but he must have been born during the first World War, which would have made him in his early fifties when we first met him. At some point he had joined the Parachute

Regiment — Michael belonged to that section of Anglo-Irish society which would never have contemplated joining other than the *British* army. He had been taken prisoner by the Japanese and had spent some years in one of their prison camps — an experience about which he seldom talked, but it was possible to guess a little of what he had been through. It showed at times in such things as his reaction when one of the children left something unwanted on her plate at the end of a meal: he leant over to remove the plate and finished up the scraps, explaining apologetically: "I'm never able to see food wasted since my stay with the Nips."

After his marriage broke up he continued to live in Achill, and in order to help fill his time he worked every day in the slaughter house run by one of the local farmers. A rather odd occupation, perhaps, not only from the social angle but for someone who had such a strong love of animals — but then Michael was always a realist. Characteristically, for he would never be beholden to anyone, he refused to accept any payment for his work, but would instead take his mid-day meal with the farmer and his family. He also had one peculiar perk from the job, in that he was able to remove offal from the slaughter-house, and he would regularly bring home the guts of sheep which would then be hung up to dry in the enormous shed adjoining his house. These gruesome and smelly relics made — or so he insisted — wonderful fire-lighters. And I'm sure he was right, although I rather boggled at being presented with some to take back to the cottage!

Not surprisingly, Michael was to become an important figure in the lives of our two daughters, who were only five and seven when they first knew him. Nowadays, sadly, people might feel mistrustful about this. But Michael unquestionably had a love of children that was absolutely genuine; and he often used to take our two with him on expeditions around the countryside and to visit various acquaintances in his ancient green Morris Traveller. Even these trips had their unusual side, for the car-door was held on literally, not figuratively, by string; with the result that on going round corners it would occasionally swing open and Michael would have to lean across his passengers in order to shut it!

One way and another we would have thought that by 1973 most of the Major's past history was known to us, since he appeared always to have talked quite openly about his earlier life. But we should have been wrong, as was revealed when he wrote that summer in answer to my letter telling him the dates of our planned visit. We always sent him this information well in advance, and usually we would simply get a card of acknowledgment that everything was in order. This year he wrote a letter — quite short, but startling in its contents. Something on the lines of: "I shall particularly look forward to seeing you this summer as my daughter Judith will be staying with me, and your knowledge of German will be useful as she doesn't know much English." Well — wham! Not only had we been completely unaware that Michael had a daughter, but there seemed no particular reason why, if he did, she should have spoken German rather than English. It was all very confusing.

I don't recall now what we expected, but what we found on meeting Judith was a small, determined and rather wary eight-year-old, with fair hair and brown eyes, whose short life had been spent against an extraordinary and bohemian background. Her mother (we'll call her Anneliese) was Austrian, an artist who had had numerous affairs; one result being that she had at this point five children by three or four different fathers, Judith being the third in this unusual family.

The connection with Ireland had come about during the 1960s when Anneliese had arrived in Achill Island to act as housekeeper to the famous German writer, Heinrich Böll, who owned a house there which he used to visit at irregular intervals. (Today, 'Mr Ball's house' — as it's always known locally — has been turned into a kind of holiday retreat for writers and artists.) And at some point, presumably in around 1964, there had been a liason between Anneliese and Michael De Vere White.

Naturally we never sought to hear the details of this. But we learnt that Judith had been born in Ireland and had spent nearly all her first year in Achill Island, being looked after for much of this time by Michael himself. According to him, there was nothing specially complicated about caring for a baby — bottles and nappy-changing were just a matter of organisation. But then, without warning, Anneliese had announced that she was giving up her job in Achill and taking Judith with her back to Vienna. When Michael tried to protest, she unkindly assured him there was no proof that Judith was his child — after all, plenty of others could have been the father . . .

Anneliese had then removed herself forcibly from Michael's life and had returned to Vienna, where she continued her *Vie de Bohème*; and during the next couple of years she had produced twins with yet another father. These were named *Brendan und Sheila* (the latter pronounced in the German way as 'Shyler'), in an apparent tribute to her time in Ireland. After that, and until the summer of 1973, seven years later, Michael heard no more from Anneliese.

The letter suggesting that it was time he took some notice of his daughter — oh yes, Judith was now definitely *his* daughter — had come as a complete surprise. But Michael had agreed the child should come over and spend a month with him — the journey to be made at his expense, of course. And he had personally driven to the airport in Dublin to collect Judith and bring her back to Achill Island.

Alison, Catriona and me with Judith.

Most eight-year-olds, sent off like this on their own, would have found it an intimidating experience; but the five children who made up Anneliese's assorted family had clearly been brought up to fend for themselves, not to mention looking after each other while she got on with her painting — or whatever. Judith was fiercely independent: she settled down immediately in Michael's far from luxurious cottage, and set out to do everything for herself, including washing her own clothes and even expecting to prepare her own meals. All this, in a matter-of-fact way that Michael found heart-rending (as also her habit, if startled, of immediately protecting her head from possible blows . . .). And although her English at this stage was only basic, she had soon picked up enough to hold her own with others, both children and adults.

She went everywhere with Michael; and from the beginning Judith's coming was to work a near miracle in his life. For, in accordance with the best Irish traditions, no eyebrows were raised about the child's origins, and the welcome accorded to her by local people everywhere was so warm and spontaneous that gradually many broken bridges were mended; and friends with whom Michael had fallen out, and with whom things 'had never been the same again', were reinstated, because they 'had been so kind to Judith'.

At the end of that summer Judith was to return to Vienna, but only temporarily. The following year she reappeared, and this time on the basis of making a permanent home with her father. Michael began proceedings to adopt her formally; he obviously adored her, and although at times Judith was still quite a prickly little person, she clearly had grown fond of him. And, as she grew older, the likeness between her and Michael was so striking that no one could have questioned the relationship.

Sadly, they were not to have many years together. Michael's health had been undermined by his prisoner-of-war experiences, and in the mid-1970s he became seriously ill. Probably he was well aware of the situation, for when he died (in October 1976) he had made every conceivable provision for Judith's future: financial trusts had been set up, her guardians were appointed, and arrangements had been made for her schooling at the renowned King's Hospital School outside Dublin. And during that last year Judith had finally agreed to drop her mother's surname, by which she'd always insisted on being known up to this point, and become Judith De Vere White. That would have made Michael very happy.

For various reasons we didn't get to Achill Island for about three years after Michael's death. Then 1979 saw us making two visits, of which the second was to be the last for the original Kelly family group of four. During the next decade it happened that Alex and I began more and more to take our main summer holiday abroad — in Greece, Italy, Austria or Switzerland; and for us it was to be ten years before we made our way back to Achill. But in the meantime our elder daughter, Catriona, had continued to make regular visits to the cottage. She had always loved it dearly; and when Ian, her future husband, came along and also fell in love with the place, Alex and I decided that it made sense for us to turn over the ownership of the cottage to them; especially as they were by now making at least three or four visits a year, sometimes even spending Christmas or New Year.

Today, as described earlier, Catriona and Ian have transformed things at Kellys Cottage from the point of view of creature comforts, and have acquired some good furniture. But they have succeeded wonderfully in preserving the essential character of the little house; and of course the dramatic beauty of its situation is unchangeable, as I found once again in the summer of 2001, which saw a family reunion when Alison and I and her two children, Alexander and Camilla, were able to join Catriona and Ian for a glorious ten-day holiday. During it we were lucky enough to have a spell of the most lovely weather I have ever known in Ireland; and for me it was a strangely nostalgic experience to see my grandchildren enjoying the mountainside and the same glorious beaches where my children had played thirty years before.

Alex and me beside Lake Thun in the Bernese Oberland, about 1989.

In the course of this visit we were also able to make an important decision. For a long time we had discussed in the family the question of where Alex's ashes should be interred. They had remained with me at the house in Barnes ever since his funeral in October 1996, and at one time we had thought of burying them in the garden there. But now, finally, we decided that there could be no better and more beautiful resting place than the slopes of Slievemore behind the cottage.

Alex had always loved Achill Island, and our view across the loch to the cliffs and sands of Keel beach; and for some reason, although no actual connection can be traced, he had always felt a special affinity with Ireland. Accordingly it seemed right to place the casket in a little grave on the mountainside, pointing in traditional fashion towards the east.

Under the wide and starry sky, Dig the grave and let me lie.

XVII: World of Words

Finally, with this chapter we come to the all important worlds of reading and writing. Happy the children who grow up surrounded by books; and I have no complaints on this score — our Edinburgh house was all but knee-deep in them. Nor was there any lack of books in our North Berwick holiday home; and despite not having learnt to read until about the age of seven, I can hardly recall a time when books weren't important.

Among the first to make a lasting impression were the *Winnie-the-Pooh books* of A.A.Milne — the first of these having been a Christmas present from my sister's husband, Eddie, who was one of my childhood's favourite people. The *Pooh* books were to remain at the top of my list for many years, and I could at one time have repeated most of the stories from memory. Other books, recalled with particular pleasure from this early stage, include most of Beatrix Potter's tales with their charming illustrations — apart, that is, from *The Tale of Samuel Whiskers*, for in this I found both Mr Whiskers and his horrid wife, Anna Maria, simply terrifying, and suffered nightmares about the idea of all that secret life going on behind the wainscoting.

Once launched into reading independently, I quickly made the acquaintance of a variety of literature at many levels. However, it's difficult when looking back at this early stage to remember which books I read for myself and which were read to me. Among those that probably overlapped both categories were the Andrew Lang collections of fairy stories — the *Red Book*, the *Green Book* and the *Violet Book* in particular, as well as Lang's *Book of Saints and Heroes*. Folk tales obviously dominated the scene, for there were also books of Norse and Scottish legends (in the former, some evil-doers met the gruesome fate of being put in a barrel lined with spikes, which would then be rolled down a steep hill . . .). Most importantly, there was a volume of Hans Andersen's stories, of which my top favourites have always been 'The Wild Swans' and 'The Little Mermaid'. The former I associate particularly with my nanny, Monica Bond, indicating that at first it would have been read to me. Before long I was making the acquaintance of Susan Coolidge's Katy books (*What Katy did at School* was the favourite); and the stories of Mrs Ewing, Mrs Molesworth, and Louisa Alcott soon came my way, often being introduced to me by Aunt Georgina. 'The Water Babies' and 'Lorna Doone' followed a little later — and the latter, with its vivid description of the hero's first climb up the waterfall to the Doone Valley, was definitely read to me for the most part by my mother.

At ten I tackled *Jane Eyre* for myself, and genuinely loved it though I question now how much I understood. My taste in reading, like that of most children who are able to 'free range', was remarkably varied. If asked around the age of twelve to nominate my most loved books, the list would have been a patchwork quilt both long and wide-spreading. Milne's 'Winnie-the-Pooh' stories would still have been included, happy bedfellows with Dickens' *Bleak House*, *Great Expectations*, and *A Tale of Two Cities*. Masefield's *Box of Delights* would certainly have been there, alongside various Guide and Brownie stories of Mrs Osborn Hann, many of Edith Nesbit's books — the two *House of Arden* stories in particular — Ransome's *Swallowdale*, *Pigeon Post* and others. George Eliot's *Mill on the Floss* and Frances Hodgson Burnett's *Secret Garden* were both much loved; as were Noel Streatfeild's *Ballet Shoes*, John Buchan's *Huntingtower*, Elsie Oxenham's *Schoolgirls and Scouts*, E.E. Cowper's *White Witch of Rozel*, Sir John Fortescue's *Story of a Red Deer*, and Elinor Brent-Dyer's *Jo of the Chalet School*. And undoubtedly there was a hotch-potch of others now forgotten.

At much the same time, or perhaps a year or so later, my two favourite plays were simultaneously *Peter Pan* (in the original version, not the story) and *Hamlet*, of which I used to memorise chunks on the bus-journeys to and from school. And soon I was meeting several of J.M. Barrie's other plays, having discovered that we possessed a complete edition of them in one huge volume. I also browsed over quantities of poetry; ranging as time went on from Chaucer and Dunbar, all through the following centuries — and lingering over the nineteenth-century romantics — to Yeats, Robert Bridges, A.E. Housman, Edwin Muir and T.S. Eliot among those from more recent times; with the *Oxford Book of English Verse* being my constant companion by the time I was fifteen or so. An addiction to this particular anthology was shared by my oldest friend, Elsie Gibbs, then Hamilton-Dalrymple, and we used to enjoy testing each other by reading out at random short extracts which had to be identified.

The curriculum at Craiglockhart did lay emphasis on the now outmoded practice of learning poetry and speaking it aloud from memory — an experience in communication that I would still rate as being entirely beneficial. Then in the course of time I was to become familiar with poems not only in English, but in French and German (the latter at home, not at school, and often introduced by the Lieder of Schubert, Schumann and Brahms), as well as with many of Shakespeare's plays. As a result of this, and of the reading-aloud sessions at home, I was lucky in having a fair grounding in literature during my growing up years. And this continued to expand; partly because, due to family circumstances, I had to spend so much time on my own that reading was always my main leisure occupation. Endless happy hours were spent with the Brontes, Trollope, Jane Austen, Elliot, Hardy, Stevenson, Kipling, John Buchan, C.S.Lewis (the adult books — *Narnia* didn't yet exist), J.B. Priestley, E.M. Forster, Dorothy L. Sayers, Agatha Christie, Ngaio March, Daphne du Maurier, Angela Thirkell, Elizabeth Goudge, and countless other greater and lesser writers. Interestingly, though, when my mother at one point had recommended Galsworthy's *Forsyte Saga* I barely struggled through the first book.

My access to reading was in fact almost without limit in those days, because my father enjoyed a wonderful privilege that had been extended to all those who were members of the Faculty of Advocates when, in the 1920s, the collection known till then as The Advocates' Library was given to the nation and became the National Library of Scotland. This entitled him for life to have, at any one time, up to twenty books sent home in the bag that was delivered daily to our house with his legal papers. The only condition was that the books must have been published for at least six months. From quite an early age I was allocated three of these twenty, and I made full use of them. No doubt the librarians were gently amused when the order for Lord Moncrieff included, among the learned legal tomes, requests for *Peg's*

Patrol, or *The Return of the Scarlet Pimpernel*, or *The New Chalet School*.

Today I can't be certain at what stage the girls' school-story had entered my life, but probably before I was nine. Certainly a number of Angela Brazil's books and some of Elsie Oxenham's, which had all belonged to my half-sister, were available in a bookcase at the North Berwick house. These shelves also contained several volumes of an annual, *Little Folks*, dating from between 1912 and 1920, and featuring stories by many popular school-story writers: Christine Chaundler, Doris Pocock, Ethel Talbot, and May Wynne were among the regular contributors. In particular there were two books, *Betty's First Term* and *Betty's Next Term*, by a barely remembered author, Lilian Wevil, that I specially liked — partly because the eponymous heroine was only ten and hence nearer my age than the main characters in school-stories commonly were. All these I duly devoured, along with Jean Webster's tales of *Patty and Priscilla* — so much more enjoyable and amusing to my mind than the better-known *Daddy Long-Legs*; as well as the *Tarzan* books of Edgar Rice Burroughs, which had rather surprisingly found their way into this bookcase.

Some of Angela Brazil's books I enjoyed — especially *A Fourth Form Friendship*, and *The Leader of the Lower School*; while the early *Dimsie* stories of Dorita Fairlie Bruce appealed strongly, as did a few books by Dorothea Moore, including *Septima Schoolgirl* and *A Brave Little Royalist* — the latter not a school-story, but a romantic tale of Cavaliers and Roundheads. Then, two among the E.J. Oxenham stories — *Schoolgirls and Scouts* and *Rosaly's New School* — became long-term favourites. I liked the former especially because of its being mainly set in the Scottish Highlands. However, for some reason Elsie Oxenham's Abbey books, which are probably the most admired and generally popular of all her stories, have never really attracted me. At least a couple came my way then, but neither as a child nor in later life (when I read many of the series during my researches for the Brent-Dyer biography) was I captured by them. Perhaps this was due to what strikes me today as the quintessentially *English* nature of the Abbey stories (I know another Scot who feels the same way). But more likely it happened because the characters in the Abbey stories were too old for me as a child and later when I was grown up it was the other way round.

In any case, as regards the school-story genre, the chief milestone came unquestionably in a brown paper parcel I received from Aunt Georgina on my ninth or tenth birthday: for this contained the first story in Elinor Brent-Dyer's Chalet School series, *The School at the Chalet* — only a second-hand 1930s reprint, but containing all the N.K.Brisley illustrations. This book, with its slightly worn red covers, was a gift of far more significance than any of us could have realised at the time. For me the Chalet School books, right from the beginning, belonged to a different category from all the other school-stories. Part of the fascination was undoubtedly the Tirolean setting of the early books — and thanks to my aunt I read all the stories (so far as they then existed) in the correct chronological order. But it was the characters that made the greatest appeal, and they were to become very much part of my life in those far gone days.

Aunt Georgina, as already explained, was an unashamed devotee of children's books with a strong leaning towards the girls' school-story. She had a quite special fondness for the Brent-Dyer series, and she would sometimes choose one of the books for our reading-aloud sessions. We used then to take turn-about as reader; and a memory lingers that, rather than confessing I didn't always know how to pronounce the German words that are a feature of the stories, I would look ahead and substitute the English equivalent. Hence, on my days as reader the Chalet girls were doomed to have <u>breakfast</u> in the <u>dining-room</u>, rather than the authentic *Frühstuck* in the *Speisesaal*.

The Chalet School always provided a link between me and my aunt. Throughout my youth she would regularly present me with the latest story as a Christmas or birthday present; and it was probably thanks to her example that I continued to read the books after I left school. Not so very often, perhaps, and always in secret; for in those days grown-ups simply did not read children's books — or at least not publicly and avowedly. Today it seems questionable whether, even at that time, Aunt Georgina can really have been the only one?

Eventually, more than thirty years later, it was to be the Chalet School that opened my path to becoming a published writer. But my interest in writing began far earlier; at the latest by eight years old, when I remember committing a school-story to paper in execrable handwriting. The school was called St. Joan's, its principle character had been born in India in the best school-story traditions, and there was a mistress with a deplorable number of 'favrets', but the manuscript of this effort has now disappeared. A play with a murder theme followed: the heroine for some reason was called Imelda, and the villain Mr Whittaker; and there were other plays, as well as many short stories and efforts at uncompleted books.

One way and another, over the years I almost always had some writing project on the go, and from these efforts I learnt a lot. Some of it was learnt the hard way: as when, at about twelve, I showed the first chapters of a book I'd started (well, don't we all?) to an older and far more sophisticated friend. Her comment on the dialogue was devastating: "But these characters all talk the same," she protested, "They're all you — they're all *Margaret Moncrieff.*" That was a painful lesson; but I've always been grateful to have had attention drawn so early to the vital importance of establishing different speech patterns for different characters — something I try to keep in mind to this day.

Both the Chalet School and writing in general were crowded out of my life during much of the 1950s and '60s. At this period I was, to begin with, a struggling young cellist trying to find enough engagements to keep my head above financial water; and later a struggling not-quite-so-young cellist with a husband and two children and much the same financial anxieties. But as soon as our children reached the age of becoming interested in books — in each case well before the age of two! — both Alex and I used to enjoy reading aloud to them.

They too, just as I had, lapped up an endless variety of books; and once again not only those addressed primarily to children. The most astonishing example was Tolstoy's *War and Peace* — no, I'm not suggesting that they read this for themselves, or even that we read it to them. But in the winter of 1968-69, when they were respectively nine and seven, Tolstoy's masterpiece was serialised on BBC Radio Four. To this, throughout the twenty episodes, both children would listen with every appearance of interest and involvement. (It may be worth mentioning that at this stage the Kelly family had no television.)

During the 1960s there was of course a great flowering of children's books, with such well-known writers as Philippa Pearce, Alan Garner, William Mayne, Leon Garfield, Jill Paton Walsh, and K.M. Peyton among those making their mark, and Antonia Forest already well established — by the mid-60s she had published six of her twelve highly esteemed books, including two of the *Kingscote* series. As one result of this abundance the children of our daughters' generation had a greater choice of new, specially written books than we had had, as well as inheriting those of earlier times. Not surprisingly, both Alex and

I chose for our reading-aloud sessions some of the books that had been, or in some cases were, our own special favourites. Mine included *Winnie the Pooh* and many of the Nesbit stories; his, some of Richmal Crompton's *William* books, Macdonald's *At the back of the North Wind* and Tolkien's *The Hobbit*. We both also enjoyed reading Dickens to them, rather as my parents had. And I made an interesting discovery about Dickens. When reading aloud the more old-fashioned books — Marryat's *Children of the New Forest*, or Blackmore's *Lorna Doone*, for example — I would often find it possible (and indeed desirable) to skip the odd passage here and there, and could do this without the listener being aware that anything was missing. But this never worked with Dickens: his writing may at times appear to contain superfluous details, but this is deceptive; and my attempts at skipping almost always meant that something vital was left out, which then had to be re-instated later. In our turn, Alex and I were introduced to many of the more recent books that were rapidly becoming children's classics; in particular to C.S. Lewis's seven *Chronicles of Narnia*, which had arrived on the scene too late to be childhood friends but were now, for both of us, to join the ranks of our own best-loved reading.

It was not until the summer of 1971 that I decided to see how our children would view Elinor Brent-Dyer's Chalet School stories. That June Alex had departed on a four-and-a-half month tour of the Far East, and his absence made this a suitable juncture, as I wouldn't at that point have expected him to take the remotest interest in the stories. I began reading them the first book, *The School at the Chalet*, quite tentatively; after all, it had been written nearly half a century earlier, and my own childhood enthusiasm for the series belonged to such a different world that I fully expected the Chalet books to seem outdated, and possibly even boring to children of the 1970s. To my initial surprise, the first story was so well received that I had to produce copies of any of the other books that could be found; and for the next few years Chalet School books were always among those in high favour.

It turned out, too, that a number of our children's contemporaries were fans of the Brent-Dyer series. And when I learnt from a friend who worked at Collins (now HarperCollins) that more than 150,000 Chalet School paperbacks were regularly being sold each year, it struck me that there must surely have been something interesting about the author of a series that had remained popular for nearly fifty years (as it was then — now nearly eighty), and could appeal to children whose world was so different from that of the 1920s and '30s when the stories first appeared.

At this stage, then, it was mainly curiosity about the woman behind the stories that sparked off my interest in the idea of writing about Elinor Brent-Dyer. A further stimulus came in May 1972 with the first of what would eventually be six memorably enjoyable family holidays in the lovely Tirolean village of *Pertisau-am-Achensee* — the '*Briesau-am-Tiernsee*' of the early Chalet School books, which may be regarded as the cradle of the whole series. And Pertisau is in itself an enchanting place, quite apart from any connections with Brent-Dyer and the Chalet School.

Alison (left) and Catriona, looking south across the Achensee May 1972.

Situated about twenty miles to the east of Innsbruck, and gloriously placed beside the five-and-a-half-mile expanse of the Achensee — the largest, and often thought the most beautiful lake in all the Austrian Tirol — it lies three thousand feet above the Inn valley, surrounded by mountains of wonderfully varied shapes and sizes. Moreover the journey to Pertisau can in itself be an adventure; especially for those who choose to travel by rail to Jenbach, the little town far below in the valley which is the nearest mainline station. For here begins the dramatic ascent by a rack-and-pinion railway-line that slowly clambers up the precipitous mountain slope to Seespitz, a minuscule hamlet at the head of the lake. From this point a steamer completes the journey, in a course zig-zagging from shore to shore across the luminous waters of the Achensee. Of course, for those who prefer cars, there is

The Kostenzer twin sisters: Nanni (Anna) and Hanneli (Johanna) as pictured on their memorial cards.

also a wide modern road built in the 1960s, with a splendid viewpoint near the top known as the *Kanzelkehre* (literally pulpit-bend). This major road continues along the side of the lake opposite to Pertisau, eventually crossing over the Achenpass into southern Germany — a beautiful journey in itself.

During all but the first of our visits to Pertisau we had, and quite by chance, the good fortune to stay with a delightful Tirolean family, the Kostenzers, who ran a working farm and also took in a few paying guests during the summer season. To enlarge a little — for our friendship with the Kostenzers added so much to the enjoyment of our Pertisau holidays — the family consisted of the twin sisters Hanni and Nanni, two immensely characterful though completely different women who were then in their late forties, and Nanni's grown-up children — Erika, who had a variety of jobs, including that of ski-instructor, and Anton who worked full-time on the farm. There was also Andrae, a cousin who lived with them and was employed by the Achensee Forestry Commission; he was a kindly and delightful man though one of few words, but then his cousin Hanni made up for that! Later, Erika's small son, Manfred, arrived to join the family.

Hanni, also known as Hanneli — both diminutives for Johanna — was fractionally the elder of the sisters, and the more down-to-earth and forceful-seeming of the two. She was in many ways the archetypal peasant woman who had laboured all her life on the farm, and who when younger had thought nothing of climbing up twice a day to one of the high alms where the cattle are pastured during the summer — a distance of around eight miles there and back, not to mention the steep ascent — and returning each time with a load of butter weighing many kilos. In our day Hanni, apart from such times as the haymaking season, was mainly busy around the house; while her sister, Nanni — christened Anna — did most of the farm work. Nanni was gentler in manner and softer-spoken, and was rightly considered by family and friends to be a '*Seele*' — a German word that defies translation; the literal meaning is simply soul, but its use describes a person with a touch of unworldliness, even innocence, and a kind of unassuming spirituality.

The Kostenzers' home, *Untertuschenhof*, where their family had farmed for at least three generations, was one of the most picturesque chalets in Pertisau. Dating from the 18th century, it was a listed building, the upper part constructed of the darkest vandyke-brown wood. The lower walls were plaster-clad in brilliant white, and decorated with frescoes that included a prayer to St. Leonard — one of the patron saints of Pertisau — while the balconies were always a riot of colourful window-boxes. Best of all, the chalet commanded the most spectacular views of the lake and mountains (and the bedroom we were regularly allocated had four windows, two looking out in each direction). Not that the interior of the house was luxurious — indeed far from it; this was a classic old-time farmhouse, with the living rooms to one side of the entrance hall, and the cowshed, complete with cows, horses, hens, and a goat, on the other. There were definitely no mod cons — just the one cold water tap in the kitchen, and an earth closet that's the only one I've ever known to be situated on an **upper** floor, with a

Me outside the Kostenzers' chalet. September 1978.

Untertuschenhof viewed from the lakeside.

long chimney-like structure descending in the direction of the midden in the cowshed below (something I might feel less than enthusiastic about today). But the house was spotlessly clean, the linen on the four beds in the large square room we all shared was exquisitely embroidered; and the breakfasts provided each morning by Hanneli were both ample and delicious, with unlimited quantities of fragrant coffee, new-baked crusty rolls, and amounts of freshly churned butter greater than the greediest person could ever have consumed.

The Kostenzers were a lovely family: kind, warm-hearted and full of humour, much respected locally, mines of local knowledge and local gossip — some of it definitely **not** repeatable. Over the years they were to become dear friends, who would welcome us with literally open arms when we arrived for our return visits and shed tears when we departed. They made us feel almost like family; and in their old-fashioned kitchen we were able to share with them and their friends many a 'Tiroler Abend' that was undoubtedly more authentic than most of those on offer at the local hotels. For us it was an added bonus that no one in their household could speak more than a word or two of English, since we enjoyed being thus compelled to use our German. Nor did we worry about the lack of mod cons; and even if the '*Klo*' did sometimes become rather less than sweet-smelling as the day for its emptying approached, this was always treated as more of a joke than anything else.

For some years my daughters and I did not reveal to my husband that Pertisau had any connection with what he often referred to rudely as 'The Shilly Shally School'. Long before he found this out he had grown to love the whole Achensee district — which is in every way an ideal place for family holdays — and he also had become a tremendous favourite with the Kostenzers. In particular with *die Hanneli*, who always had a special smile — or a piece of *Apfelstrudel* — or a gently risque joke — saved up for *Herr Kelly*.

In any case, Alex was by then accustomed to my strange obsession with Elinor Brent-Dyer, and would even show some interest in the progress of my researches. Especially when he learnt that not only had Brent-Dyer herself been a teacher — as clearly indicated in her books — she had actually founded and for ten years run her own school. That immediately painted a fascinating picture of what amounted to a double life. On one hand, the idealized world of her fictional Chalet School, where difficulties and even sorrow may have to be faced but a remedy will always be found. On the other, a real-life school with all its inevitable ups and downs, and the probability that not every problem will be solved in the final chapter. How had she coped with the dichotomy?

My original idea was simply to write an article — perhaps, three or four thousand words — about Elinor Brent-Dyer and her books; and with this in mind I contacted her two main publishers: W. & R. Chambers who had produced all the hardbacks of the Chalet series; and William Collins who since 1967 had been issuing Chalet School paperbacks under their 'Armada' imprint. But, to my surprise, none of the various editors to whom I talked could tell me much. All could testify that Miss Brent-Dyer had been a colourful personality, and they recounted various amusing anecdotes, but no one could supply any real information.

However, Armada was at least able to give me the address of a Mrs Phyllis Matthewman, an old friend with whom Elinor Brent-Dyer had shared a house at Redhill in Surrey during the last years of her life. And when, late in 1974, Mrs Matthewman kindly invited me to lunch with her, I set off in high hopes. The two had apparently known each other since childhood; surely there would now be answers to my many questions. In this interview I had hoped to learn the basic facts about Elinor Brent-Dyer's life; but it turned out that Mrs Matthewman's recollections were decidedly sketchy. Not that they weren't entertaining, for Phyllis proved to be an interesting person, who was herself a writer; she specialised in romantic novels but had also published a number of school-stories and even two short biographical booklets for young readers — one about Sir Alexander Fleming, the other about Malcolm Sargeant.

Later she became a friend in her own right, but regarded as an informant Phyllis was unreliable. Very few hard facts emerged during that first interview, with even fewer actual dates; moreover, some of those she gave me turned out to be inaccurate. She did manage to find the addresses of a few other people who had known Brent-Dyer at various times, but, all round, it was soon clear that tracking down the real Elinor Brent-Dyer would be a long and arduous business, and one in which Phyllis would be of little assistance.

From this point began a quest for information and a project that was to occupy much time during the almost five-year period from late 1974 to the summer of 1979. However, the story of the frustrations and fascinations of my searches along the Brent-Dyer trail has been told several times elsewhere. Notably in the magazine *SIGNAL* ('The Quest For Elinor') and in my contribution ('In Search of Elinor') to *The Chalet School Revisited*, the book of essays edited by Rosemary Auchmuty and Ju Gosling and published by Bettany Press to commemorate Elinor Brent-Dyer's centenary in 1994.

Here, I shall mention only that the task of digging for biographical, social, topographical and other details proved unexpectedly congenial. I found that I hugely enjoyed spending hours in libraries and other places of reference, hunting through street directories, maps, registers, wills, census forms, electoral rolls and all manner of documents. Meeting and collecting information from people around the country was also thoroughly rewarding; especially as a number of these meetings would lead to valuable new friendships. And afterwards, the piecing together of all those tiny details so laboriously acquired was highly satisfying. This was a treasure hunt that combined some of the elements of detective stories, crossword puzzles and jig-saws — all of which I enjoy — even if the clues here were invariably in the wrong order and many of the pieces missing.

At the same time I began to realise my life-long ambition to write a full-length work of fiction. Oddly enough it was that concept, *full-length*, that had for many years inhibited me, for I had always imagined that to write something involving that quantity of words would be impossible — I should never find time to complete it. But in 1969 I had made a discovery almost by chance. That year my husband went off in May for a tour of New Zealand which was spread over six and a half months, and during the separation we wrote an aerogramme to each other at least three or four times a week, mine always being typed edge-to-edge in single spacing. And, just before Alex returned home in December, it happened that I was invited to a party attended by a large number of journalists. For some reason the subject of my letters to New Zealand came up in conversation, and one of these professional writers casually remarked that this number of aerogrammes, densely typed as they were, represented more than a full-length book. Which suddenly made it plain that quantity was not in itself a problem.

Thus encouraged I managed during the second half of the 1970s, in addition to researching and writing the Brent-Dyer biography, to complete two full-length children's stories. One was a reconstruction of a 'missing' Chalet School book; the other, a period novel, *Breath of Autumn*, which was set in the year 1939, partly at a fictional convent school, partly in an unnamed but undisguised North Berwick.

It must have been around this time that I decided to adopt the name of my maternal grandmother, Helen McClelland, as my writer's name. For some reason neither my married name of Margaret Kelly, nor my maiden and professional name, Margaret Moncrieff, seemed really suitable for a writer. And clearly there are advantages in having different names for the different sides of one's life. I have only to look at an envelope to know whether a letter will concern personal or family affairs (Margaret Kelly, or sometimes Margaret Moncrieff Kelly); business matters, (Mrs H.M. Kelly); music, either teaching or performing (Margaret Moncrieff); or writing and book friends (Helen McClelland). Then the tiresomely many envelopes that arrive addressed to Mrs **H** Kelly (with the H on its own) immediately betray their lack of any personal connection, and can straight away be binned, since no such person actually exists. And, no — oddly enough this is all helpful rather than confusing. Of course I did once, when writing a letter to explain my daughter's absence from school, notice just in time that I'd signed it Helen McClelland. But, apart from always demanding care when signing cheques, the different identities seem to sit quite easily.

However, writing books — under any name — is one thing; getting them published, as I soon discovered, is quite another. And by ill fortune it happened that the 1970s was a particularly difficult time for writers of anything connected with the girls' school-story, this genre being then considered in critical circles to be stone-cold dead and deservedly so.

Attitudes to the whole matter of writing for children were changing; political correctness was becoming important, with publishers growing ever more socially conscious and editors looking for stories that were not only unisex — or certainly not slanted to girls — but covering only subjects considered relevant to the 1970s. Our daughters were happy enough to include examples of this up-to-the-minute genre in their reading (we nicknamed such stories 'oil rigs and rape', later shortened to O.R.& R.). But they found these books often had a limited appeal, and would never have placed any of them on a level with, for example, Lewis's *Narnia*, or Pearce's *Tom's Midnight Garden*, or the Nesbit stories, Arthur Ransome's books, or Margaret Lovett's *Great and Terrible Quest*. They also continued for many years, as well as ranging freely over the classics, to enjoy the Chalet School and other stories of the kind so despised by the experts.

By the summer of 1979 the first version of *Behind the Chalet School* was completed, but I had so far been unsuccessful in placing either of my children's novels. Both had drawn some hearteningly appreciative comments from editors, in particular from Margaret Clark, then at Bodley Head; also from one well-known literary agent, Mrs Osyth Leiston. But no one wanted actually to publish either. (My Chalet School story was eventually to be published in 1995 by Bettany Press and republished in 2000 by HarperCollins, but *Breath of Autumn* is still languishing on the shelf.)

At this point the manuscript of the biography had gone through several phases, and I shall always be full of gratitude to one person in particular for helping me to reconsider certain things about the early versions. I had been given an introduction in the mid-1970s to a quite unlikely fan of Elinor Brent-Dyer and the Chalet School series, the late Mr Hilary Maurice Bray, who came from a literary background and had a lifetime of publishing connections. He had been most complimentary about my reconstruction story — originally titled *Grange House visits the Chalet School* — and I had ventured to send him a draft of the biography and ask for his comments. Now Hilary Bray came from an older generation and an era when manners were more formal. He would never have condemned anything outright. Instead, his long detailed critique was couched in the most elegantly diplomatic language (and in rather elegant handwriting). But, despite the punctilious politeness, he nevertheless made it quite plain that this first version was dangerously over-loaded with details — the kind of material that might be interesting in itself, but, in this context, was neither intrinsically significant, nor was it advancing the main theme. I still treasure one remark of his on the perils of inflating small details: "If it could be definitely established [he wrote] that **Homer** had an aunt with red hair, this might be of interest. It isn't quite the same with Elinor Brent-Dyer." A lot of pruning had to follow that comment! The first 40 pages of the original were reduced to 23, with a whole chapter bodily removed, and many valuable lessons were learnt.

The obvious first choice of publisher for *Behind the Chalet School* was the Edinburgh firm, W.& R. Chambers, who had produced all the original hardbacks of the Chalet School series, as well as many of Brent-Dyer's other titles. Memories can get blurred — mercifully, perhaps — but I recall that Chambers considered the manuscript on two separate occasions, more than a year apart; that the second time it was by their own request; and that both times they retained the MS for several months. But in the end, despite sending me extremely flattering reports, they declared themselves unable to publish the book.

After the first rejection from Chambers, I next tried William Collins, who at this point had been bringing out Chalet School paperbacks for about twelve years. And at least my dealings with them were speedy: one of their editors, who had sounded greatly interested on the phone, invited me to bring the manuscript along and to have tea at their office which was then near St James's Street, Piccadilly; and I duly delivered the manuscript to her, trying not to have any high hopes. Just as well, too; she had presumably been expecting something quite different, for as early as the following afternoon she wrote a letter explaining that, among other things, she didn't think *Eleanor* [sic] had had a very interesting life . . .

That was in about February 1980. It inaugurated a period of frustration, for during the months that followed I made several more unsuccessful attempts to place the biography. This was just about the worst time that I, as an unknown writer, could have chosen, with the general climate of opinion being so vitriolically opposed to the girls' school-story genre. Even my friends would enquire with raised eyebrows: "But what in the world makes you want to write about *Elinor*

Brent-Dyer? — and who was she, anyway?" And, as expressed by my husband, who was normally most supportive of my writing efforts, "People who want to read well researched in-depth biographies don't want to read about Elinor Brent-Dyer. And vice versa . . ." He was later to be proved wrong in both parts of this statement; and during the 1990s he even enjoyed reading some of the early Chalet School books. But at that time he was undoubtedly voicing the opinion held by a majority of editors and publishers. Without question the general view was that I had better just give up the attempt.

Probably it was in the late autumn of 1980 that I noticed an advertisement by a small publisher called New Horizon; it could have been in the *Spectator* or the *New Statesman* or the *Tablet*, all of which my husband regularly bought. This firm was offering to publish manuscripts on a subsidy and royalty basis; something I'd never heard of at that time, but on impulse I wrote to ask for details; and when their reply came I was sufficiently interested to send them a copy of the manuscript. One copy still remained at Chambers awaiting their verdict, but fortunately I had made two carbons of the original typescript, so was still able — in accordance with all the best instructions — to retain one for myself.

At this point I cannot remember the exact chronology of events, but it wasn't many weeks later when, by coincidence, two letters arrived in the same post on the same morning. One was from W. & R. Chambers, finally informing me with much (and I think genuine) regret that they were unable to publish the biography, which would now be returned to me under separate cover. The other was from New Horizon, accepting the manuscript for immediate publication and setting out their terms.

It didn't take long to decide. For in view of all the circumstances, this offer from New Horizon seemed likely to be the best I should get. Either I could now agree to conditions such as they suggested, or I could continue an almost certainly unsuccessful campaign with the mainstream publishers. I chose the former alternative, and agreed to invest £1200 in exchange for a forty percent royalty on all sales of the book. It was a decision I've never regretted. The various publishers reports had established that the biography did in itself have some merit; and not only did the New Horizon project offer me a start as a writer, there can be little doubt now that the book has played its part in changing attitudes to the whole matter of girls' school-story fiction.

Apart from anything, as revealed in countless letters I received after the biography appeared, *Behind the Chalet School* has helped to uncover the existence of innumerable devotees, all of whom had till then thought themselves alone in their fondness for the Brent-Dyer and similar series. Again and again, people would use words to the effect: "I always thought I was the only one"; and the letters came not only from all over Britain but from numerous parts of the globe, with Australia particularly well represented. (It was in fact an Australian fan, Ann Mackie-Hunter, who in 1989 founded 'Friends of the Chalet School'; this, the first of two now flourishing Brent-Dyer fan clubs, was joined in 1995 by 'The New Chalet Club', and today the two societies represent between them a world-wide membership of around fifteen hundred, with many fans belonging to both.)

Of course, I was in many ways extremely lucky in my dealings with New Horizon. First, in being able at that point to advance the necessary money. But, above all, in that my contract with the firm was drawn up for me and carefully vetted by a tough legal friend in Edinburgh, who made certain that I was covered in every possible direction, and that the money I paid as subsidy could not be used for any other purpose than the publication of my book. (I've learnt since of other writers who fared badly with New Horizon and lost considerable sums.) And I have no complaints about the firm's design of the book, nor about their marketing of it during the first two years after its publication. Unfortunately, though, just when I was about to begin making a profit on the sales, New Horizon, like so many of these small publishing firms, went into liquidation — it seems the director took himself off to Spain, leaving a good many unhappy creditors.

Rather surprisingly, another small firm, Anchor Press, bought up all New Horizon's stock, and since this included the plates of *Behind the Chalet School* they asked if they could bring out a second printing of the book. Sadly, it wasn't long before they too became bankrupt, but by this time I was actually getting a little ahead financially in the project.

During its first year the biography had sold quite well in a modest way; but the real boost to sales followed a broadcast in the BBC Radio Four *Woman's Hour* programme which was first given in January 1983, and then had two repeats later that year, one on August Bank Holiday and the second in top-rate listening time on the evening of Christmas Day. This fifteen-minute feature consisted of extracts from the Chalet School books read by Kate O'Mara (who had connections with the series through her mother, Hazel Bainbridge, to whom Brent-Dyer's first book is dedicated), and an interview with me about the writing of the biography. That the programme was so successful is largely to the credit of a BBC producer, Pamela Howe, who at that time held an important position in the *Woman's Hour* team. Pamela was herself a fan of the Chalet School and of other school-stories, but she had had to work hard for more than a year to convince the BBC authorities that this was a programme worth making. Perhaps it gives some indication of the change in attitudes that gradually took place during the late 1980s and early '90s that when, in the summer of 1995, my reconstruction story, *Visitors for the Chalet School*, was published by Bettany Press, it was the subject of six radio interviews in about ten days, as well as receiving an excellent review in the *Independent on Sunday* — one moreover that took the story seriously, something that would have been quite unlikely a few years earlier.

In this new climate of opinion HarperCollins had also begun to take a different view of the Chalet School books. Until the late 1980s their attitude, despite the excellent selling record of the series, had been more apologetic than enthusiastic. Then in 1988 a new editor, Sarah Asquith, arrived and everything changed. During the next few years I received several commissions: first, to provide the text for *Elinor M. Brent-Dyer's Chalet School* — a large format paperback with numerous attractively produced colour illustrations which appeared in September 1989. Next, to revise this material and expand it for *The Chalet School Companion* — published in 1994 as part of the firm's celebration of Elinor Brent-Dyer's centenary. (The latter event was itself a most important factor in spreading the Brent-Dyer cult — more of this in a moment.) Then came requests to write Introductions or Afterwords for various publications. Finally, in March 2000 my reconstruction Chalet School story, *Visitors for the Chalet School* (previously published in 1995 by Bettany Press) was added to the HarperCollins complete series of Chalet School paperbacks.

The long-delayed acceptance of this story by Collins represents a real victory, and could serve as an encouragement to others. For *Visitors* had in fact been considered, and rejected, by them on at least **three** previous occasions — once in the 1970s, and twice (possibly even three times) during the early and mid-1980s. Moreover, on the last unsuccessful attempt the story had even been personally sponsored by Mary Cadogan, the well-known authority on girls' stories, who had generously offered to approach one of the editors she knew well. In this belated triumph some of the credit must unquestionably go to Bettany Press for having ventured to publish *Visitors* in the first place, thus bringing it to general attention. Here, very special thanks are owed to Ju Gosling and Rosemary Auchmuty (who were then joint owners of the firm) and their editor, Joy Wotton; especially for all their splendid suggestions which undoubtedly helped to transform the original story.

Further confirmation of today's changed attitudes to the school-story genre came in 1999, when HarperCollins chose to include *The School at the Chalet* in their new series of *Children's Modern Classics*. Yet another accolade being the invitation I had received in 1996 to contribute an article on Elinor Brent-Dyer to the forthcoming revised edition of the *New Dictionary of National Biography*.

Looking back, it can be seen that a major turning point was the Brent-Dyer centenary in 1994. During that year a remarkable number of events commemorating the life and work of Elinor Mary Brent-Dyer were organised, not only in many parts of Britain, but as far afield as Australia. Numerous Brent-Dyer fans contributed to the running of these, but foremost among them were two dauntless enthusiasts, Clarissa Cridland and Polly Goerres, who devoted their time and enterprise for over a year to arranging the main celebrations, which were all held in places associated with Elinor Brent-Dyer. Things began appropriately on the sixth of April 1994, exactly one hundred years from the author's birth and in her birthplace of South Shields. There followed a lively weekend gathering in Hereford during April attended by over 160 fans, many of them from abroad, including several from Australia. (This proved a particularly enjoyable time, providing as it did the opportunity to put faces to many of those previously known to me only as correspondents.) Then in June fans met in Edinburgh — home of W. & R. Chambers, Brent-Dyer's main publishers; and in September it was the turn of, first Guernsey, then Reigate in Surrey. Here a thanksgiving service was held at the church Elinor had attended regularly during the last years of her life when she was living at Redhill; and afterwards a specially commissioned headstone, paid for by Chalet School fans around the globe, was unveiled at her grave. Finally a Christmas party was held in London, preceded by a school-story conference which saw the launch of the

Chalet School fans assembled at the Centenary gathering organised by Polly Goerres and Clarissa Cridland in Hereford, April 1994.

special commemorative book of essays, *The Chalet School Revisited*, published by Bettany Press. The events in both South Shields and Hereford had the backing, interest and support of the local councils, and in both places memorial plaques to Elinor Brent-Dyer were erected, while — more remarkably — a commemorative tablet was placed outside the library in the Tirolean village of Pertisau-am-Achensee which had been the inspiration of her Chalet School series.

All in all, the various happenings that year were an astonishing tribute to the Chalet School's author. And although no one would claim for Brent-Dyer the status of a great writer, it cannot be denied that her books have given and continue to give pleasure to countless readers. Nor — allowing for the limitations of the particular genre and period within which she worked — that these books include some first-rate school-stories, many of them among the best examples of their kind.

Returning to 1981, which had seen the eventual publication of *Behind the Chalet School*, this was also the last year that we were able to make any kind of family visit to Pertisau — and in this case without our elder daughter who was occupied elsewhere that summer. Before my next visit in 1998 seventeen years were to pass. Alex had died in October 1996, and both our daughters were married and living independent lives. Not only that: in the course of 1997 both the Kostenzer sisters, Hanneli and Nanni, had died. So many of my Pertisau memories were associated with them, as well as with my own family, that it's doubtful if I would ever have revisited the Achensee, had it not been that in the summer of 1998 sixteen members of the New Chalet Club had organised a ten-day holiday based at the

Bergland Hotel in Pertisau. After a lot of thought, and being subjected to a little kind persuasion, I decided to go there for part of the time; although, having always preferred smaller set-ups to hotels, I actually stayed in a neighbouring farmhouse and joined the NCC party for evening meals at *Bergland* and for various enjoyable expeditions, including some to places I'd never previously seen.

To revisit Pertisau was a decision made, not with reluctance — for I looked forward greatly to being with the group — but with a certain amount of apprehension. Never, since my very first visit to the Achensee with my mother right back in 1951, had I been there without Alex and/or at least one of our daughters. Nor had I stayed anywhere but with the Kostenzer family at *Untertuschenhof* (which is now unoccupied). But in the event the wonderful Achensee magic did not fail to work. Of course, there had inevitably been changes during the seventeen-year absence. Not so much in Pertisau itself; but some fairly horrendous new building has, sad to say, been allowed to disfigure parts of the neighbouring village of Maurach. Even in Pertisau hotels have expanded, restaurants have grown and have changed hands, new shops have appeared, and new gondola lifts now offer exertion-free trips up the Bärenbad mountain. Nevertheless, it would be impossible to alter the extraordinary beauty of Pertisau's mountain and lakeside setting; and much of the old atmosphere can still be recaptured. It was good too, if sad, to be able to visit the graves of Hanneli and Nanni; today they lie side by side near their grandparents in the beautifully tended little graveyard that encircles St Nothburga's Church in Eben — a neighbouring village. And it was touching to find, when I visited Nanni's daughter Erika, that there was still a photograph on the mantlepiece of our younger daughter, Alison, clasping the tiny Manfred — Erika's son — in her arms.

Back in the 1980s Alex, too, had been busy storming the literary world, though in another direction. He had always written poetry off and on, ever since his schooldays; and I still treasure the various highly romantic poems he wrote to me in the early days of our relationship (all of them in Scots, rather than Queen's English). After that, due to the pressures of work there was a quite long interval during which he wrote little or nothing. Then, at some point in the mid to late '70s, things started blossoming again. He began looking through various youthful efforts, which he was stopped from consigning to the wastepaper basket by our younger daughter, Alison. She encouraged him not only to save them but to go on and write more; the result eventually being a book of poems, *Visitations*, that was published in Dublin by the Elo Press in May 1986. The collection covers an extraordinarily wide range of longer and shorter poems, on many subjects — serious and humorous, personal and otherwise. Perhaps I'm not in a position to give an unbiased opinion of the collection, but I'm able to state that it has been outstandingly well received.

During this period — mid-1980s to 1990s — my own writing had taken new directions, including a handful of short stories and a number of articles for various publications. Among them the quarterly magazine *SIGNAL — Approaches to Children's Books* (editor Nancy Chambers), which published two of my articles at different times; *news & views*, the magazine of the European String Teachers' Association; and *The British Music Journal*. Some were biographical — including articles on Hans Gál, Antonia Butler, and Donald Francis Tovey (the last named with much assistance from Mary Firth); others had a technical slant.

Then, around 1990, I set to work on a novel with a musical setting, *Time and Again*. In this I was able to fulfil two long-held ambitions: to write a time-slip novel; and to use a music-school as the setting for a story. I've always been fascinated by stories involving time-travel — from Edith Nesbit's numerous examples, the plays of J.B. Priestley, and various books by, among others, Esther Meynell, passing through Alison Uttley's *Traveller in Time* and Elizabeth Goudge's *Little White Horse*, to Philippa Pearce's *Tom's Midnight Garden*, Penelope Farmer's *Charlotte Sometimes*, and Jill Paton Walsh's *Chance Child* — to give only a few examples. And C.S. Lewis's books, both those addressed to children and those to adults, have revolutionised my whole ideas on the subject of time. For me it is no longer hard to believe that, somewhere out there in the universe, the end of the 21st century could long ago have come and gone.

One of the things people frequently ask about a work of fiction is where the writer's ideas came from. Yet it's often difficult to answer this, for it may have been such a small and apparently insignificant spark that ignited the flame. I once got the idea for an entire ghost-story just from noticing the strangely intent way a one-year-old baby would sit gazing into space: what could he be seeing that was invisible to us but appeared so entrancing to him? And then one thing led to another . . . As regards *Time and Again*, the first spark was provided by a random discovery that in the year 19<u>89</u> the days of the week and the dates in the month had exactly coincided with those in 19<u>39</u>. As one obvious example, the third of September in 1989 fell on a Sunday, just as it had on that fateful morning fifty years earlier when the lacklustre tones of Neville Chamberlain announced to the nation that Britain was now at war with Germany. This discovery could have meant anything or nothing, but for me it immediately suggested two possible periods for a time-slip story. Various things had always held me back from following the most usual formula of sending present-day characters back to some period in the historical past. Mainly it was the thought that so many examples already existed, both classical and modern, including the work of authors who were by far my betters. But the idea of all the hours that would be needed for historical research was also daunting. Then it suddenly struck me there was no reason why this standard formula should not be reversed, with a character from the past somehow finding a way of reaching the present day.

Approached from this angle, the necessary research would not be extensive, since most of the story would take place in the present. And anyway, as things turned out I much enjoyed spending a few days in Edinburgh's Central Public Library, discovering many interesting details about the early part of World War II, which had passed over my head at the time. (I was specially interested — although this was not directly relevant to my researches — to find in a *Scotsman* of October 1939 a long and quite detailed report about the atrocities in the German concentration camps. So people *could* have known about this if they had wanted to . . .)

Before long *Time and Again* began almost to write itself. The local topography gave no problems — this was the land of my childhood. Nor did the musical setting, though I was careful not to include any real-life professional musicians among those in the story. I also deliberately avoided using any real country house as a model for Pennyriggs — the site of the fictional music-school. Discovering the real-life location of fictional sites can be a happy pastime, and one in which I've often joined with enthusiasm. But this can at times cause readers to become obsessed with a determination to identify every single place described in a story, which seems a little insulting to the author's imagination. In any case, various things in the plot of *Time and Again* absolutely demanded a custom-built setting.

With the manuscript completed, it was once again a matter of trying to interest a publisher. Or rather, of trying to find one who was ready to translate interest into action. I did in fact have a surprising number of encouraging letters from the various publishers I tried, up and down the country, and from two literary agents. With one exception, they all made extremely complimentary — if sometimes contradictory! — remarks about the story. But at this stage no publisher was actually prepared to take it on, and neither of the agents was able to place it, although one in particular (Robin Denniston, formerly of OUP) made great efforts to do so. Thus, once again I have to thank Bettany Press for deciding, early in 2001 to publish the book (which is now generally available).

The latest venture has been the writing of these memoirs. Started in June 2001, they were completed in the early summer of 2002, although it might be more accurate to say that this particular random selection of memories is now finished. There are many gaps; and many past events that clamoured for mention have not been recorded. Among them — at random — a memorable fortnight in 1953, when some friends (Hubert and Frances Somervell and Tom Ram) took me on a cruise in a thirty-foot sailing yacht, during which we had many adventures, crossing and re-crossing the seas between harbours in England, France and the Channel Islands. And I would love to have included something about the inspiring if exhausting sessions that our original piano trio (Alex, me and Jackie Bower) used to spend being coached by Isolde Menges, the famous violinist — an extraordinary person whose teaching about the art of ensemble playing was quite simply a revelation. Her lessons, which would continue literally for hours and were punctuated with endless cups of black coffee, were always given totally for free.

It may be noted that I have written little about family life and personal matters during the years since coming to Barnes in 1961. But then, writing about the past and its people is one thing. For me, it's important that our children's lives are their own; as are those of the many present-day friends I'm fortunate in having.

At least this final chapter does manage to bring things more or less up-to-date on the writing front. In my case, anyway: although it happens that during recent years both our daughters have become involved in writing, to different degrees and in different ways. Catriona already has many published books to her credit, all in the field of

Russian literature and culture, including translations of Russian poetry. At the moment she is writing a history of childhood in twentieth century Russia; and she has also acted as an adviser to Cambridge University Press — a considerable feather-in-the-cap for an **Oxford** don! (Catriona still keeps the surname Kelly; as does her sister, although the latter uses the form Moncrieff-Kelly to distinguish her from another Alison Kelly, a well known violinist.)

Alison, after taking a two-year course and a diploma in creative writing, has now herself been invited to **run** a similar course, and plans somehow to shoe-horn this into the crowded life of a professional cellist, both performer and teacher, and the mother of two children. It seems that Alison's personal account of growing up in the Kelly household was one of the highspots in the class she attended — to date I haven't been given the opportunity to read it. That will be among many new experiences eagerly awaited — perhaps in 2003/4? Hopefully, the World of Words will hold much to interest and to challenge all three of us in the future.

Me with Alison and Catriona at my granddaughter Camilla's christening party, December 1995.

Afterword

These memoirs began with reflections on the theme of 'Worlds Apart', and the significance of a marriage that took place on the sixth of June 1957 — now more than forty-five years ago.

An appropriate Ending might be the poem, Silver Wedding Greeting, that Alex wrote for me to mark our twenty-fifth wedding anniversary in 1982.

Silver Wedding Greeting

As
Once
Monks
From
The
Oratoried
West
Took
Pliant
Coracles
To
Unimagined
Corners
Of
The
Grim
Brooding
World

Afterword

Faith
Surviving
Tempests
And
An
Endless
Fear
Of
Menacing
Ice
Where
Later,
Ships
Of
Oak
And
Even
Iron
Would
Founder

So
We
Too,
Dear
Love,
Pilgrim
Voyagers
After
So
Many
Years
Of
Seas
Far
Stormier
Than
Any
We

Opposite: Catriona (wearing my 'going away' dress) at our Silver Wedding party, June 1982.

Me with Alison, Alexander and Camilla, 2001.

Had
Reckoned
On,
Still
Together
Hand
In
Hand
Guide
Our
Frail
Craft
Through
Uncharted
Seas
Of
Lasting
Love.